POOR PUSS

A Social History of English Cats

Medieval to Millennium

Marilyn Crowther

"Alas! Poor Puss comes last and least."
William Gordon Stables 1874

ISBN 978-1-912419-57-9
Printed and bound in Great Britain.
Published by Art Circus Books 2019
An imprint of YouCaxton Publications.

www.artcircusbooks.co.uk

Contents

Dedication

I dedicate *Poor Puss* to my late husband and collaborator Kenneth Crowther
who wrote the first draft manuscript for his innovative idea:

'A Social History of English Cats'.

His professional research and keen observation have supported me in my pleasurable
task; to re-write and up-date the book for discerning cat lovers of today
– and their eight million pet cats.

A contribution from the sale of this book will be made to Cats Protection.

Acknowledgments

I am grateful to all who have given me their generous help and support in preparing *Poor Puss*.

Special thanks go to Colin Knipe for transcribing my inscrutable manuscript into book format; to
Amoret Tanner for her fund of knowledge about ephemera that proved most useful in compiling
the Love and Kitties chapter; and to Caroline Davidson for her invaluable literary expertise and
encouragement.

How The Cats Made Me Write It

The Author at Long Mountain House, Jamaica with pet cat Fluffers, one of the kittens that danced by moonlight

We didn't know much about cats when *we went to live in Jamaica, but our little 'rescues' stole our hearts and led us on to uncover Puss's largely unknown and fascinating social history.*

We lived on Mona Heights, an area of natural beauty, below the Blue Mountain range on the campus of the University of Jamaica where my husband had a senior research post to study some of the fascinating aspects of Caribbean history.

There, waiting to greet us in our new home at Long Mountain House, was resident cat Mum-puss – a feline of great character with a streak of the Orient – who had been cared for over the years by a series of expatriate occupants.

As we busied ourselves settling in, we began to notice that we were under scrutiny; each day as we came and went, a grey striped tabby cat watched us from the edge of the thick, impenetrable 'bush' that bordered our property. At our approach, he – or she – disappeared in the bat of an eye. Did our feline observer want food, or was he a hopeful suitor for Mum-puss? We put out food. It soon disappeared, so did our charming little spy but eventually she (Mata, after the famous spy Mata-Hari) was confident enough to eat at our back door and stretch out contentedly in the shade of our Pau-Pau tree.

Some weeks later as I sat indoors writing home, something soft and warm was placed gently on to my foot, Mata's kitten. She returned with three more bundles, their eyes only just open and, like their Mum, beautiful. We placed a box in a quiet corner and there, happy at last, she nursed her kittens and kept them scrupulously clean.

In common with most cats, Mata was a pragmatist. Her careful observation of us – which most would dismiss as mere cat curiosity – was a survival skill. She had her own list of boxes to tick; could we be trusted with her precious family; was it safe and was there food. Mata had saved her kittens from a dangerous environment in the bush where there were numerous predators, including the mongoose for whom a small kitten would provide a tasty snack.

There were more rescues like Mata. Some possibly belonging to departing expatriates, had probably been re-homed, but the disruption of losing their owners often led them to hunt and roam the mountain side, usually with fatal results. One starlit night on our patio as we sipped our drinks and listened to the whistle of tree frogs, we saw in the soft dark of the garden what appeared to be a group of fluffy kittens dancing a rapturous ballet; their silvered fur luminous in the moonlight as they jumped and leaped at the flutterings of nocturnal moths. We were spellbound. Could we be dreaming or was there something in our rum punch? It took very little detective work to find that the kittens belonged to our resident cat Mum-puss, sired by a neighbouring Siamese, mother cat having kept them carefully hidden for six weeks.

Our rescued cats varied in number as we re-homed them, but there were often as many as twenty cats and kittens relying on us for food and care; unfortunately, neutering was not an option in those far-off days and it was vital to bring the kittens in to socialise them as early as possible. Our cat family lived together in harmony and affection, which disproves the conventional view of cats as aloof and solitary; living with so much space may have allowed them to bond together. Mum-puss was the matriarch of our feline family and earned our deep respect. She moved around her domain with the assured poise of an early movie star and any kitten stepping out of line got a smart box on the ears. She adored my husband who often helped deliver her kittens, so when she explained to him that she had sustained a nasty bite and was unable to feed them for a while,

she knew they were in safe hands. When a large Alsatian dog appeared in the garden we rushed to her aid. There was no need; with claws firmly fastened to his neck ruff, she rode him round the garden rising up and down rodeo cowboy style; her victim yelping for mercy. We never saw *him* again.

When the hurricane came most of our cats hurried indoors and we fastened our storm shutters. Hours later Fluffers, our half Siamese became fidgety but we had no litter trays. Thankfully the wind had dropped but rain was still lashing down. Sheltered under a large umbrella, cat and I walked to the gravel path by our patio and there gratefully, he squatted. Others came forward, eager to take advantage of this unique opportunity. Disaster struck at three in the morning when I awoke to a scratching noise and alerted my husband to the fact that there was a very soggy patch on his side of the bed. He begged to be left in peace; he did not care, he said, all he wanted was to sleep! Traditionally it is the role of dogs to go walking with their owners. However, the cats of Long Mountain House were always keen to accompany us on a walk, which started from home along our secluded road with around eight or ten cats; some scampered ahead, most walked sedately alongside. Our companions were probably some of the more extrovert of our bunch: Moll, our cat-burglar who was able to open and enter the ground floor bathroom window; Blackers, whose speciality was raiding the refrigerator; and our little red puss Brandy, who was gay. Happily he never brought home any

kittens. There were some hazards. Local fierce guard dogs often emerged and on seeing the cats, chased up close behind barking and growling. My husband – always our rear guard – brandished a walking stick which despatched them home pronto. Meanwhile I walked on with the cats, who – with touching faith in our powers of protection – never panicked, but continued at a gentle trot, tails up. Or they may have been confident that they could easily see off a couple of pathetic dogs!

Eventually, our lotus-eating days with our cats came to an end and it was time to return to the UK; happily there was continuing care for our resident Mum-puss. All our remaining cats were re-homed, except Fluffers, one of the kittens that had danced by moonlight. Feeling unable to part with him forever, he headed home and into quarantine. Saying goodbye to our cats was the hardest thing we ever had to do. As human beings we felt privileged to have been accepted into their unique family. They had given us their love, loyalty and trust and shown bravery and ingenuity in their fight for survival.

On a cold November day, our cat Fluffers left quarantine; he loved summer when he could sleep in the sun but in winter he stayed close to hearth and home. For family reasons, we needed to remain in the UK where we both worked in communications; print, past and present would remain a defining interest both in our careers and in our private lives. We continued to offer any homeless cat a shelter, and our remarkable 'Muffin' –

streetwise and battered – found his final retirement home with us. He loved to go walking and always led the way along our quiet Close, picking up his front paws as smartly as any trotting circus pony. To the amazement of neighbours, my husband followed at a leisurely pace (feet firmly on the ground), a cigarette in his left hand, a gin and tonic in his right. They made an eccentric looking pair.

Cats were still at work in our lives when by chance, our local Inn was undergoing renovation and we spotted some old colour prints on a rubbish skip parked outside. Most were advertisements for wine and tobacco but one was for household soap featuring a black cat at a tub, paws deep in soapsuds and captioned 'THOM'S CASTILLE SOAP – BEST IN THE WORLD' (featured in chapter 8). On examination we saw that the coloured dots were not regular but applied randomly like a rash. It was our first original piece of cat ephemera, printed around 1895 by chromolithography.

Why would a Victorian advertiser use a cat to sell soap, we wondered. We recalled how our lovely cat Marta tried to lick the stripes off her kittens; cats have always been thought of as cleanly. A black cat is also a good luck symbol and, for the customer, Thom was the kind of familiar kitchen mouser they knew. At the time, cat images were being used to promote every kind of household product.

The search was on to find out more. By following in the paw prints of Puss, we uncovered a staggering amount of material in books, newspapers, magazines, letters and diaries; some buried deep for hundreds of years waiting to be discovered amongst the archives of libraries and museums. Ephemera fairs, auctions and flea markets yielded up many seductive images. Our collection grew into an impressive social record of the ever changing role of cats over the centuries.

Poor Puss is an attempt to tell that story.

Chapter 1

Who Do You Think You Are Puss

A Case of Mistaken Identity

Imagine you are a cat living at the beginning of the sixteenth century, earning your keep in the libraries of medieval monasteries and cathedrals just as your ancestors had done before you. Your job, to protect valuable vellum manuscripts from the teeth of predators. You are cared for by kindly monks and if you are lucky there are rabbits to be had in the meadows and woods surrounding the abbeys and priories where you may be living. You play a useful role in society and you are sure of your own identity. It sounds like a good life, unfortunately it isn't going to last…

CATS WORK FOR THEIR LIVING

Cats are contemplative creatures, so they felt at home and lived on friendly terms with their pious hosts. Many centuries later, the French poet Théophile Gautier wrote an appraisal of cats which reads as the perfect monastic job description:

'these charming creatures, tranquil, mysterious and gentle with velvet tread. They like silence, order and quietness and no place is so proper for them as the study of a man of letters'.

In an affectionate tribute, an Irish monk of the 8th or 9th century wrote verses in praise of his white cat, Pangur Bán. Scholar and cat, says the author, both persevere with their tasks, he in pursuit of knowledge, the cat of its prey:

I and Pangur Ban my cat,
'Tis a like task we are at:
Hunting mice is his delight,
Hunting words I sit all night

In a 13th century 'rule book' nuns were not allowed pets – but an exception was made for a cat which could be kept for company and possibly mousing duties – bearing in mind the alleged antipathy

Grey striped cat holding mouse.
The Lutterell Psalter, c.1325–35.
© The British Library Board. Add. 42130, f.190

that women have towards mice. But there was a warning: she must control it from being a nuisance to others and she must not allow herself to get so fond of the worldly creature that she might be drawn away from her spiritual vows. But the nun was safe; only her cat knew her secret and of course cats never tell.

Records at Exeter cathedral reveal an unbroken succession of resident cats from the early 14th to the late 15th century. All came within the remit of the cathedral treasurer, who allotted half the money from the collecting boxes to pay the wages of four vergers, a grave digger, a seamstress, a laundress – and the cat. The cat's stipend was separately itemised and throughout this long period it stood at 13d a quarter, or 4s.4d. a year – one penny a week. During the 1360s and '70s accounts show a doubling of the allowance with a reference to 'cats' in the plural. In 1384 the cathedral cat was the focus of a complaint from the treasurer to the Archbishop of Canterbury that the dean and chapter were withholding its wages. The chapter made an attempt at an excuse by disparaging the cat – it was, they said only a 'catulo' – a little one!

Cats on anti-rodent patrol in a monastery.
Bodleian Libraries, University of Oxford.
MS. Bodl. 533, fol. 13r

Nun & cat with spindle. Maastricht Hours.
© *The British Library Board. Stowe 17, f.34*

The beauty of the images in a medieval bestiary draws us into a dream-like world of seductive shapes and colours that enchant the eye and calm the senses. The written text however is brief and to the point, reflecting the contemporary view of cats as no more than useful killing machines:

'This creature is called mouser because she kills mice. The common word is cat because she captures them. They have such sharp sight that the brightness of their glance overcomes the darkness of night. Catus is the Greek word for cunning.'

So cats were useful mousers but cunning – and even more disturbing, their eyes glowed in the dark, which came to be construed by later generations as a sinister characteristic. In the margins of their manuscripts these medieval artists found freedom, as if the margin itself was an extension of the world, a place where animals could dance and indulge in light-hearted fun. One cat

Puss fiddling to mice.
The Renowned History of Dame Trot and Her Cat.

Chap book woodcut 1820.

beats time on a tambour to accompany a donkey piper, another plays the fiddle. These are our images to come, the cat and the fiddle will return down the centuries in children's stories, nursery rhymes and on inn signs.

Cat playing a rebec, forerunner of the fiddle, used to accompany dancing. Book of Hours. c.1320–30.

© *The British Library Board. Harley 6563 1.40*

GAMMER GURTON'S NEEDLE
Published 1575

'And Gib our cat, in the milk pan she spied, over head and ears,
'Ah, whore! Out thief!' she cried aloud, and slapped the breeches down;
'Up went her staff and out leapt Gib at doors into the town'.

In this bawdy Elizabethan domestic comedy Gammer Gurton is patching up her manservant's breeches when she spots Gib thieving the milk, causing her to lose her one and only precious needle. She picks up her 'staff' (a 16th century version of a walking stick) to threaten the mischievous puss, who makes a speedy exit; the entire play is spent searching for the needle. Gib loses one of his nine lives when, thinking his tail is set alight, there is general panic in case he sets fire to the thatch. A Gib or Gyb cat is a tom cat and a real one would have been difficult to stage manage. However, a pantomime cat actor may have played the part in this fast-moving farce, alternatively a stuffed animal with plenty of miaowing noises from the wings may have sufficed.

John Aubrey in his *'Brief Lives'* has some interesting observations on the colours of 17th century cats:

'W. Laud, A.B. Cant was a great lover of catts. He was presented with some Cyprus catts i.e. our Tabby-catts which were sold at first for £5 a piece, this was 1637 or 1638.'

The remarkably high price quoted, must have reflected rarity value at the time. It appears that the introduction of the new tabby-cat soon outpaced the indigenous English cat population – a change which Aubrey greatly regretted:

'I doe well remember, that the common English catt was white with some blewish piedness: sc. a gallipot* blew. The race or breed of them are now almost lost.'

* Gallipot: a traditional dish or jar used by the apothecary for mixing ingredients.

THE DISSOLUTION OF THE MONASTERIES

By the 1530s the cats that once stalked the monastery libraries and refectories were gone – like their masters – made redundant. Even worse, having lived with the monks for many years, they were seen as 'papists' and liable to prosecution, while their alleged association with witchcraft further damaged their faltering identity.

In 1469 the church warden of St Michael's church, Cornhill, noted in his accounts book that prayers had been said *'for three rat trappes'* for the church. It was a break from tradition to use traps instead of cats and experience over centuries had shown that rats soon learn how to avoid them. Around the same time cats suddenly disappear from the sumptuary records of Exeter Cathedral. The significance of these two unrelated events point to a growing restraint on cats in the discharge of their traditional duties; they are no longer welcome in places of worship.

MALEFICIA – THE WITCHES' FAMILIAR

Although a witch might be young or old, male or female, many of them were frail elderly women no longer able to support themselves who lived on the parish and were generally regarded as scroungers. They probably led solitary lives and a cat was an ideal companion, it gave out furry warmth and cost little to feed. The stereotypical old witch woman, ragged poor and living with her cat became a fixed notion that has lived on in popular culture ever since. So how did cats fall into such bad company that they were branded as the witches' 'little helpers'? Although there is no clear answer, clues point to the church dissenters – breakaway Christian groups denounced as heretics by the Roman Catholic Church and alleged to be cat worshippers. Such a group was the Cathars who held the 'dualist' belief that God and the devil are equally powerful in the world, whereas Church doctrine teaches God is above, and can overcome the devil. French theologian Alain de Lille asserted that the name Cathars came from the word

THE OLD WOMAN AND HER CAT.

The witch and her cat take a flight to the moon.

Hand coloured illustration,
Dame Dearlove's Ditties. c.1820.

cat; that they worshipped it in the form of a large black cat – the devil in disguise – and *'kissed his arse'* when black masses were held. Superstition, fear and the need for a convenient scapegoat swept poor puss along in the ensuing holocaust.

A WINDOW ON WITCHES.
York 1622

'Tell me catte, cannot the bird speake?' The cat told her the bird's name was *'Tewhitt'* and *'she'* (Margaret Waite) *'hath had it for ten years'*.

This strange conversation took place between Hellen Fairfax and a large white cat named Fillie when Hellen, under the spell of local witches had fallen into a trance. A window on this bizarre world from the archives of the British Library covers one year, October1621 to December1622, in a detailed diary kept by Edmund Fairfax, Yeoman farmer, Latin and Greek scholar and writer. He claims his two daughters Hellen age 21 and Elizabeth, 7 were frequently 'possessed' by witches, saw apparitions, fell into trances and underwent physical and mental abuse. Hellen had nightly visits from all sorts of satanic creatures including a large black dog. Cats made frequent appearances seeming to have a social life of their own, many were black, in all over 40 cat visitations are recorded. Fairfax's accusations and those of his neighbour John Jaffray, whose 12 year old daughter was also afflicted, resulted in the trial of six local women at York assizes in 1622.

Although unpopular and despised, these women, some elderly, were often much feared. Jennit Dibble was said to be descended from a family of witches; she was served by a cat named Gibbe *'who hath attended her now above 40 years'*. Margaret Waite, a woman of *'lewd behaviour'* kept a safe house for thieves; her 'spirit' was a black and white spotted cat named Inges. In court, the Fairfax's neighbour Thomas Forest testified that riding late near her house he was:

'assaulted by so many cats he could hardly defend himself from them, but did ride away with all speed and yet they followed him a great way'. The cats it was alleged were 'witches who desired to have pulled Forest from his horse that they might have a touch of him and afterwards bewitch him'.

All six women were acquitted.

ERGOT POISONING – A CLUE

Ergot poisoning or ergotism is caused by eating a fungus contained in mildewed rye bread or other cereals. Outbreaks recorded throughout Europe for centuries were linked with mental illness, hallucinations, psychosis and mania, some of which the Fairfax sisters endured. Although in 1670 a French physician, Dr Thullier, made known his theory that the ingestion of mouldy rye could cause convulsive ergotism, it was not until 1988 when serious research began on the Salem witch trials of 1692 that the connection finally made.

A badly behaved or uncontrollable animal was considered to be 'delinquent' and could be brought to trial by its owner and executed for its actions. So it is not surprising that when the domestic cat was accused of Satanism it led to the custom of burning them live in baskets over a bonfire. It was a popular event practised throughout northern Europe on festival days. In his book *The Golden Bough*, J G Frazer gives us a glimpse of the sun King's participation:

'In 1648 Louis XIV crowned with a wreath of roses and carrying a bunch of roses in his hand, kindled the fire, danced at it and partook of the banquet afterwards. This was the last occasion a monarch presided at the midsummer bonfire in Paris.'

Handsome, well cared for cats, or exotics, shared a cherished place among the French aristocrats and 'people of quality' (as Samuel Pepys might say). Those cast on the bonfire were of the mangy street cat variety, referred to in France as 'singed cats'.

CATS AT THE COURT
OF VERSAILLES

While cats were being burned alive at religious festivals for public entertainment, others were already scaling the social ladder even into the corridors of power. Louis XV, unlike his father, was fond of cats and of the many that roamed the grand Palace of Versailles one, a white Angora was his special pet. His name is not known but he enjoyed the protection of the King from the teasing of unkind courtiers and servants. The palace of Versailles was a cats' playground; the entire court had a passion for gambling and the room which housed the lotto tables was also home to an extended family of grey Angoras which frolicked among the pieces. When the King died suddenly of smallpox in May 1774 his whole household, fearing contagion fled to the palace of Choisy, leaving Versailles almost abandoned. A party of English tourists arrived and were allowed to view inside where, in one of the apartments they found a 'majestic cat' whose silver collar labelled it as the pet of Madame Victoire, one of Louis XV's daughters and still being cared for by some loyal retainer.

Although Louis XVI did not like cats, his wife, the Austrian born Marie Antoinette adored them. There is a strong tradition that our popular American Maine Coon cat of today is the result of cross-breeding between local shorthairs and six Persians which the queen had shipped across the Atlantic to New England in the hope that she would be able to join them in exile. As we know, she met her executioner before she could make her escape. Although this story is contested, it appears that a longhair gene was in some way introduced, enough to leave an imprint on the indigenous felines. Today in rural Maine, large longhaired semi-feral farm cats (known as 'foundation stock') are still to be found. But as their ancestors are unlikely to have appeared on the cargo list of the ship that carried them from France, the question may never be resolved.

The first longhaired cat to arrive in France, was alleged to have been a black and white Persian smuggled in to Paris in 1700, having been stolen by a 'gentleman's servant' travelling from Rome. However, it appears that two earlier travellers, Nicolas-Claude Fabri de Pieresc and the Italian Pietro Della Valle introduced Persians and Angoras to France at some time during the 17th century. Exotic longhairs came at a price, the preserve of the wealthy and as objects of conspicuous consumption they were not kept as common mousers. The native shorthaired variety was still to be found on the hearth of many French homes as portrayed in the painting by Francois Boucher *'La Toilette'* (1742) where a small red cat of the boudoir is luxuriating among the frilly underwear of his owner.

A dreamlike scenario is enacted on the roof tops of the Palace of Versailles, where aristocratic shorthaired cats perform an opera-ballot.

Illustration from Les Chats by François-Augustin de Paradis de Moncrif, 1727.

THE FRENCH CULT OF THE CAT

A lively network of aristocratic writers and intellectuals at and around the court of Versailles were inspired by their cats to write poetry, plays and even love letters on their behalf to other cats owned by friends. Madame Deshoulières, (1638-94) a poetess of some standing – praised by Voltaire as the French Calliope – had a female cat named Grisette, who was in touch with at least three hopeful feline suitors. Madame's daughter also penned a heroic tragedy *'La Mort De Cochon'* with cat choruses; a parody in the manner of Corneille about the passion of Grisette for Cochon the dog of the Duc de Vivonne – an entertaining diversion for friends. Letters flew back and forth between the cats – they were lively correspondents. Although a translation can never do justice to the cats' elegant French, here is Tata the cat of Madame la Marquise de Montras who writes of the lovely Grisette:

'Never was a cat so beautiful, Never was a cat so pleasing.'

Dom Gris, the cat of Mme La Duchesse de Bethune writes endearingly in his love letter:

'I may be just a tom-cat but I have a sensitive soul.'

While Mittin, the cat of Mademoiselle Bocquet joins in with his own heartfelt tribute to a lovely creature who lives in luxury and never has to demean herself by hunting:

*'You are never seen soiling your
Innocent and delicate paws
With the blood of mice and rats.'*

When an adored cat lived a privileged life amongst the aristocrats of Paris, she might expect to be honoured in death. Ménine, the pet cat of The Duchesse de Lesdiguières was commemorated with a very fine tomb, said at the time, to be one of the sights of Paris.

The tomb of Ménine in Paris.
'Here lies a lovely cat'.

The Book of the Cat.

THE GREAT DEBATE

It was not a good time to be a cat, adored and versified by some, persecuted by others. The French anti-cat lobby was vociferous, cats were treacherous they said, they suffocated babies and were linked with the devil. French philosopher and intellectual René Descartes (1596-1650) published his chilling doctrine regarding animals, that they were unfeeling objects and mere machines for the use and pleasure of man.

A century later Georges Buffon, the leading naturalist of his day writing in his best-selling *'L'Histoire naturelle'* (1749–67) stated:

'The cat is a faithless domestic and only kept through necessity to oppose another domestic which incommodes us still more and which we cannot drive away'. He goes on to accuse cats of being cunning, servile thieves and further reveals his personal puritanical view that 'we pay no respect to those who keep cats for amusement'.

Cats might have been forgiven for thinking that the day of the age of enlightenment was a long time dawning, but it was on its way. Cat hater Buffon's generally accepted view regarding cats was later challenged by his contemporary, naturalist Antoine Fee who wrote in support of the much-maligned feline race. Cats, he said were:

'capable of profound attachment. It is difficult to win its affection; and easy to forfeit it: in this consists the great difference between the cat and the dog.'

LES CHATS
A BOOK OF THEIR OWN

'I shall write a history to the glory and honour of cats.' It was the first-ever book devoted entirely to cats. *Les Chats* by François-Augustin de Paradis de Moncrif was published in 1727, thirty-three years after the death of the poet and cat lover Mme Deshoulières. It was a firm riposte to the growing condemnation of cats by the anti-cat lobby of the time.

He was a man of many parts, member of the Académie française, musician, playwright and poet. There was also a whisker of tom-cat about him; lithely athletic, a brilliant fencer, popular with men and women alike. Voltaire described him as *'my very dear Sylph'*. In *Les Chats* he gives an insight into the sacred cats of ancient Egypt, drawing on his exhaustive knowledge of Greek and Roman texts.

There are humorous revelations regarding the personal relationships of cats with each other and some amusing anecdotes regarding the eccentric behaviour of several cat devotees of recent times. It seems there were cat lovers whose behaviour verged on paranoia; the wealthy lady who, without the comfort of a cat in her room at night became ill and often fainted. This was a problem when travelling and on occasions an entire sleepy village had to be searched from end to end in the middle of the night for a suitable candidate. Another eccentric, Mademoiselle Dupuy, a celebrated harpist always practised in the presence of the more discerning of her two cats to improve her technique. She found that

THE ANGORA.

The Angora Cat. Line drawing from Our Cats

by Harrison Weir.

the style most approved by her cats also pleased her human audience. In her Will she left her cats a pension of thirty sous a month *'that they may live well'* – along with elaborate advice on their menu. Unfortunately her legacy was quashed on appeal by her family.

A FITTING MONUMENT FOR KOULI-KAN

In England there is evidence that by 1800 Persians and Angoras had become fashionably collectable among the well-to-do. Before then information is limited. One cat we do know a little about is Kouli-kan, a Persian belonging to the Anson family of Shugborough Hall, Staffordshire, from whom the present-day Earls of Lichfield are descended. It was speculated that Kouli-kan may have been acquired by their famous relative Admiral Anson, and accompanied him on voyages on his ship the Centurion. It seems much more likely however, that Kouli-Kan was the last of a line of Persians introduced at Shugborough by Sir Thomas Anson.

In November 1749 Lady Anson writes to her husband Thomas from Bath where she has just had a conducted tour around a large quarry with the stonemason. She sounds excited at having had a privileged viewing of their latest technology:

'We have admired the power of Mechanism in the Crane at the Stone Quarry, the engine for engraving Seals, and that for turning stone vases, the largest and most magnificent of which – and they are indeed stupendous – are but six pounds (£6) the pair so I should think if you had fixed on a Design, you might have Kouli-Kan's Monument made here, and afterwards break and colour it as you please.'

So Kouli-Kan's memory was honoured, as that of Ménine, the pet of the Duchesse de Lesdiguières had been before her, with an impressive stone monument.

Stone Monument to Kouli-Kan a Persian cat belonging to the Anson family of Shugborough Hall, Staffordshire 1750.

GOTTFRIED MIND A BORN CAT ARTIST

'He was often to be seen at his desk with a mother cat on his lap and two or three kittens perched on his shoulders or on the

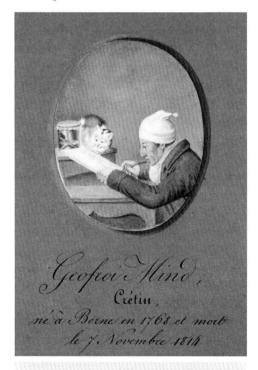

Gottfried Mind self portrait with Busi. Watercolour.

nape of his bowed neck, avoiding any movement which might make his beloved animals uncomfortable.'

Sigmund Wagner: Obituary for Gottfried Mind 1814.

The self portrait of Gottfried Mind has the following explanatory caption:

'The portrait could only have been done using two mirrors. He is dressed in a night cap – the common custom of the people of his rank in Berne.'

(George Fairholme 1829)

The tortoiseshell cat pictured is Busi, his favourite in later life, which dates the work to the early 1800s.

Mind was autistic, born to poor Hungarian immigrant parents living in Berne (Switzerland) in 1786. It was not the best start in life but his paintings of cats would one day bring him international recognition. As a teenage lad, Mind's skill with the brush was spotted by Herr Freudenberger, a businessman who owned a small print publishing company. Gottfried started work there hand-colouring Swiss scenes for the tourist trade. He never learned to read and write and, other than any training he may have been given in his work he was entirely self-taught. Social graces did not come easily to him, although always kindly towards animals and children, he could be offhand and surly with strangers.

One who did penetrate his gruff exterior to become his friend and patron was an aspiring young civil servant, Sigmund Wagner and it was probably their mutual fondness for cats that led to the friendship. Wagner kept two handsome white shorthaired cats which Mind portrayed perched on a mahogany table beside fine leather-bound volumes, probably in Wagner's study. Perhaps to ensure 'little Friedli' as he was called, had a good meal he was invited to dinner every Sunday at Wagner's house. But he always put his pets before himself and from time to time Wagner would get a message *'Busi is ill'* or *'Busi is expecting her kittens so I can't come today'*.

Busi was the matriarch of Gottfried's extended feline family and as a former colleague of Mind recalled, she was:

'his very dear friend of many years standing who strolled nonchalantly among his brushes when he was painting as if she knew what he was doing, but for her master she would never have become famous, and she was proud to be so honoured'.

Her name, Busi, is the German form of 'pussy' and she is easily recognisable as the tortoiseshell and white cat playing with her kittens on many of Mind's drawings. On his self-portrait she sits beside him looking on with proprietorial satisfaction. Mind saved Busi's life and some of his other cats by hiding them when in December 1809 magistrates ordered a local cull of cats in Berne following a rabies outbreak. He never got over that terrible disaster and grieved all his life for those that were lost.

THE RAPHAEL OF CATS

Fame found 'little Friedli', in the form of Madame Vigée Le Brun; celebrated artist, court painter to the Royal family and friend of Marie Antoinette. When Madame's latest canvas was rejected from the Salon she knew that her friendship with the Queen had placed her life in danger and she wisely left France for a four year painting tour on the Continent and Russia where she was eagerly commissioned by European royalty. Her husband, an art dealer had remained in France and his wife regularly sent work back to him to sell. Meanwhile, Sigmund Wagner had become influential in Berne where he launched the *Alphirtenfest*, a national Swiss festival. It was there that

Busi and Her Kittens.

Watercolour portraits of Mind's favourite cat.

Kunstmuseum. Berne.

he met 'the famous Mme Le Brun'. She visited them he said:

'to obtain some of our Mind's work, shrewdly observing that these masterly pieces would be acknowledged as such, even in Paris. It was she who described him as 'The Raphael of Cats' a name which has stuck'.

Once the celebrated Mme Le Brun had given Mind her generous accolade, the picture buying public could not get enough, his prices shot up and his work gained entry into many noble drawing-rooms, including the King of Württemberg and the Emperor of Austria.

Probably unknown to himself, Mind achieved a shift in the perception of the role of cats in art. He moved them from the position of stage prop in genre paintings or children's portraits to centre stage – as single subjects deserving their own space. His studies of children with animals and those of his own cats including Busi mothering her kittens reveal remarkable technical skill as well as a touching innocence. Some of his pictures set in a fantasy world may have been produced to order, perhaps to satisfy a less earnest market. In an Arcadian setting of architectural arches and artistically crumbling ruins of dream like beauty a bemused tortoiseshell cat (with familiar Busi markings) pauses in mid-strike on a mouse. There are mice everywhere so has she really captured the fattest, the juiciest? This is a dilemma in a cat's paradise. The tables have turned in a companion work where a cat is imprisoned in a golden cage while mice play around Tom and Jerry fashion, to

tease him. The parent mice have even brought their little ones to see the big captive beast.

When Herr Freudenberger died, his widow took over the everyday running of the business and Mind continued to occupy his small Spartan, garret room on the premises. No doubt, the people who made big profits from Mind's artistic talents were Frau Freudenberger and the Le Bruns. But to 'little Friedli', who had given so much, money was of no interest; he didn't understand it or want it. He had his art and his cats.

Gottfried Mind died of a brain haemorrhage at the age of 46 in November 1814. The Press honoured his passing with the same amount of coverage as a head of state.

Busi with her kittens. Watercolour portrait.

Swiss National Library, Prints and Drawings Department: Collection Gugelmann.

In England towards the end of the eighteenth century, animal welfare was becoming a contentious issue. Campaigners were eager to remind the public of unpalatable truths, but traditional attitudes of rights of ownership and power were difficult to overcome.

THE ANIMAL WELFARE CRUSADE

In October 1772 the Reverend James Granger preached a sermon from his pulpit in Shiplake, Oxfordshire against the everyday cruelty inflicted on animals; he spoke from his own personal convictions with no backing from the Established Church. His congregation, mostly small farmers and landowners was outraged and viewed his homily as interference in their proprietorial rights over their animals. The Reverend Granger's outburst was followed in 1776 by Humphrey Primatt's *Duty of Mercy and the Sin of Cruelty to Brute Animals,* suggesting for the first time, that cruelty to animals is a sin. At the time, bulls and bears were commonly baited for entertainment; horses worked until they dropped, dogs made to draw heavy carts and work treadmills, cats caught and skinned alive for the fur trade. Influential artists and writers joined the campaign in a bid to nudge the public conscience. William Hogarth produced his set of controversial illustrations 'The Four Stages of Cruelty' as if to hold a mirror to the depravity and gratuitous cruelty to be seen everywhere saying, *'If my pictures have the effect of checking cruelty to dumb creatures, I am more proud of being their author than I should be of having painted Raphael's cartoons'.*

As there was no legislation for the protection of cats, prosecutions against fur traders could only be brought under a 'Paving Act' when it was proved the offender had thrown carcasses into the street, consequently many of those involved got off free. The welfare of cats – and dogs – had little priority for legislators at the time committed to the banning of higher profile events such as bull and bear-baiting rather than the horrors of the slaughter house and slum street. It was difficult enough to get a sympathetic hearing in a parliament dominated by the landed gentry but the mere hint that domestic animals might be next on the agenda was to invite ridicule – and did! In a House of Commons debate in 1821 on the treatment of horses and cattle one member remarked that if such lunacy were to become law, he would not be surprised if it were followed by a Bill for the protection of dogs – *'and cats!'* added another, *'to laughter so loud'* reported *The Times* correspondent *'that the rest was drowned out'*.

FORMING THE HEARTS – AND MINDS – OF CHILDREN

The slogan of the early animal welfare campaigners *'catch 'em young'* was defined in James Granger's *'An Apology for the Brute Creation'*. 'This discourse is not only intended for such as have the Care of Horses and other useful Beasts: but also for children and those that are concerned with forming their hearts'. Similarly, from Humphrey Primatt in 1776:

'The minds of children are both tender and susceptible and are open to instructions by which parents may lay a sure foundation for reverential love, but if they suffer the child to commit acts of cruelty they harden them.'

What is the use of tantalizing that poor cat, Mary. page 2.

Sophia and Mary by E Wallis. 1820.

Caption: 'What is the use of tantalizing that poor cat Mary' said her twin sister Sophia, 'You had much better learn your lessons'.

Mary: 'I wish to teach pussy to beg; look how tedious the little animal is; as often as I put her up does she scratch and struggle to break loose from me'.

Forgotten Children's Books, A W Tuer 1898.

The unpalatable truth, that children at the time were not being taught to respect their pets but looked upon them as a live extension of their toys – expendable and easily replaceable – was about to be addressed.

Authors – mainly women – were ready to meet the challenge of persuading children to show compassion for small

Two Cat Authors. Early picture postcard

creatures through their books; garden birds, trapped and sold to live in cages and pet dogs and cats often mistreated in the nursery. In 1786 Mrs Sarah Trimmer was first off the mark with her best seller *Fabulous Histories for the Instruction of Children in Their Treatment of Animals*. A rambling story of the Bronson family and a nest of garden robins with the Disney World names of 'Dicksy', 'Flopsy' and 'Pecksy'. Mrs Trimmer has no mercy for the two bad boys next door who are depicted as vicious and depraved. Boys are usually the 'baddies' in these stories where they either get their just punishment or sometimes they may even be converted.

The way that children treated their nursery pets, is illustrated in a story dated 1820 where a little girl torments her pet cat by trying to make it perform tricks like a dog. This was by no means unusual; kittens were commonly dressed up in clothes or pushed around strapped into prams as if they were merely an extension of their nursery toys.

CATS PICK UP THEIR PENS

Cats were given a voice, the opportunity to write in the first person and narrate their own adventures through the growing number of popular cat books of the time. In Mary Pilkington's *Marvellous Adventures* (1802); Elizabeth Sandham's *Adventures of Poor Puss* (1809); and the anonymous *Felissa, or The Life and Opinions of a Kitten of Sentiment* (1811), the stories are inventive and contain shrewd observations on contemporary society. In *Felissa* there is an amusing 'send up' on the snobbish social pretensions of Persian cats. Most of these books follow a similar pattern; our cat heroines begin life with well-to-do families, are condemned and victimised for crimes they did not commit and after many wanderings, at last find loving homes. All follow the tradition of the 18th century picaresque novels as in Henry Fielding's *Tom Jones*. Our feline heroines would have recognised the world of Jane Austen except that Miss Austen's morally impeccable people and romantic images of love and marriage are replaced by some unpleasant glimpses of Georgian

Dame Dearlove's Ditties for the Nurse.

'So wonderfully contrived they may be either sung or said by Nurse or Baby'.

Published 1820 by John Harris,

Life and Adventures of Poor Pussy. Pussy Tells Her Tale.

Hand coloured from Illustrations by Cruikshank.

Read's Story Books, 1856.

upper middle class dysfunctional family life. Husbands rarely at home, wives continually off to parties and balls, children pampered, disobedient and left to run wild under the casual protection of uncaring servants.

In *Dame Dearlove's Ditties* we are given a good example of an attempt to brainwash toddlers in their nurseries to be kind to animals with a lullaby about a little girl who wants to protect her favourite cat from being savaged by their guard dog, Towzer. Fond of her cat and a sensible girl, she points out the practical benefits of keeping her larder free from mice.

Considering that all these stories were written by upper middle class authors for upper middle class children, the rural poor come out well. Perhaps the odd scoundrel here and there, but the majority are represented as hard working, God-fearing and good natured; willing to offer a home and a bite to eat to a cat down on its luck. In *Adventures of Poor Puss*, Tabby, who sounds rather prim, stays with a group of beggars, two men a woman and three children. The men, ex-sailors in the Royal Navy have been badly crippled in action and unable to work:

'They led very orderly lives' she reports, 'the woman was teaching her children to read. They lived in a barn till the owner turned them out and after that in a tent. But what little they had to eat poor Tabby came in for a share, nor did anyone offer to ill-treat me all the time I was with them'.

A later publication but still on the same theme of kindness to animals; you do not need to be rich to show mercy and give charity. Pussy relates to her friends how her wealthy owners turned her out in the snow for killing their pet canary. Pussy no doubt overstepped the mark when she did the dreadful deed and she confesses that her motive was jealousy because her young mistress was neglecting her in favour of her pretty new songbird. Pussy wanders about and is found by some rough boys who tie a saucepan full of pebbles to her tail and laugh heartily at her struggle to get free. Old Hodge the ploughman comes to her rescue and takes her back to his wife to share in their modest fare and catch the mice in their cottage.

Any Victorian child lucky enough to own a copy of *Read's Story Book,* with its forty hand-coloured illustrations, would probably have a magic lantern in the nursery as well. Pictures were projected from glass slides with the aid of limelight, on to a wall or screen. Here we see Poor Pussy as she shows her lantern slide – *'Greeting Old Hodge With a Friendly Purr on his Return From Work'.* Using the parlour table gas lamp for illumination, we have the latest technology, as well as a happy ending:

'When Hodge from his ploughing would come home at eve,

'I'd run out to meet him, nor would you believe;

'How gently he'd stroke me, how pleased he would be,

'As I purred him a welcome then jumped on his knee.'

Pussy Welcomes Old Hodge As He Returns From His Work.

Life and Adventures of Poor Pussy. Reads Story Book. 1856.

With hand-coloured illustrations.

Frontispiece: Dame Wiggins of Lee and Her Seven Wonderful Cats, a humorous tale written principally by a lady of ninety, with hand coloured illustrations. 1823.

While she ran to the field,
To look for its dam,
They were warming the bed
For the poor sick lamb:
They turn'd up the clothes
All as neat as could be;
" I shall ne'er want a nurse,"
Said Dame Wiggins of Lee.

For their kindness he had them
All drawn by his team;
And gave them some field-mice,
And raspberry-cream.
Said he, " All my stock
You shall presently see;
For I honor the cats
Of Dame Wiggins of Lee."

To shew them his poultry,
He turn'd them all loose,
When each nimbly leap'd
On the back of a Goose,
Which frighten'd them so
That they ran to the sea,
And half-drown'd the poor cats
Of Dame Wiggins of Lee.

Dame Wiggins of Lee and Her Seven Wonderful Cats.
With hand coloured illustrations. A K Newman and Co., 1823.
a.- The sick lamb.   b.- Riding with the farm team.   c.- Riding the geese.

The early feline friendly 'moralities' were not the only cat stories on offer. The rise in the popularity of cat books from 1800 onwards produced some classic gems, mostly rhyming fantasies with tom cats the boisterous heroes of many. *The Comical Adventures of Old Dame Trot and Her Cat* and *Dame Wiggins of Lee and Her Seven Wonderful Cats* went through many later editions; both are comedies in a domestic setting about genial old women and their pet cats. Dame Wiggins dances a jig in spite of her gout along with her multi-tasking pets. Dame Trot's cat rises first thing and makes breakfast. She shaves the dog who she decides is far too furry and spends the rest of the day admiring herself in the mirror in her fashionable clothes. Dame Wiggins' cats are all boys living in a happy pantomime world, having killed all the mice they are employed around the house, till she packs them off to school. They rescue a sick lamb which they lay tenderly on the Dame's own bed with a warming pan. They go flying on the backs of the local farmer's geese and so delight him with their antics that he presents the Dame with a ham.

Some of these fictional cats were long familiar characters from the past such as *Dick Whittington and His Cat*, first published as a ballad in 1641 and many prose versions later, seems to have caught the English imagination: Moncrif (the French author of *Les Chats*), when in London in 1713–14 on a diplomatic mission was amazed at the number of 'Whittington and Cat' inn signs.

Dick Whittington and His Cat.

Hand-coloured Illustration

Dick purchases his cat for a penny from a woman who assures him it is a very good mouser.

Grant and Griffith London 1854

Puss set sail on a merchant ship bound for the Barbary Coast where he caught all the mice in the Palace of the ruling Sovereign and Consort. Dick was generously rewarded with 'chests of gold' from their grateful majesties.

The Surprising Adventures of Puss in Boots or The Master Cat.

Puss traps rabbits for his master who becomes 'Marquis of Carabas' by dint of his clever cat.

John Harris, London c.1830.

Puss in Boots, loveable rogue and cat super hero was originally an old folk story and yet another favourite, *The White Cat* was the invention of the Comtesse D'Aulnay. Both were translated into English and Puss went on to become a children's classic. *The White Cat* was often adapted for pantomime in the late 19th century but is now largely forgotten. Between them, Whittington's cat, the White cat, and the macho booted Puss embody the feline prototypes of their time – consummate mouser, cunning rogue, possessor of magical or black-magical arts. By comparison, the early 19th century cat stories reflect a fuller and more sympathetic understanding of feline nature. But this hardly prepares us for what was soon to come – the emergence of the native short-haired cat as a symbol of cosy Victorian domesticity.

Chapter 2

The Great Leap

From Stable to Drawing Room

***Times have changed Puss, you have** found some good friends and you are welcome amongst the celebrities and trend-setters of the day and even better, they are not afraid to stand up and say so. You have seen off those tiresome chattering pet monkeys and yapping lap dogs from the parlour. From now on it will be your turn to take your place on the couch beside the lady of the house – dozing on her lap, or warming yourself beside the fire. No nursery is considered complete without an incumbent kitten. As a patriotic cat you are at the scene of war in the Crimea, comforting home-sick troops. As you doze contentedly, seated on top of a tea chest in your billet, you have become a symbol of Victorian hearth and home.*

* * * * *

Over the many years of Queen Victoria's reign cats did something remarkable; they clawed their way up from stable to drawing room. The aspirations of a growing middle class – particularly in London – required no less than the ownership of a house with a horse and carriage in the stable. There, snuggled warm amongst the straw was a cat – often nursing kittens – whose job it was to keep down the vermin. The cat, male or female that fulfilled this important duty, would have been fed regularly by the servants working in the house. Many a fluffy kitten made the move upwards from stable to nursery in the arms of a young master or mistress to become a favourite household pet. Queen Victoria herself was a committed animal lover; her views are on record and they were forthright:

Kitten Worship.

Fashion Plate for Cassells Magazine
January 1888

'No civilization is complete which does not include the dumb and defenceless of God's creation within the sphere of charity and mercy.'

As far back as 1813 when she was only sixteen, she and her mother the Duchess of Kent, had *'very readily'* agreed to become patrons of the newly formed Society for the Prevention of Cruelty to Animals; and in 1840, three years after her accession to the throne, the Queen granted the Society the title of 'Royal'.

Cats had never been entirely without friends and admirers, but in the late 18th and early 19th century these were few enough that when they were also well known public figures like Samuel Johnson, Horace Walpole, the philosopher Jeremy Bentham, or 'the father of English pantomime' John Rich, it was seen as an eccentricity which attracted attention. Samuel Johnson who famously fed his cat Hodge on oysters had another cat named Lily 'the white kitling' and while Hodge was 'a very fine cat' Lily was described only as 'very well behaved'. She was possibly the house cat that preferred the kitchen while Hodge was Johnson's special companion.

Philosopher Jeremy Bentham's puss had the grand title of Sir John Langbourne, who ate macaroni at his master's table and was a known philanderer, having seduced all the she-cats in the area where they lived. In later life he repented, took holy orders, to become the Reverend Dr John Langbourne and was highly respected by all.

John Rich, actor manager of both Lincoln's Inn and Covent Garden Theatres earned the name 'father of pantomime' because of his innovative comedic slapstick and magical effects which moved pantomime a big step closer to the unique entertainment we know today. Rich was devoted to cats and on a visit to his lodgings by the famous actress Peg Woffington, she was amazed to see the great man surrounded by them, he was:

'lolling at ease holding a play in one hand and in the other a teacup. Around him were seven and twenty cats of all sizes colours and kinds. Toms and tabbies, old cats and kittens, tortoiseshells, Maltese, brindles, white, black and yellow cats of every kind. Some were frisking over the floor, others asleep on the rug; one was licking the buttered toast on his breakfast plate, another engaged in drinking the cream for his tea. Two cats lay on his knee, one was asleep on his shoulder and another sat demurely on his head.'

Not all puss's friends were famous, Mathew Cook was an old ferryman on the River Lea at Edmonton – sometime in the second half of the 18th century – where he played a vital role in a community dependent upon his services to see them across the water. Although described as living alone, he had for company sixteen cherished cats:

'all of whom he taught tricks.' Every morning and evening was practice time – before and after his work – one by one they would *'leap over his hands, joined as high as his arms could reach, and this afforded him much pleasure.'*
When the river rose, his home flooded and had to be visited *'over the meadows partly by cart and partly in a boat'* where he was found *'dangling a bit of scrag mutton before the best fire existing circumstances could produce in a room on the ground floor knee deep in water. All the time he called out to reassure his cats in the room above, where he had huddled them for safety.'* A true cat lover!

(Book for a Rainy Day. J T Smith. A Dictionary of Cat Lovers, by Christabel Aberconway)

Another true cat lover and contemporary of Mathew Cook the ferryman was Christopher Smart or Kit Smart as he was known amongst his intellectual peers. Smart was a poet, scholar and Fellow of Pembroke College Cambridge, when he developed mental problems and in 1756 was committed to Bedlam lunatic asylum and later to a debtors prison where he died in 1771. Smart's greatest consolation and only source of affection was from his cat companion Jeoffrey to whom he was deeply attached. In his fascinating and sometimes obscure poetic tribute to his friend *'A Song From Bedlam – For I will consider my Cat Jeoffrey'* there are two lines which never fail to charm today:

*'For he is of the tribe of Tiger.
For the Cherub Cat is a term of the Angel Tiger.'*

Poet Laureate and writer Robert Southey, made no secret of his love for the feline race; he wrote at length about their fortunes and adventures both in letters and in his book, *The Doctor* (1834) where they feature as the *'Cats of Greta Hall'* the house in Cumbria, where he and his family and that of his brother in law, the poet Samuel Coleridge lived. All his cats were given eccentric names such as 'Hurleyburleybuss' and 'Marquis Macbum' who had no less than six other official titles. Macbum as he was known, was dearly loved and when he died, deeply mourned by everyone, even the servants. When their black cat named 'Zombi' (after the Chieftain of the Palmares negroes in Brazil) disappeared, he was replaced by a 'Black Tomling' named Prester John but following a gender discovery, his name was hastily changed to Pope Joan. 'Hurleyburleybuss' had eyes

A Christmas Family Party.

Illustrated London News. December 1847

'*of a hue between chrysolite and topaz*'; he was a mysterious cat that came and went – more of a lodger than a resident. The mystery was solved however, when he was spotted one day '*walking towards the Hill*' but they never found out who else had '*the honour to be his (other) owner*'.

(A Dictionary of Cat Lovers by Christabel Aberconway).

The English – who were known to prefer their dogs – were now making space in their homes for a more manipulative newcomer – the cat – and he knew exactly where he was going.

Just like Queen Victoria at that time, the well-to-do luxuriated in domestic life and enjoyed nothing more than to assemble their extended family to join them on special occasions such as Christmas and New Year. In the Christmas issue of *The Illustrated London News* of 1847 a picture entitled *A Christmas Family Party*, shows a cat and kittens in the centre foreground; a small girl sits with a cat on her lap and on the right another child appears to be stroking a cat seated on granny's lap.

A REMINDER OF HOME

Even more significant is the cat that appears on a painting with a very different background by John d'Albiac Louard, a freelance war artist with the British forces in the Crimea. In his picture *The Welcome Arrival*, later exhibited at The Royal Academy, two officers on the left are sheltering with Luard himself seated right,

in a barrack hut. A crate of provisions, a gift from relatives in England is opened up and there are pictures from magazines pinned on the wall. One man is gazing intently at an image of a dear one back home but the focal point is the little tabby cat, rescued as we know, from the ruins of Sevastopol – now basking in the warmth of the stove. Taken as a whole, the picture encapsulates the domestic virtues and values of Victorian middle England, steadfastly maintained even on a foreign battlefield and a reminder of Sir Henry Bishop's still familiar song '*There's No Place Like Home*'.

In a letter home to his father in 1855 from HQ, Sevastopol, Luard wrote:

'*My rat trap has been very useful in the stables, but a nice old Russian cat has just increased our establishment by four kittens. I think she will keep the rats off, however, I only wish she could do the same for the fleas.*'

A WELCOME GREETING. (See p. 165.)

The New Arrival.

Children greet their newly-arrived kitten which had come by rail; a common means of transporting cats and other small animals especially to and from cat shows.

Little Folks Magazine 1880.

The Welcome Arrival. John d'Albiac Luard. 1857.

National Army Museum

CATS AT HOME

The silent entry of cats into the hearts and homes of Victorian England went largely unnoticed. But in 1852 *Chamber's Edinburgh Journal*, a popular magazine with a family readership, mentions this domestic change as an established fact:

'*In this country, at this time, cats have superseded parlour favourites decidedly more mischievous in their habits. It is not the least merit of the cat that it has banished from our sitting-rooms those frightful mimicries of humanity, the monkey tribe; and as to the little dogs,*

Tray, Blanch and Sweetheart, although we are not insensible to their many virtues and utilities, we care not to see them sleeping on our hearth-rugs, or reposing beside our work-tables.'

The first cat show in 1871 was almost twenty years in to the future when an anonymous correspondent drew attention to the wretched lives of London's feral cats and their more affluent domesticated relatives. The letter appeared in the *Illustrated London News* 1853 and the writer notes the different faces of the 'house' cats and the 'yard' cats:

'the affable faces of cats which are noticed – perhaps playfully talked to, – and the fierce and moody countenance of those neglected creatures which in London and elsewhere grow half or wholly wild, among gardens, yards, and outhouses, picking their living as they can. The two classes seem to belong to different species. The well kept and well

treated house cat seems rather civilized than tamed; the neglected and too often persecuted brute outside the window has relapsed in to a skulking savage, the natural playfulness of their species having entirely vanished.'

In a gardening article which appeared in *Cassells Magazine* in 1891 the subject of these wretched semi-wild creatures is once again raised:

'Cats are the bane of London gardens. It is impossible by any cleverly contrived system of wire netting or barricading to keep them out. Really there should be a London cat tax. This would prevent the howling hordes of hungry animals, making day as well as night hideous by their cries. The London cat cannot be happy. It is not in the nature of things that he should be so. It is often a kindness to put him out of his misery. He has – I am speaking now of the common or garden-wall cat – a hunted slinking look and his poor mangy coat shows, alas! traces of the brutality of London Street arabs.'

This does not make comfortable reading. The lives of country cats however, sound much better. In *A London Child of the 1870s* the autobiography of M V Hughes, she describes a much more benign and complex feline hierarchy on a country estate in Cornwall, owned by relatives, where she and her family used to holiday each summer:

'Artistic homes and how to make them.'

Article in The Lady's World. 1886–7

"FORGET YOURSELVES A LITTLE WHILE."

Forget Yourselves A Little While.

The Girl's Own Paper 24 December 1881

'The first charge on the estate was a personal visit to every animal. Cats first. These were divided into four distinct classes, and the cats seemed to be as snobbish as the humans. The parlour cats were Persians, sat on laps and best chairs, and would never recline in the kitchen, although they would stroll casually about when a savoury smell was prevailing. The kitchen cats seemed to be always having kittens in the fathomless linen cupboard at the top of the stairs. If they ventured into the dining-room it was to hide under the table in the hope of gain. Orchard cats prowled round the yards and stables, quite self-supporting, never *venturing indoors unless under stress of hunger… Then there were the office cats. The 'office' was a side wing of the old house, where accounts were kept and where the farm-men were paid on Saturday. Behind it was the 'slaughter-house' which I never had the courage to explore… a few lean and humble-minded cats managed to exist in this borderland, despised by both parlour and kitchen cats.'*

Christmas in the New Hospital for Women.

The New Hospital for Women at 222 St. Marylebone Road, London, was not only devoted exclusively to the treatment of women, but was staffed by women doctors, administrators and nurses. In the illustration, a small black cat wearing a collar is visiting patients.

The Girl's Own Paper. 1883–4

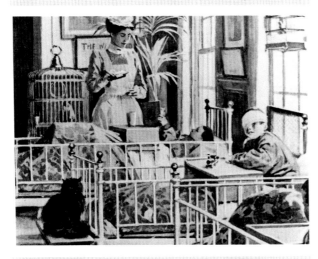

A ward at Cheyne Walk Hospital for Children in Chelsea where a resident fluffy black cat makes himself very much at home, in keeping with the Florence Nightingale tradition. Founded in 1875 'in one of the pleasant old river-side houses and known as the little hospital by the river'.

The Sphere - Supplement, November 1901.

Many educated Victorians took the sensible view that owning a pet not only kept children amused but taught them an awareness of personal responsibility and a kitten was often the preferred choice. *'In an ideal nursery'*, writes an authority in *The Lady's World* magazine, *'pets, flowers, toys and a good sofa should always be found.'* The accompanying illustration includes the resident cat.

CATS AS THERAPY

In her influential – and at the time contentious – essay *Notes on Nursing* (1858), Florence Nightingale recommends domestic pets as therapy for invalids. As a semi-invalid herself in later life, she put her theory in to practice; cats were her constant companions and consolation. From time to time she gifted a kitten or two from her own family of cats to London hospitals under her own patronage to brighten the lives of patients on the wards. *'The tortoiseshell pussy has gone to rejoice Kings College Hospital'* she notes in a letter to her father

Sketch by Edward Lear of himself and Foss, 1885

in 1861. Nine years later when her cat loving Parisian friend Julius Mohl fell ill on a visit to England, she offered to lend him some of her *'rumbustious boys'* (tom cats) to amuse him while he was confined to bed.

(Letter to William Edward Nightingale 12 December 1861. Wellcome Institute, and letter to Julius Mohl, September 1870 Public Record Office.)

THE OWL AND HIS PUSSY-CAT
The Love Story of Edward Lear and His Cat Foss

'The problem here is the mice.' A remark made by the Abbot of a remote monastery perched on the cliffs of Mount Athos to Edward Lear – who was on one of his sketching tours in northern Greece – may have been the inspiration for Lear's most famous nonsense poem *The Owl and the Pussy-cat*. The Monks had a strict rule – no female creature was allowed within. Unfortunately, the message hadn't reached the mice and the place was overrun. To get rid of them the abbot had decided to import twenty score of male

Last photograph of Edward Lear, 1887

cats which had to be ferried over from the mainland. Lear was enchanted and, as the personification of the owl of his poem, his cat Foss is undoubtedly the pussy-cat. At their Italian home, Villa Emily in San Remo, as Lear sketched, sunned himself and picked the caterpillars from his stocks and passion flowers, a contented Foss was his constant and often sole companion.

Before the arrival of Foss, Lear had a cat named Potiphar or Potta for short, a gift from Madame Poplawska, a near neighbour. Clearly a cat of parts, his behaviour was *'truly exemplary, he disports himself around the room sits on one knee quietly or rushes out and climbs up an olive tree'*. In a matter of weeks he

was *'Potiphar the excellent, an unrivalled person in this establishment'*. Later in the summer of 1872 Lear went to England while Georgis, his Greek manservant, visited his family in Corfu taking Potiphar with him for safekeeping. But there the cat somehow wandered away and got lost. Back home at Villa Emily, Lear resumed work and began *'thinking about cats'* but Georgis, no doubt conscience stricken at having lost Potta wasted no time. In Lear's journal for 4 November 1872 he records the arrival of Foss and that Madam Poplawska again was *'pleased to have found the twin brother of Potta disposable, who is to come tonight'*. A Greek word for brother is 'aderphos' so the newcomer was called Foss for short. So began the loving lifelong relationship between the artist and his feline companion to be immortalised in Lear's many affectionate caricatures.

Like many another eight month old cat, Foss was tooth and claw happy. He was discovered ripping up Lear's letters and papers and was banished to the kitchen but within weeks he had *'insinuated himself back to the fireside. He climbs up the chimney but comes down again on his own and he catcheth grasshoppers.'*

THE TALE OF A TAIL

Foss was a tabby with bold tiger-like stripes, but he had another distinguishing feature; he was minus part of his tail. Lear's first mention of this was in a letter written with characteristic wry humour to his friend Chichester Fortesque in February 1873 inviting him to stay for a few days at his villa in picturesque

San Remo. Lear then teasingly offers to show him *'an infant school and the Municipality, a lemon grove, a railway station and several poodles,'* (Lear detested dogs), *'not to speak of my cat, who has no end of a tail—because it has been cut off.'* The superstition that docking a cat's tail will prevent it from straying seems to have been fairly widespread in continental Europe. Lear himself had remarked on it when he was in Milan in 1838 where it was a common sight. But in Lombardy, where cats were *'better treated,'* he found an even more eccentric custom where all the cats had their ears pierced *'with little bows or tassels of blue or pink ribbon depending therefrom!'*

Sixty years later Helen Winslow *(Cats for Pleasure and Profit 1911)* also encountered the practice of tail docking in parts of rural France. Foss was already eight months old when he arrived at Villa Emily so his tail was probably docked while he was still a tiny kitten. In the last photo of Lear ever taken, purposely contrived to show Foss curled up on his lap we are left with hardly any sign of the celebrity feline; only the end of his tail shows as he makes his hurried departure. So it must have been a very small cut and not quite the hatchet job we see in cartoons of Foss. But Lear was a born humorist and shrewd enough to spot a good idea. The unforgettable stumpy tail became Foss's personal signature.

Like many cats, Foss was perceptive and seemed to sense when his master was planning to leave on another work project. In the autumn of 1873 when Lear left for India he wrote *'Foss would persist in following me right down the steps and into the road'* and had to be carried back by Bernardino, the gardener who was to look after him. Foss must have felt abandoned, for on Lear's return eighteen months later he would have nothing to do with him at first, preferring to camp outside. But within a few days he had forgiven and forgotten and it was *'dinner, Foss assisting'* once more at Villa Emily. When in June 1878 Lear left for Genoa, *'poor old Foss came to see me off, keeping close to me and butting me with his head.'* Lear undertook these sketching expeditions to exotic locations in order to supplement his modest investment income. His work sold well to a market ever eager for novelty. But to arrive at these far-flung beauty spots was physically demanding and often dangerous. He longed for peace and quiet, to potter in his beloved garden and work at leisure on his paintings. In a letter to Fortesque he mentions that Georgis is on holiday: *'I am alone with Foss my cat in my big house, where I am writing this at my open window in sight of the bluest sea and sky and Ipomoea flowers possible.'* Georgis was also feeling his age and unwell so Lear sent him home again the following year to recover. He was as fond as Lear was of Foss, and wrote little messages for him from his sick-bed: *'Tell him I will bring him a triglia fritta'* [fried red mullet].

Disaster struck in 1879 when property developers acquired land in front of Villa Emily and began to build a new hotel, blocking the view of the sea. Although Lear's property was greatly reduced in value, he managed to raise enough cash

to move further along the coast and build Villa Tennyson – named after the poet laureate as Villa Emily had been named after the poet's wife. Their new home was built to the same design as Villa Emily *'so that Foss should not become confused'*. Lear was visited in 1882 by Henry Strachey who left a detailed and touching description of Lear's ménage towards the end of his life:

'At breakfast the morning after I had arrived, this much-thought-of, though semi-tailed cat, jumped in at the window and ate a piece of toast from my hand. This was considered an event: when visitors stayed at Villa Tennyson, Foss generally hid himself

'Foss Dansant', from Edward Lear's 'The Heraldic Blazon of Foss the Cat'

in the back regions, but his recognition of me was a sort of 'guinea stamp' which seemed to please Mr. Lear greatly.'

Strachey recalls how, at the end of his visit Lear took out some old envelopes and drew on the back of them a series of heraldic pictures of his cat. These were for Strachey's sister then eight years old.

'After he had done seven, he said it was a great shame to caricature Foss, and laid down his pen.'

Lear struggled on but when his friend Franklin Lushington visited him in November 1885 he found him *'sadly aged and feeble, – very crippled at times with rheumatism – totters about within his house'*. *'Fell over Foss and hurt my nose'*, Lear notes, but his diary entries became fewer. December 30th 1886: *'dined with Foss only, rather good mutton'*, and the following April 30th: *'Foss is a comfort!'* *'Foss is dead'*, he writes to his friend and patron Lord Aberdare on 29 November 1887:

'and I am glad to say did not suffer at all – having become paralysed on all one side of him. So he was placed in a box yesterday and buried deep below the fig tree at the end of the orange walk.' *'My poor friend Foss'*, he continues, *'who ever has known me for thirty years, has known that for all that time Foss has been part of my solitary life… all those friends who have known my life will understand that I grieve over this loss.'*

Lear's grief at the loss of his friend must have confused his mind over Foss's age which was probably no more than sixteen years. With Foss gone, Lear's loneliness and isolation were complete. He died on 29 January 1888. So the Owl and his Pussy-Cat passed away – to be reunited, who knows? *'To dance hand in hand'* in some whimsical other world.

Another cat loving author, Charles Dodgson, better known as Lewis Carroll, cast eight year old Alice Liddell as heroine

Pussy's London Life. - With Madge / The Rescue / Irate Milkman / A Fierce Dog.
From Aunt Louisa's Birthday Gift Book, published by Kronheim & Co., 1865,
with chromolithographic illustrations.

are Arthur, Amy and Emily?' he asks. 'Do they still go up and down Finborough Road and teach the cats to be kind to mice? I'm very fond of all the cats in Finborough Road.'

('A Selection from the Unpublished Writings and Drawings of Lewis Carroll', ed. Stuart Dodgson Collingwood, 1899.)

THE FASHIONABLE FELINE

Long haired cats were still rare enough in the early 1800s that they cost more than most people could afford. A longhair was seen as a luxury, giving rise to snobbishness and a 'must have' culture amongst the nouveau riche. Here was an opportunity waiting to be exploited by cat breeders, photographers, writers of juvenile fiction and many others who saw a way to turn an honest penny.

In 1832 Sir Walter Scott thought it worth noting in his journal that he had seen a Persian cat at Lord Yarmouth's home. Charles Dickens's fondness for cats is well known from his daughter Mamie's biography, but she does not say what variety they were. However, Dickens himself, in an article in his magazine *Household Words* in 1857, writes of his 'cherished Angora tom'.

Children's fiction writers soon began to introduce the new longhaired breeds of cats in to their stories. The hapless Persians were typecast as spoilt, pampered and vain; this provided a convenient nail on which to hang a plot and also as a cautionary tale for children – as we see in '*Pussy's London Life*'. For a more discerning market, books were often illustrated using the latest technical

of 'Alice's *Adventures in Wonderland*' (published 1865) where she encounters the famous disappearing Cheshire Cat of characteristic feline mystery. Alice worries continually over her own real life cat, Dinah and as she descends the rabbit hole she hopes '*they'll remember [Dinah's] saucer of milk at tea-time*'. Dodgson had

a fondness for cats and in his letters to another child, Agnes Hughes, he invents stories about her three cats who invite themselves into his house where he gives them rat-tail jelly and buttered mice for breakfast. They try to help him by opening all his books at page 50, but unfortunately, spill glue on them. '*How advances in chromolithographic print which greatly enhanced the beauty of an exotic feline heroine on the page.

Mary Pilkington saw both humour and irony in these thoroughbred cats whose owners claimed a Persian pedigree from long ago. In her *Marvellous Adventures or the Vicissitudes of a Cat* (1802) she attempts a satirical send up where an aristocratic 'Milord' – no less – presents the heroine, Tabs to her Ladyship:

"Permit me Madam, to offer one of the most valuable of the Persian breed."

"Beautiful creature!" exclaimed her Ladyship in raptures at my appearance, "I declare I never saw so lovely an animal."

In the anonymous *Felissa, or the Life and Opinions of a Kitten of Sentiment* (1811) the opening sentences are again written to ridicule the pretentions of those who consider themselves superior because they follow the fashion for longhaired cats. Felissa, the heroine, begins her story:

'I can assure my readers that I was born of an illustrious race, that their time will not be wasted in reading the Memoirs of a cat "whom nobody knows". My mother was a native of Persia, and named Lily on account of the exquisite whiteness of her fur, which was said to rival the snow.'

Lady Grilda is a titled, vain and beautiful white Persian cat who goes to London with her mistress for 'The Season'. Grilda escapes through a window in order to show off her 'graceful form and beautiful snow white coat' to the London cats. Once on the street, she is chased by a fierce dog; she escapes only to find herself

shut in overnight in a basement coal shed and on her release she is pelted with stones by some boys. She tries to drink milk from a pail, falls in and gets a smack from the irate milkman. She wanders lost and hungry, her white coat now matted and soiled. Eventually she meets beggar girl Madge Dunlee, who sits and shares her morsel of bread with the little stray. As it happens, they are right opposite Grilda's home – where she is spotted. Madge is rewarded with food and is to be 'clothed and taught'. Grilda is a wiser cat.

LA GRANDE MADEMOISELLE and the NIGHTINGALE CAT DYNASTY

As one of the most famous women in British history, Florence Nightingale led an eventful and often dramatic life. She always remained true to her cats; they were her lifelong companions and her loving friends who calmed and consoled her as she struggled bravely against poor health. In spite of her heavy work load she found time to correspond about her cats, in particular with her great friends Julius and Mary Mohl in Paris. With no quarantine restrictions, there was regular two-way traffic in desirable kittens across the English Channel between Florence and the Mohls. As we read her letters to and from family and friends we realise what a big part her beloved cats played in her life – and sometimes even that could be eventful and dramatic.:

'I broke down all at once and fled to Malvern with a little cat' wrote Florence Nightingale in a letter to her close friend Mary Mohl. Her work with the

British war-wounded in the Crimea had damaged her health and although her most lasting achievements lay before her in the reform of nursing care and public health, she never fully recovered her own. As a genuine cat lover, Florence often gave a home to a needy stray, but many of her cats from 1859 onwards were descended from one which her friends, Mary and Julius Mohl had imported from Persia to their home in Paris. 'La Grande Mademoiselle' writes friend and biographer Kathleen O'Meara, 'was an important member of the family:'

'She had her supper every evening in the drawing room but sometimes on a Friday evening when Mary held her salon she was forgotten or kept waiting. She would then take it uninvited, out of the milk jug. One evening, a lady who was unaccustomed to the ways of the house, exclaimed 'Oh dear! Look, the cat is lapping the milk!' 'Yes, she is making a nice little supper' smiled her kindly old hostess indulgently, and went on with the conversation.'

La Grande Mademoiselle arrived sometime in the early 1850s. She had a long life but sadly died of starvation during the siege of Paris 1870–71 along with many other animals and Parisians, while the Mohls were taking refuge in England. Mary and Julius sometimes looked elsewhere for kittens to send to friends or family in England if none of their own were available. A letter from Mary to Hilary Bonham-Carter in Winchester reveals the details of one of their searches:

'We have all been kitten-hunting. I have

found one not more than five or six weeks old; it is not as pretty as I could wish because it is white with a few spots but it will have a bushy tail; it is the very short tails when they are very young that turn out the best. But it will be a pretty kit; it has a very high forehead, the hair is soft and good, I think it is the best we have seen. Your kitten was born at an artist's, perfectly mad about cats. I will put it in a basket with a bottle of milk, poor love.'

'Poor love' indeed. There were no quarantine restrictions on cats entering Britain before 1886, and rail links with France were already fast and efficient. A few years later Mary herself was able to travel from London to Paris in around twelve hours. But by freight, to the Bonham-Carters' home near Winchester can hardly have taken less than thirty-six hours. A long stint for a six week old kitten in a basket with a bottle of unaccustomed cow's milk, handed out, presumably by any railway employee who happened to concern himself. Why go to the trouble when cats were just as available in England? *'The hair is soft and good'*, Mary wrote, *'and this one will have a bushy tail'*, so perhaps it was a Persian cross.

The kittens which the Mohls sent to Florence Nightingale are variously described as 'fine Persians' and as 'yellow and striped, almost like tigers' which again suggests hybrid longhairs. They were born of or directly descended from Mary and Julius's Grande Mademoiselle, for Flo refers to her in a letter of 25 February 1871, (directly after the siege of Paris) as *'the great ancestor of our family's cats'*. Some of these cats were certainly installed in Flo's lodgings at Hampstead by September 1859, when her mother, Fanny, visited her there. She found Flo lying in bed with a fire and the window open… *'reclining on pillows in a blue drifting gown, her hair picturesquely arranged'*. There were *'several pussy cats'* in the room and one was *'lying on her shoulder'*.

The problems Florence had with some of her other cats are on record in letters to Mary and Julius Mohl, such as bad boy Thomas in 1856:

'I do not like to give Thomas away. He is stupid, ignorant, thievish and dirty. I don't think anyone would keep him and be kind to him as we are. He is so handsome that people come from afar to see him. It was a shock to find he was not contented with one wife. Pussy had four kits more beautiful than herself, of which Thomas killed one and then hit his eldest daughter a tremendous whack on the side of the head, which she survives. However the only reason which makes the servants bear Thomas is that they think that Pussy would pine without him.'

At one point she did find what she hoped was a suitable home, but *'he did nothing but disgrace himself, climbed up the chimney and had to be put in the bath-tub; quarrelled with another cat in the garden.'* So she took him back. Thomas turns up again some months later, rehomed at Embley Park (the Nightingale's country estate in Hampshire) with at least one other of Flo's cats. She had sent them at a time when her health was causing concern. *'I can only lie quietly in bed'* she wrote to her uncle, Sam Smith in June 1861. *'If I tempt myself by getting up I am entirely laid aside for three or four hours by the exertion of dressing.'* At the family home at Embley Park it seems Tom finally settled to a happy life because in August her father returns to the subject:

'Can you bear to hear of the two waking, sleeping, insinuating creatures who alternate between the two sides of the window sill. Tom, the now familiar one – the other more occupied with its field-mice which it seems to treat as if it loved them.'

In 1865 Florence moved into her own house – 35 South Street in London's West End, bought for her by her parents who felt it preferable to paying bills for her rooms at the Burlington Hotel. (In spite of her dedicated services to the nation she never received any personal financial support from Government.) Here she began to rebuild her little cat family. In a fragment of a letter from Mrs Mary Watson, possibly housekeeper at Embley Park in reply to an unknown enquirer, *'the last two kittens sent from here to Miss Nightingale were thorough bred, Topsy being the mother and Tom the father.'* (From the Verney family papers.) Writing to Julius Mohl in February 1868 she tells him how *'the little cat'* – the one she had taken with her when she fled to Malvern:

'wanted to get married. So I presented to her the two greatest parties in England, Messrs Bismark and Benedek. She would have neither of them. She wants me to invite a hideous low cat out of the street – I won't.

But I said she might go out if she liked. But she is too shy.'

In January 1871 Paris surrendered and the Prussians lifted their siege. Julius Mohl returned to their home in Paris to find some bombs had fallen along the windows in the garden but the house was spared. 20,000 citizens had been slaughtered or died of hunger, public buildings demolished or burnt down and for the Mohls, their Grande Mademoiselle was a sad casualty of the war. On her return home, Mary Mohl writes to her friend Minnie that she is feeling better, but:

'if only I had a kitten to kiss I should be better still. Florence has a beauty for me; if you can find anyone that will bring me my kit in a basket I will do everything in my power for them, so pray set your fertile brain to work.'

Minnie was quick off the mark, for a week later Mary writes again:

'Thank you my dearest Minnie, for getting me my kit. Oh, if you knew the feverish longing I have for it! … Don't be angry; it is a fact and can't be helped.'

The courier was a Monsieur Liebreich, who was on a brief visit to England and it must have been quite a stint both for him and the kitten for, after collecting it from Flo in South Street he travelled to Bath to see his daughter before returning to France via Dover. Mary Mohl was ecstatic:

'Dearest Minnie, Liebreich brought the lovely creature last night at seven o'clock,
and it began to play as soon as it got out of the basket. I was in perfect raptures. He, poor soul, brought it straight from railroad, and had so much trouble, I felt remorse, and expressed it. He said there was nothing he would not do for me.'

Julius Mohl died in 1876 and Mary lived on until 1883 and died cuddling her favourite cat, a beautiful white Angora who was said to dote on his mistress, although he was polite to others. He was found a comfortable home with some friends where he seemed very happy; but at the end of a year he *'took himself off'* and everyone was in great distress about him. It was found that he had *'fixed himself in a Bonapartist family, having very ungratefully, changed his politics'*. Mary of course, had detested the former Emperor Napoleon III, whom she nicknamed 'Celui-Ci' or 'The Great I Am'.

A RAILWAY DISASTER

In 1885 Florence was travelling back to London by train with her cats after a stay with her sister Parthenope and brother-in-law, when she lost a kitten.

At Watford station, her kitten 'Quiz' jumped out of the window on to the line and scampered off out of sight. Florence immediately 'pulled rank'. *'I summoned all the station masters in England'* she declared. *'He of Watford'* was sent back along the line to find the missing kitten and he telegraphed Florence later that evening: *'Cat found, not hurt.'* Quiz spent the night in the Euston parcels office and returned to her grateful mistress next morning *'shocked but alive and singing'*.

Flo's victories over entrenched bureaucrats in the army, the government and the medical profession had been won not by open confrontation but by persistence in the face of continual setbacks and disappointments. In 1891 she reflects – *'I learn the lesson of life from a little kitten, one of two. The old cat comes in and says, very cross, "I didn't ask you in here. I like to have my Mum to myself!" And he runs at them. The bigger and handsomer kitten runs away. But the little one stands her ground and when the old enemy comes near enough kisses his nose and makes peace. That is the lesson of life, to kiss one's enemy's nose, always standing one's ground.'*

FASHIONABLE PHOTOGRAPHY: CARTES-de-VISITE

Proud owners naturally wanted to preserve a record of their cats, but cats are notoriously fidgety in front of the camera. The problem was not helped by the slow exposure times of the emulsions used in early plate glass cameras so cat subjects needed to be calm and composed. The Carte-de-Visite was an innovative form of visiting card with a photograph to replace the traditional name and address. These quickly became a popular collecting craze. Kept and mounted in to a multitude of Victorian albums, they eventually outstripped their original purpose. These delightful small cards covered a wide variety of subjects and competition for custom between photographic studios was keen; most used the reverse side of the card as an advertising space where they printed their own business details.

Whitie at Home

WAITING FOR MILK   ROTARY PHOTO

'Waiting for the Milk' by E Landor.

A picture postcard published by Rotary Photo.

Fading images of cats long ago on cartes-de-visite, c.1870–80.

In the group of domestic pet cats shown here, Whitie and the black Persian are both longhairs and probably rather special. The others are obviously also much loved pets, the little girl bears an uncanny resemblance to the young Alice Liddell of 'Wonderland' fame. Framed in the oval and probably a tom, is a cat that appears to be in charge. The cat nursing her kittens, although not a very clear photograph, is a touching picture of cat contentment. All these images are affectionate tributes made by the Victorians to their cats.

PICTURE PERFECT

How to pose frisky, obstinate cats to their best advantage must have exercised the minds of the early cat photographers who did not have the advantages of today's fast cameras. Their methods were slow and laborious, but somehow they managed it. One of the first, according to his own account, was Thomas Fall, who had his own studio in Baker Street in central London. Interviewed for *Lady's Realm* magazine in 1897, he claimed to have been photographing pet animals for forty years. He attended all the London cat and dog shows and had recently snapped some of Queen Victoria's dogs at Windsor, the Princess of Wales' pets at Sandringham and the Prince of Wales' hundred year old cockatoo. He believed he possessed hypnotic powers to make his sitters feel at ease. The firm of Russell and Sons also of Baker Street and with a second studio at Windsor, specialised in cats; a number of their shots of famous show winners and their famous owners, were published in contemporary books and magazines. The negatives survived as late as 1955 when Russells went out of business but sadly, the original plate glass negatives ended up on a tip.

Landor picture postcards:

Five O'Clock Tea./Celebrating Queen Victoria's Birthday.
Two's Company, Three's None./Swing High, Swing Low.

PATIENCE, PERSEVERANCE AND PROMPTNESS

This was the mantra of the most famous and the most fashionable of these virtuoso Victorian snappers of celebrities and their cats; Edmund Landor is on record as a photographer at a studio in Knightsbridge, London in 1905 having moved on from his premises in Ealing. By modern standards Landor's pictures look contrived but in his own day they led to endless speculation. How had he managed to take them? Were they faked in some way? Landor relates how on passing a shop window where some of his cat photos were on display:

'I chanced to overhear a lady remark to a friend "Yes they are very good, you know how they are done of course, stuffed kittens placed in position and photographed that's the way".'

Other theories, that the cats were hypnotised, that they were held in position by hidden assistants, were all denied. Landor disclosed some of his professional secrets in *Penny Magazine* July 1904 with '*How I Catch My Cats for the Camera'*. In fact he used whatever new techniques he had to hand at the time, so he was able to combine

Special Offer.

Barkers Photographic Department, Kensington

two or more photographic prints – trimmed, patched together, artist retouched and re-photographed – to create a 'second generation' negative. One obvious example is his picture of some 25 cats, posed in rows on a staircase, which nevertheless called for considerable technical skill in synchronising the images.

In reality the logistics were challenging. First, to obtain the right sort of cats – or more often, kittens. Ordinary 'moggies' wouldn't do and owners of pedigree cats were reluctant to lend them out, odd kittens borrowed from different sources often didn't hit it off. In the studio they were hell bent on exploring; so to attract their attention, an assistant armed with an array of interesting rustling objects such as pampas grass was a good start. Meanwhile, the photographer had to *convey the idea that you are their best friend on earth and not a monster luring them to destruction*. So Landor's motto had to be *patience, perseverance and promptness*. Perhaps Landor's historical importance lies not so much in the development of 'pet art' photography, where others in Britain and America were also involved, but exploiting the commercial potential. Recently introduced colour process printing for the newly booming picture postcard market sold his cuddly pedigree kitten images in such vast numbers that over a hundred years on they are still easy to find.

Many professional studios found it profitable to offer a print service to

A picture postcard dated January 1913 from a breeder in Surrey to a Mrs Challis in Ongar Essex:

'Are you still considering black kitten to breed from? I may part with my last one. It's a good one, but not very cheap, because', she adds, it had gained a 'Reserve' – a minor award – at a recent show.

'A Glamorous Miss MarCooley' on a Picture Postcard

supply copies of amateur snapshots as picture postcards. Prices were amazingly low at Barkers even for the period, 144 cards works out at less than a penny each. Barkers were out to catch 'Business men and Hotel and Boarding House Proprietors'. However, professional cat breeders found it an ideal way to advertise their latest thoroughbreds while proud owners also wanted pictures to show off their handsome, often prize winning animals.

Others took a more 'entrepreneurial' approach, as revealed on a picture postcard dated July 1906 seemingly from one teenage cat enthusiast and picture postcard collector to another. Pictured, is Miss MarCooley a blue or Chinchilla Persian owned by the sender; her intention is to sell further copies to her friend, who will then sell them on at a profit to friends of her own. The message reads:

'Dear Maxey, shall not charge for this card, it will do for your album. If you only have 6 they will be 3/6 [three shillings and sixpence] and you can have 12 for 4/6. Can you do with that many? We can get them thro' by the 24th.'

There is no shortage of cute cats pictured on sheet music; often published as piano accompaniment for dances held mostly at private family parties. Availability of gramophone recordings helped promote new dance rhythms but sheet music sales continued with such novelties as *The Old Cat's Whiskers Are Turning Grey* – a sad tale of a pet moggie who no longer pulls the local toms – a novelty Fox-Trot of 1923. Felix the Cat and his surreal adventures – on the theme that cats have nine lives – featured in numerous cartoon films. The 1924 Fox-Trot *Felix Kept On Walking* was a smash hit, recorded in 1927 by the Paul Whiteman band, then at the height of its fame.

On the theatrical front the Theatre Museum lists only one London production of *Puss in Boots* up to 1873.

SCENE FROM THE BURLESQUE OF "WHITTINGTON AND HIS CAT," AT THE LYCEUM THEATRE.

Whittington and His Cat at the Lyceum Theatre 1845.

Illustrated London News.

CHRISTMAS CATS.

THAT Cats can be taught is well known,
But still it some wonder arouses,
To see the three Pussies here shown,
All three, at one time, drawing houses.

There is first the *White Cat* at the Lane,
And then *Puss in Boots* at the Garden;
While the Surrey brings *Whittington's Cat*
'Tother two the stage-race to run hard in.

'Christmas Cats.'

Punch Magazine Jan.19.1878.

This was at Covent Garden in 1818 when for some unexplained reason, the audience not content with booing the performance, wrenched up the seats and tore down the curtain. *Whittington* fared better: it was produced at least six times between 1814 and 1853 and as the century moved on kept a permanent place in the annual standard repertoire. *Puss in Boots* seems to have been less popular with three listings, 1873, 78 and 87. Cat themed productions peaked between 1891 and 1900 with fifteen London showings of *Whittington* and at least four of Puss also the inspiration of six new comic or sentimental 'cat' songs, six 'cat' dance titles and numerous polkas and quadrilles. By the early 20th century the tide had turned with only five London productions of *Whittington* and four of *Puss in Boots* between 1901 and 1914. The *Puss in Boots waltz* in 1903 ended the long sequence of cat titles. The next did not appear until 1914 and they were both one-steps. The 20th century had arrived.

Punch Magazine comments on a unique event when at Christmas 1877 for the first time and probably the last, the three classic cat stories are being presented simultaneously at London theatres: *The White Cat* at Drury Lane, *Puss in Boots* at Covent Garden, and *Dick Whittington* at the Surrey.

That Cats can be taught is well known,
But still it some wonder arouses,
To see the three Pussies here shown,
All three at one time, drawing houses,
There is first the White Cat at the Lane,

Cat-themed dance music:
a) *The Pussy Quadrille. 1857* ©*The British Library Board, h 911.*
b) *Impudence Schottische. 1893* c) *Our Pet Pussy, Easy Set of Quadrilles.1874*
d) *Les Chats Quadrilles. 1847.*

And then Puss in Boots at the Garden;
While the Surrey brings Whittington's Cat,
'Tother two the stage-race to run hard in.'

Songwriters were kept busy churning out material for the benefit of a new generation of amateur after dinner entertainers. There were also comic music hall hits of the time like *'Pussy had another Sardine'* (1900), *'She lives on the Isle of Man – Where the Cats have got no Tails'* (1907), and *'My Wife's Sister's Cat'* (c.1909) popularised by the comedian Harry Champion and available through the new medium of recorded sound. Others had already begun to satirise the sentimentality of the previous half century. The later Victorians would probably not have approved of poking fun at their revered Laureate, Tennyson's lines with *'Come into the garden, Maud, Where the Black Cats snarl and moan.'*

THEY FLY THROUGH THE AIR WITH THE GREATEST OF EASE THOSE DARING YOUNG CATS ON THE FLYNG TRAPEZE

From a popular song
first published 1867

By now, cats were pursuing their own theatrical careers. A hundred years after the old ferryman Matthew Cook had taught his cats their clever tricks in his flooded riverside cottage, feline acrobats were pulling in the crowds with their elaborate stage performances at venues in Britain, Europe and the United States. The German trainer Herr Techow was internationally famous; his cats were dressed as circus clowns with pointed

Leaping through a fiery hoop.

One of Professor Frederick's Performing Cats.

hats; walked on their front paws and stepped across a row of Indian clubs. At the time, concerns for animal welfare were being raised generally, but when writer Helen Winslow interviewed him and his cats in the late 1890s at Keith's Theatre Boston in the United States she reported '*His cats seem particularly fond of him; uniting in a chorus of purr-miaows and scrambling all over him when let out of their cages.*'

It was not uncommon for these showmen to give themselves bogus titles to impress a gullible audience. 'Professor' Fredericks, a well known impresario had a cat troupe that often performed at popular London venues such as the Oxford Theatre and the Royal Aquarium. Fredericks had begun his career as a lion tamer with a circus in South America and earned a reputation for his bravery and 'mystic power' over animals, but admitted that domestic cats made him more money. The 'Professor' who was interviewed by Louis Wain in 1888 for an article in the Illustrated London News, said that his assorted team of cats included all breeds and sizes, from English tabby shorthairs to white Persians as well as Portuguese and Spanish cats.

Their performance began with an act called 'Climbing the Pole' performed by Arco, a Portuguese puss who, having reached the top, disappeared inside a small box conveniently placed for a titbit. The 'Pole' the Professor said, was the hardest trick in the repertoire because the higher the cat climbed, the further he was from his master's control; sometimes declining to go up at all! Nevertheless, on this occasion, Arco went up and down like a seasoned trouper. The star of the show was Sloper, a big black shorthair who was his master's pride and joy though he had only cost sixpence. Training began by teaching the cats to sit up and beg, but, said the Professor, '*only one in three is trainable and blacks take most readily to the work. Cats are willing to work, but are unreliable; Sloper may walk the tightrope five nights in a row, but on the sixth he refuses. When the fit is on them, I let them rest, I never use force and never strike an animal.*'

'I THINK I WILL JUST WATCH THE SHOW TONIGHT'

The unreliability of cats is amusingly recalled by contemporary writer Agnes Repplier who saw at the Folies Bergère in Paris, a troupe of performing animals with just one cat. '*The cat condescended to leap twice through a hoop and balance prettily on a large rubber ball. After that she went up a ladder, had a wash, then curled up and went to sleep. Twice the trainer spoke to her but she took no further*

Walking over champagne bottles

Professor Frederick's Performing Cats

interest in him or his entertainment.' A friend who saw the same cat on another night reported *'she did wonderful things, came down the ladder on her rubber ball, played the fiddle, and stood on her head.'* But the night another friend saw her *'she did nothing at all except to cuff one of the monkeys that had annoyed her – I presumed she was there for decoration!'* Cats enthralled Victorian audiences with their remarkable acrobatics and it all had to be stage managed. The 'Professor' used two large boxes or 'safe houses' placed either side of the stage; from these, the cats made their entrances and exits. Harrison Weir gives a detailed description of the opening act when the cats walked along the tops of a row of chairs placed across the stage. The process was repeated with variations several times, with two cats crossing together, one passing over and the other under the horizontal rung between the seat and the top of the chair. The stage cleared and a plank was raised in position with a row of champagne bottles standing on it at intervals each with a flat disc on top. The cats stepped out confidently *'from disc to disc without displacing or upsetting a bottle'* while their companions on the plank below *'threaded in and out between the bottles'.*

A STAR PERFORMANCE

Then it was the turn of Sloper the Spanish black shorthair to thrill the audience by walking the tightrope, but an even greater challenge awaited him; white rats were produced to sit at intervals along the rope. Carefully lifting his feet over each rat, Sloper completed his journey and remarkably, they were so pleased to see their old friend that they leapt on his back and rode home in triumph to deafening applause. The grand finale featured a spectacular jump through the fiery hoop by leading stars of the show. All now ghosts from the past. Fascinating curiosities of cat history for cat lovers everywhere. Raise your glass to the memory of Sloper, Arco and all the cool cats of the Victorian Variety Theatre.

Sloper, the skilful black cat and his 'ratty' friends all performed with 'Professor' Fredericks' troupe at the Royal Aquarium London.

Drawn by Harrison Weir from his book 'Our Cats and All About Them', 1889.

Chapter 3
The Cult of the Cat
The First Cat Show and The National Cat Club

Now Puss, you are the star turn; the centre of attraction at the first cat show in 1871 where you enter a glitzy 'showbiz' world. Pedigree breeding is a pastime enjoyed by royalty and aristocratic ladies, who spare no expense in providing luxurious living quarters for cats that can sometime sell for as much as a racehorse.

These admired breeds are popular with the public who flock to see them at cat shows – followed up by reports in the Press and reviews in popular magazines.

For the first time, cat breed characteristics are defined by Harrison Weir, organiser of the first cat show and registered by the newly formed National Cat Club.

*****

A PET CAT FOR A PRINCESS

We know that Queen Victoria liked dogs; they travelled with her from one royal residence to another and throughout her reign she accepted gifts of rare breeds. This did not mean, as has been claimed, that she disliked cats. There is ample evidence that both she and Prince Albert shared the view of their contemporaries that cats made good companions for small children. Their eldest child

Victoria, the Princess Royal, was just two years old when they gave her a cat as a Christmas present. On 25 December 1842 the Queen notes in her journal:

'Pussy came down with me [from the nursery at Windsor Castle] and was quite enchanted with a large black cat, a sort of Persian cat, with long silky hair'.

['Pussy' was the nickname given to Princess Victoria and was a pet name commonly adopted by Victorians for very young children.]

The Cult of The Cat

Lady's Realm Magazine 1900

Photos of Silver Lotus and Dossie by Landor of Ealing; and Lavender Blue by Goshawk of Harrow

The following day she continues:

'Pussy was at our luncheon, so happy with the really beautiful black cat we had bought for her; it is so tame that it will eat out of her hand, and lets itself be caught and played with, being very gentle and good'.

Just where this black Persian came from is a matter of speculation. Although the Queen uses the words *'bought for her'*, in the 1840s thoroughbred cats were not yet commercialised in Britain. There were a few amateur breeders, mainly aristocratic ladies. One of these hobbyists was Lady Mary Cust, the pioneer writer on cat care who kept a small breeding cattery. Lady Mary had been Woman of the Bedchamber to the Queen's mother [the Duchess of Kent] and her husband Sir Edward Cust was the Queen's Master of Ceremonies. It is quite possible that Princess Victoria's cat – the first known to hold an appointment at the British court – was from Lady Cust.

Many years later, Lady Aberdeen told a charming story of a royal visit to Haddo House, her husband's family seat, in the late 1840s or '50s. As a boy he and his brothers and sisters had a cat called Shelley and they were under strict orders to keep her and her kittens out of the way of the visiting royal party. But Shelley escaped and rushed out of the house pursued by the children and Prince Albert who joined in the chase. She recalled: *'Shelley was captured and brought back to be presented to Queen Victoria, one of the few cats who ever had so great a distinction.'*

Artist Friedrich Keyl started as a protégé of Edwin Landseer and was commissioned in 1848 to draw and paint some of the horses, animals and domestic pets on the royal estates. Among the pets in the collection is this fine study of an Angora cat belonging to the royal children.

In fact, all the royal children seem to have shared their parent's fondness for animals, and cats in particular. Prince Leopold, the Queen's fourth son is to be seen with one on an archive photograph.

An Angora cat. A pet of one of Queen Victoria's children.

Drawing in crayon and coloured chalks by Friedrich Wilhelm Keyl, c.1850.

Royal Collection of Watercolours and Drawings. Royal Collection Trust © Her Majesty Queen Elizabeth II, 2019

In later years both King Edward VII as Prince of Wales and Princess Helena were both caught up in the Cult of the Pedigree Cat… of which more later.

THE GAMEKEEPER MENACE

Princess Victoria kept dogs and cats at her home, the Neues Palace at Potsdam, after her marriage to Crown Prince Frederick of Prussia in 1858 and corresponded with her mother about their pets. To judge from these letters the German aristocracy were far less indulgent towards domestic animals than their English counterparts. Gamekeepers were a threat everywhere it seems and even Florence Nightingale lost her beloved 'Muff' to a gamekeeper's bullet at her family home at Embley Park. On the 17th of August 1880 the Crown Princess Victoria writes to her mother:

'I am quite ashamed to feel as upset as I do today, but we have a tame pussy that belonged to Waldie [Waldemar her youngest son died the previous year at the age of eleven] and of which we are all extremely fond. A quarter of an hour ago a stupid Jager goes into the garden and seeing the dear little thing sitting on the road shoots her, then hangs her against a tree and cuts off her nose. I cannot help crying, she has been our constant companion for three years. We took her when a kitten. This morning as usual she was lying on my bed and purring and rubbing her head against my cheek. She always shared my tea of a morning and this morning she was particularly affectionate. She used to know Waldie's step so well she always ran to meet him. It seems the keeper gets a little money for shooting cats. Poor little animal, I was so attached to her and loved to feel her sitting on my lap or shoulder – or on my pillow and with her pretty purring sound! I am foolishly fond of cats you know. The girlies are in great distress. I shall not take another pet certainly. People are so brutal here with poor dogs and especially cats. They think nothing of ill-using and killing them and I cannot bear it. The children are comforting themselves by burying her in Waldie's garden by the side of his favourite dachshund who was driven over in May 1876 if you remember. He was dreadfully unhappy about it.'

Three days later she resumes:

'The man [the keeper] was neither punished nor reproved. Count Eulenburg only laughed and Wille [her eldest son, Kaiser Wilhelm II] who does not understand a sentiment for pets thought it was laudable zeal in pursuance of his duty, as cats might harm pheasants, so I got very little sympathy.'

These letters brought a prompt response from her mother who writes back on August 11th:

'… and now let me say how horrified and distressed I am about your cat! It is monstrous… and the man ought to be hung on the tree. I could cry with you as I adore my pets. When they belonged to a loved and lost object it must be quite a grief!… Our

keeper once shot a pet one of Beatrice's [her youngest daughter]. Keepers are very stupid but none would dream of mutilating an animal here! I think it right and only due to the affection of dumb animals who (the very intelligent and highly developed ones) I believe to have souls, to mourn for them truly and deeply.'

On a more practical note she adds,

'We always put a collar with V.R. on our pet cats and that preserves them' [from the attentions of trigger-happy gamekeepers].

BREEDING FOR PLEASURE – AND A LITTLE PROFIT

In 1869 an advertisement was placed in the 'Exchange' column of *The Queen* magazine, one of many that began to appear around that time:

ANGORA CATS.

Very handsome, longhair, one white the other tabby (female) would exchange for goat harness. Open to offers. – Monkswood.

By the 1850s, the supply of exotic longhaired thoroughbred cats began to catch up with demand as more amateur breeders and so more kittens emerged. Over the next decade, the cost of Persians and Angoras tumbled dramatically. In this gradual process of commercialization, France was some twenty years ahead of Britain where semi-professional breeders on a small scale did not emerge until the early 1870s. These advertisers, largely amateur ladies and some gentlemen breeders, kept their anonymity by using a pseudonym; in

cases where they did give their home addresses, they suggest large properties in country districts. The gentility of the time saw any kind of financial transaction made through the columns of a newspaper as vulgar and demeaning. Advertisements were carefully worded in the form of proposals to 'exchange' an item for something of equivalent value. The range of these exchanges – to acquire or dispose of a thoroughbred cat – with a price tag from £1 to £6 – gives an insight into the tastes, interests and activities of the upper middle classes. For women, jewellery was popular; rings, brooches, lockets, jet, onyx, chatelaines and vanity bags; ten yards of good black silk, an ostrich feather or collectors' items such as postage stamps, greetings cards and books by Scott and Dickens. Some more bizarre items that advertisers wished to move on included a bagatelle board, a *'light Bramah pullet of late hatch but valuable'*. *'A machine for crimping'* – and one for *'purifying butter;'* a *'good singing canary'* and *'a useful surgical enema instrument in box'*.

Some advertisers were almost too honest, like Baugh-y-Bey Millesh (24 April 1869). The writer is obviously a man, who reveals much about himself. It is to be hoped the poor old Rumpy found a kind home:

'I have a Rumpy (Manx) cat which squints with one eye, to exchange.

A good field glass or a central fire breech loading rifle preferred; but am open to offers. It must have a kind mistress, as it is a great pet; but

I am about to part with it, as I have no further use for the creature.'

However, when it came to animals of uncertain ancestry, the truth sometimes became more flexible. A Persian or Angora cross might have been worth between five and fifteen shillings, but a thoroughbred was worth much more and it was not always easy for the untrained eye to spot the difference. Many a cat with a dubious identity was passed off as thoroughbred. Mrs Kinchant, a knowledgeable fancier writing in *The Cat* in the late 1880s tells how she had been ripped-off in this way three times in a row. She paid in advance for a cat advertised as a *'beautiful Chinchilla'* which turned out to be *'a mangy brown tabby'*. Another *'lady breeder'* sent her a specimen which was neither Chinchilla nor pure bred. The third came on approval and again disappointed, as it was *'a washed out nonedescript'*.

From the early 1870s a few semi-professional breeders began to emerge under their adopted pseudonyms. The names; *'Remembrance'*; *'Vertumnus'* and *'Railway'* were among the first in the advertisement columns who regularly offered to exchange their animals for other goods. Pure bred cats imported from France, Spain, or directly from Persia were more highly rated than those of the second or third generation born over here and could fetch the equivalent of seven or eight pounds each. The following are typical advertisements in *The Queen* magazine at the time:

'Several grand specimens of the pure-bred

imported Angora cats which being so enchantingly ornamental are now prized so much as drawing room pets.' (Monks Wood. October 1870).

'I have several beautiful Angora kittens of various colours bred from foreign cats of great size and beauty with long soft hair and large bushy tails. Wanted green lancewood venetian blinds.' (Mrs Clarke, Alconbury Hill House, Huntingdon. July1870)

'I have just brought from Paris a pair pure white French cats male & female, beautiful eyes, long hair, very valuable. Exchange for rich seal and grebe furs.' (Annie, 1870)

The traditional livestock show was always an important event on the calendars of country towns, where farmers competed for trophies; showing their finest sheep, cattle and pigs. Fancy pigeons and exotic poultry were often included or merited their own show. The 'First Exhibition of Sporting and other Dogs' show was held at the Crystal Palace in 1870. A show devoted entirely to cats would have been regarded as a joke: unlike dogs, they served no sporting purpose. Nevertheless their social credentials had risen dramatically over the two decades leading up to 1870 and now they were only waiting for a 'white knight' to come to their rescue.

THE FIRST CAT SHOW

'Cometh the time cometh the man…' And in the cause of the cat the man was Harrison Weir (1824–1906). As a young man he had been apprenticed to George Baxter, famous founding father of mechanised

colour printing. However, Weir was also a gifted artist and abandoned the printing trade for book illustration and graphic design. Like many Victorians he was multi-talented; a member of the Royal Horticultural Society, a judge at poultry and pigeon shows and author of a definitive work, *Our Poultry and all about them*, said to have taken him 25 years to complete. As an artist he specialised in animals and illustrated numerous cat stories for children, notably *The Memoirs of Puss and the Captain* (1854) which went through many editions.

Weir also kept pet cats; and to judge from his still sought-after classic *Our Cats and all about them*, knew more about feline physiology and psychology than most people of his time. Perhaps it was the success of a dog show at Crystal Palace in 1870 that inspired him when he wrote in the introduction to *Our Cats*:

Cat Show Poster.

The striking cat's head motif designed by Harrison Weir for the first cat show in 1871. Printed black on yellow; a simple design with a modern look.

'I conceived the idea that it would be well to hold 'cats shows' so that the different breeds, colours, markings etc., might be more carefully attended to, and the domestic cat, sitting in front of the fire, would then possess a beauty and an attractiveness to its owner unobserved and unknown because uncultivated heretofore. Prepossessed with this view of the subject, I called on my friend Mr. Wilkinson, the manager of the Crystal Palace. With his usual businesslike clearheadedness, he saw it was 'a thing to be done.' In a few days I presented my scheme in full working order. I also made a drawing of the head of a cat to be printed in black on yellow paper for a posting bill [poster] Mr. F. Wilson the [Crystal Palace] Company's naturalist and show manager then took the matter in charge.'

So it was that the world's first-ever cat show was scheduled to take place on Thursday, 13 July 1871 and the following day. (Most early cat shows ran for two days at least.) For judging, the animals were to be divided into twenty-five classes, mainly by colour, though a few classes were reserved for longhairs and shorthairs respectively and for 'exotics' like Siamese and Abyssinians – of which there were then only a few. Each class was to be judged by 'points of excellence' devised by Weir himself and not far changed to the present day except for the final category (adding a touch of light relief) where claimants were invited for the title of the heaviest cat to turn the scales.

The entrance fee for competitors was 3s.6d. per animal per class and the total prize money was £70. Not very generous it would seem, but enough to present each winner with a silver commemorative medallion. Admission to the public was one shilling per head.

PRESS SPECULATION – A CAT SHOW GAMBLE?

It was a remarkable act of faith on Weir's part and as he said 'many were the jibes and jeers thrown at me'. He wasn't sure in advance how many cats would present themselves; an aspect crucial to the success of the show and the sole responsibility of the exhibitions manager. It was reported that this unhappy man had to boost numbers by commandeering some of the cats employed in the Crystal Palace's kitchens and refreshment rooms – fine specimens, so it was said. The final head count was one hundred and seventy animals, a most satisfactory result. *Another awkward question: how would the cats react to one another, even though they were confined to separate pens?* The Press loved it and spread news of the forthcoming event through their editorial columns, arousing widespread public interest. The view taken by these newspapers and periodicals was amusement mixed with slight irony. The event may have been seen as an accident waiting to happen… that the first cat show may well be the last. What if a couple of hundred cats were to escape and turn on each other, the judges, or the spectators? Or if no competitors were to turn up at all? The possibilities were endless.

Punch magazine couldn't resist a whole page humorous piece all about famous people of the day, known cat lovers who might be providing entrants for the show. Mr. Punch showed a cartoon of a hideous looking creature with fangs – his own darling cat, 'Black Fairy' – which he was minded to enter in all twenty-five classes, but concluded it would be unfair to the other contestants, to scoop all the:

*'Prizes that none beside ourself could gain,
Should <u>our</u> immortal Mouser take the plain.'*

The Graphic pictured a group of fashionable ladies, agonising – could they bear to be parted from their precious Puss, to send her to the show? While the Daily Telegraph urged its readers on the morning of June 13th to 'hurry down [to the show] as soon as you have finished reading these lines'.

Harrison Weir himself recalls how travelling to the show by train, he encountered a friend who scoffed at the very idea of a cat show, but who agreed to come along with him:

'Inside the Crystal Palace stood my friend and I. Instead of the noise and struggle to escape, there lay the cats in their different pens, reclining on crimson cushions, making no sound save now and then a homely purring, as from time to time they lapped the nice new milk provided for them… As we passed down the front of the cages, I saw that my friend became interested, presently he said "What a beauty this is! And here's another." 'And no doubt said I, many of the cats you have seen before would be quite as beautiful if they were as well cared for, at least cared for at all; generally they are driven about and ill-fed, and often ill-used, simply for the reason that they are cats and no other.'*

The dignity and composure of the cats amazed the press. *'Unlike our friends*

The Cat Show at the Crystal Palace.

'Can we part with Puss?' Three elegantly dressed ladies face a heartrending decision.

Graphic magazine 22 July 1871.

the dogs', wrote *The Queen* magazine's columnist, *'whose yelping, barking and howling always render guidance to their location, the cats met the gaze of the crowds of visitors with almost regal impassibility'.* The Graphic reported *'such was the crush around the pens that at times it was impossible to see a cat'.* Weir's own blue tabby was amongst the prize winners. Though she was fourteen years old she was still among the best of her type. To mark her public debut he gave her a little silver bell to hang on her collar, and after her death he always wore it on his watch chain. He himself was presented by the Crystal Palace Company with an ornate silver tankard *in recognition of his suggestions and services'* and for his *'labour of love for the feline race, and acting without any fee or reward'*.

So successful was this world's first cat show that the Crystal Palace Company followed it up with another in November the same year. This was a risky gamble. The event was no longer unique and bad winter weather could easily reduce visitor numbers. However, the public came dressed against the cold in heavy overcoats and hand-muffs while the cats reclined on beds of straw to keep them warm. The show drew bigger crowds and more competitors than the previous one.

The *Graphic* magazine of 2 December gave priority with both a front cover spread and a leading article:

'Not many years ago, a public exhibition of the cat tribe would have been looked upon as an absurdity. But why an absurdity? asked Common Sense. Why should any collection of choice creatures be viewed as an absurdity? If it be right to exhibit shorthorns, Southdowns and pigs why should it be wrong to exhibit dogs or pigeons, rabbits or babies, barmaids or cats? At all events, cat shows have met with the approval of the public, and as regards the fair sex, are perhaps more popular than displays of any other domestic quadrupeds.'

Again, comparison is made between the *'relaxed aura of cat shows'* and the *'unpleasantly powerful collective odour, barking and growling'* at dog shows:

Cats at the First Crystal Palace show 1871.

Drawn by Harrison Weir

Illustrated London News.

'Glance by comparison at Pussy in the Show – surrounded by all her admirers. She reclines as calmly in the cage as if she were on the domestic hearthrug, and she receives the homage of the admiring crowd with the most gracious serenity of demeanour, merely evincing her gratification by purring like a Lilliputian water-wheel. But what a moral ordeal it must be!... "You darling creature!" "What lovely whiskers!" "What beautiful soft fur!" "I must stroke you behind the ears!" Philosophic pussy receives these compliments with equanimity, and is morally none the worse for them; but the human dandy would emerge from the cage so puffed out with self conceit that a society would at once have to be formed for his suppression. Gentle reader, go to the Crystal Palace today, watch the cats, and decide whether you could endure to be made so much of.'

In retrospect, the Crystal Palace show of December 1871 was the defining moment when cats finally won their credentials as chosen household pets. Such was the popularity of these shows

CATS AND CAT SHOWS

Cat Fanciers at the Second Cat Show.

The Graphic magazine front cover, 2nd December 1871, designed by artist and cat show founder Harrison Weir.

'Absence Makes the Heart Grow Fonder'.

A caring owner produces tit-bits for her cat out of her 'Gladstone' bag.

The Graphic magazine, 2nd November 1889.

The Jones's cat arrives in good condition at the Crystal Palace

From a set of drawings by Louis Wain.

Illustrated London News. 1884.

that within a year or two they were attracting not only Londoners but visitors from all over the country and the railway companies were running special excursions. Cat shows soon caught on in the provinces. In Birmingham the first show was held in 1873 and in Edinburgh two years later. At the Birmingham show the list of patrons included not only several titled people but the famous naturalist Charles Darwin FRS and the pioneer writer on cat care, Lady Cust. These 'Birmingham and National' shows were held at the Old Wharf, Broad Street Corner [a canal-side warehouse] and ran for as long as five days, from Saturday to the following Thursday with a break on Sunday. Owners who lived within travelling distance were allowed to take their cats home each evening provided they were returned to the hall by 9am the next morning. But many were 'cats from the country' who had come by rail; feeding them and cleaning their pens must have been a marathon task.

It was commonplace for cats to travel to major shows by rail, often despatched from long distances unaccompanied; leaving the organisers to sort them out on arrival at the hall. A story is told that a lady sent one of her she-cats to a show and the same cat was returned to her safely, so she thought. But some weeks later she found that all her other females were pregnant.

Midland Railway handbill for the National Cat Show London. 1873.

Advertising an excursion from Bradford, Leeds, Wakefield, Barnsley and Sheffield to the National Cat Show at the Crystal Palace, Monday 22 September 1873, a journey time of 7 hours 45 minutes. The return was on the following Friday.

So Handy Labels.

Purpose designed luggage labels for containers of 'cats in transit'.

Advertisement in Frances Simpson's Cats and All About Them. 1902.

According to J G Gardner (*The Cat being my Experience of Poor Puss*, 1890) the early shows attracted a quota of cranks and oddities:

'I was much amused watching the arrival of an exhibitor [at the Crystal Palace] many years ago, with quite a collection of cats – one in this pocket, one in that; two tied together with a bit of frayed rope; one led by a string, like an Irishman's pig. A small family were in a small hamper without a lid, and a very large specimen in a dilapidated bandbox without a bottom. How he got them together, kept them together, and took them home together was a wonder.'

As in London, the organisers of the Birmingham events were overwhelmed by their own success. In 1873 the number of people through the turnstiles averaged well over 6,000 each day, besides the *'many thousands'* who had bought tickets in advance. The *Birmingham Daily Gazette* reported *'since Monday there have been many thousands of intending visitors turned away, unable to gain admittance.'* One who did get in was William Gordon Stables, ex Royal Navy Surgeon, cat fancier, show judge and in later years a prolific writer of boys' adventure stories. Like Weir two years earlier, he was accompanied to the show by a friend – a local industrialist – a *'rough diamond'* who had never shown the slightest interest in cats. He ended up buying a kitten on the spot and taking it home with him in his overcoat pocket.

The public interest in cat shows seemed unstoppable; more and bigger shows, more visitors, more exhibitors, new venues all over the country. In 1886 the Crystal Palace show attracted four hundred entrants and in 1899 over a thousand. From 1899 onwards twenty thousand visitors a year were paying at the door. Writing in 1890 the Rev. J G Gardner remarked that even at *'mixed shows'*, where cats were shown with rabbits, cage birds and guinea pigs, *'the cat exhibit is the most frequented – even when it has been an afterthought it has proved a happy thought for the treasurer when the cat has been added.'*

THE FIRST OFFICIAL NATIONAL CAT CLUB

Cat shows were not just display cases and competitions for the feline elite but shop windows for selling them; the growing demand for distinctive animals by the late 1880s gave rise to commercialisation. The Cat Fancy, originally an amorphous group of amateur breeders and enthusiasts had first formed in the 1870s, and in 1887 became the National Cat Club – the first cat-related body to exercise any effective authority. The NCC laid down regulations for shows and defined the various 'points of excellence' by which the cats were to be judged. Harrison Weir had laid all the foundations and perhaps most importantly, established a stud book. It is sometimes overlooked that previously, though there were (so called) 'thoroughbred' cats, there was no such animal as a 'pedigree' because no accurate record of lineage existed.

With bogus thoroughbreds up for sale and a gullible public eager to buy, not surprisingly crooked dealers and self-styled 'breeders' were ready to pounce on unsuspecting cat lovers. J G Gardner in his *The Cat, being my Experience of Poor Puss* 1890 gives readers a list of 'don'ts'. Don't buy from dealers you know nothing about, or salesmen who know nothing about the kittens they are selling. And above all (following Mrs Kinchant's advice) don't buy from advertisements. Even at the cat shows things didn't always run smoothly and there were instances of breeders [or posing as breeders] selling the same kitten several times over, leaving their victims to sort it out with the organisers after the show while they disappeared into thin air. Louis Wain sketched just such a scene in the Sales Office at the Crystal Palace 1887 show; three smartly dressed women are arguing over the ownership of a small kitten who sits patiently waiting for the outcome.

Apart from rare breeds like Siamese, cats were classified for competition as long or shorthaired then by colour or markings and sometimes by sex. Within these parameters all the entrants started equal in the judges' eyes, regardless of whether they were nominally thoroughbreds or not. But the adoption of the new classifications for genetically 'pure' pedigree animals from around 1890 meant that all the rest (the vast majority) were marginalised by degrees, for show purposes. Although this was unavoidable, the NCC came under fire for its alleged bias in favour of the longhaired varieties. J G Gardner pointed out that at the 1888 (NCC) Crystal Palace show, two gold medals had been awarded for longhairs and only one for shorthairs. Even worse,

Disputing Claimants.

One of a series of 'Sketches at the Cat Show' by Louis Wain.

Illustrated London News October 1887.

The craze for Persian and Angora cats was now sweeping the whole country – not only trendy London and the South-east. A writer in *Fur and Feather* magazine in April 1890 describes a visit to a pet shop in Bradford, Yorkshire where she found:

'Persian and Angora kittens in every colour, grey, blue, black, white, as well as our old friend the Tabby, which was to be found there in all the glory of his frill, brush, and long silky fur – so great an improvement upon the sleek coat and whisp-like tail of our unpretentious English cat.'

HARRISON WEIR RESIGNS

it emerged that although any cat owner was free to enter shows organised by the NCC, only those who were members of the club were eligible for prizes.

From early on, special classes and prizes were reserved for the cats of 'Working Men', no doubt to encourage working people to take an interest and to care for their cats. *The Graphic* magazine patronisingly remarked – *'good mousing qualities are more regarded than an elegant appearance on the hearthrug'.* The Working Men's classes were well supported, but how do you define a 'working man' and /or his cat? Louis Wain reporting on the Crystal Palace show of 1899, praises the high standards of the exhibits, but was:

'sorry to see that some of the cats entered in the working men's classes are also entered in the ordinary classes; these, to my mind are only bogus working men's cats, and have no right to compete in the working men's classes.'

Going Home. Bona Fide – the Property of a Working Man.

Illustrated London News, 27 October 1883.

Not everyone agreed with this condescending relegation of our British shorthair and one was Harrison Weir who had accepted an invitation to become the first president of the National Cat Club in 1888. But the liaison was short lived and ended in recrimination. Weir had done more than anyone else over the past twenty years to improve and promote the cause of cats. In the preface of his second book *Our Cats and all about them* (1892) he angrily dissociates himself from the NCC and all its works:

'In my former edition of 'Our Cats', I wrote hopefully and expectantly of much good to be derived from the National Cat Club and of which I was then President; but I am sorry to say that none of those hopes or expectations have been realised, and I now feel the deepest regret that I was ever induced to be in any way

associated with it… I found the principal idea of many of the members consisted not so much in promoting the welfare of the Cat as of winning prizes and more particularly their own Cat Club medals, for which, though offered at public shows, the public were not allowed to compete and when won by members were misled into believing it was an open competition. I therefore thought it my duty to leave the club for that and other reasons. I have also left off judging of the Cats, even at my old much-loved show at the Crystal Palace, because I no longer cared to come into contact with such 'Lovers of Cats'.

Harrison Weir, the idealist who always put Cats first, was disillusioned by the new commercial world of cat show-business mixed with human greed. Ten years later he returns to the theme. Writing more in sorrow than in anger in his preface to Frances Simpson's *The Book of the Cat,* he explains that cat shows have not fulfilled his expectations:

'Why? Because particular breeds are catered for and run after. Why such breathless talk about long-haired cats, be they blues or silvers? This is not the cat breeding I want, I wish; and if I live, I hope to see far more of the 'harmless necessary cat' at our shows; for a high-class short-haired cat is one of the most perfect animals ever created.'

FRIENDS IN HIGH PLACES

The spectacular rise of 'Poor Puss' from the role of humble fireside cat to that of star status was much acclaimed in the pages of ladies' magazines. It is noticeable that the ingratiating tone adopted by these journalists reflects the new status of cats as pets and protégées of the royal family as well as many members of the aristocracy. Here, *Lady's Realm* magazine (August 1900) eulogises under the title of *'The Cult of the Cat'*:

'It is scarcely thirty years since the first cat show was inaugurated, largely through that good friend of pussy, Mr. Harrison Weir at the Crystal Palace. Yet in that short space of time how great has been the change in conditions of life of the harmless, necessary cat! The modern champion leads a luxurious life; she is a truly gorgeous creature, that reclines on silks and satins and whose toilet is equally as important as that of her mistress. The champion of the cat world is an aristocrat par excellence, whose will is law, and whose career is one long round of sunshine… in no branch of the animal 'Fancy' have ladies been more successful than in that which has been honoured and graced by Her Majesty the Queen, the Princess of Wales, the Duchess of Bedford, and those renowned artists and naturalists Mr. Harrison Weir and Mr. Louis Wain.'

Cats as Cup Winners. An appraisal of the Crystal Palace Cat Show by Leuty Collins.
Illustrated by Louis Wain. Windsor Magazine, 1900.

'It was less than twenty years ago that the feline tribe was looked upon as simply a necessary household appendage and allowed its domicile only in the kitchen. But the National Cat Club, whose admirable show takes place yearly at the Crystal Palace has proved that a great deal of interest is nowadays taken in the cat world – so much so that it would seem the study of the cat is becoming an absolute cult in itself, and that the animal's nineteenth century descent from the Egyptian idol is not in vain.'

CATS AND CORONETS

Ever since the first cat show, the appointments of administrative posts such as organisers, judges – and even many of the competitors – were fulfilled by members of 'high society'. Into the 1890s there arose a strange new phenomenon – a cadre of aristocratic lady breeders, farming pedigree cats on a previously unprecedented scale on their country estates. Not unlike tulip mania in Holland in the 17th century, in that it involved a large outlay of money, personal vanity and prestige. In photographs of these formidable ladies, they set out to confront one another not only with superior cats but more extravagant hats. Some of them, at least, were so self-centred and spoilt that tempers soon frayed. One visitor to the Crystal Palace in 1899 noted *'Some of the women exhibitors were so rude, I couldn't imagine why the judges didn't turn round and walk away.'* *Our Cats* magazine commented on the same show:

'It is to be regretted that even exhibitors of the fair sex should be so loud in their lamentations as to attract the attention of passers-by and the scene verges on the ludicrous.'

Such was the personal rivalry that one exhibitor is said to have tipped white powder over her competitor's black cat. At another, the show manager was obliged to retreat for his safety, behind a stack of chairs when some lady competitors took umbrage at something he had done or left undone and chased him round the hall.

CUSTOM-DESIGNED CATTERIES FOR FASTIDIOUS FELINES

To be the owner of a prize-winning cat became a status symbol. Prices rose to the skies. In 1900 a much-coveted Chinchilla was valued at £200. The tales got taller and in the United States another cat was said by Helen Winslow to have sold for as much as a champion racehorse. In Britain, the register of breeders and fanciers began to read like a guest-list for a royal occasion. In 1898 The National

Mrs. Frances Simpson and 'Cambyses'.

Mrs Frances Simpson, breeder, show judge and author of The Book of the Cat with her silver male Chinchilla 'Cambyses'.

Cats for Pleasure and Profit.
Frances Simpson. 1911.

Cat Club had as its joint presidents the Duchess of Bedford and Lord Marcus Beresford; the vice-presidents included Lily, Duchess of Marlborough, the Countess of Warwick, Lady Granville Gordon, the Hon. Mrs McLaren Morrison, the Countess of Sefton and Lady Smithfield. The Dutch cat painter Henriette Ronner, then at the height of her reputation, was an honorary vice-president and the popular cat cartoonist Louis Wain, the chief executive and secretary of the committee.

Contemporary journalists seem to have been quite overawed. In 1900 it was reported of Mrs Herring of Tavistock House, Lee, that:

MRS. COLLINGWOOD AND "JAMES II."

Mrs. Collingwood and 'James II'

Mrs Collingwood of Bossington Hall, Leighton Buzzard, exhibitor and breeder on a grand scale, with her tabby shorthair 'James II'. Her male blue Persian 'Royal Bobs' was bred by Princess Helena Victoria of Schleswig-Holstein.

The Book of the Cat.

'her catteries are so extensive that one might be tempted to term the place a farm, if one did not remember that all the beautiful creatures to be seen are pets... Her fame has spread as far as Turkey and the Sultan has purchased direct a beautiful brown tiger tabby.'

Around the same date, Mrs Collingwood of Bossington Hall, Leighton Buzzard, had twelve cat houses, spread over twelve acres of grounds. At Birchington-on-Sea, Kent, Lady Decies ran a 'model' cattery; its wooden floors covered with cork and raised a foot above the ground for ventilation. *'By a series of wooden blinds, the strong sea breezes and the bright* rays of the summer sun can be regulated.' Inside her own house, two rooms were set aside for mother cats and kittens; their walls *adorned with pictures by Louis Wain*. At Kepwick Park, *'her stately home in Yorkshire'*, the Hon. Mrs McLaren Morrison bred *'some of the most perfect cats to have graced the* [judges] *bench.'*

'Mrs McLaren Morrison herself is one of the most attractive and fascinating women of the day… She has made Kepwick Park a veritable House Beautiful, with the rare curios and art treasures she has collected in the many lands she has visited. One of the handsomest specimens of the feline race ever seen is her blue Persian, Champion Monarch, who as a kitten in 1893 won the gold medal at the Crystal Palace and the next year the Beresford Challenge Cup at Crufts for the best long-haired cat.'

A true cat show celebrity and flamboyant personality, Mrs McLaren Morrison had begun showing in 1899 and by 1900 was entering as many as 25 cats in each of the major shows. When she travelled, *'some of her cats always accompanied her, whether to her flat in London or to her residence in Calcutta. She was always to be seen with her Indian attendant, at shows, taking an active interest in everything.'*

In Scotland, Lady Aberdeen's Haddo House catteries were considered *'some of the most renowned of all'* and contained *'some of the finest silver tabbies in the world'*; while Lady Alexander of Ballochmyle owned *'the largest selection of short-haired blues in the world'*.

Most celebrated of all these aristocratic breeders was Lady Marcus Beresford

whose enthusiasm for cats of all varieties was shared by her husband Lord Marcus and by his brother Lord William Beresford. Lord William held various appointments with the British army in India and it was from there he sent his sister-in-law *'a number of beautiful Persians and a pair of Siamese'*. Lady Beresford's cattery on her husband's estate at Bishopsgate near Windsor was considered a criterion of excellence for all the rest. For the American press, members of the British aristocracy seem to have been perceived as not far removed from characters in the Arabian Nights. They fantasised over her cattery as *'a cats' paradise, where one thousand cats repose on velvet cushions and drink milk out of porcelain saucers'*. Not a thousand, perhaps no more than one hundred and fifty at most, but Bishopsgate kittens were sought after all over the world. And not porcelain, but spotless white enamelled bowls and dishes stacked tidily on racks. A kitchen of their own, where their meals were prepared by a cattery maid-servant whose sole duty it was to look after them; and under her, a boy to do the rough work. This and much more Lady Marcus tells us herself in lecture notes which Helen Winslow fortunately preserved:

'Some of my pets live in a pretty cottage, covered with creepers, which might well be called Cat Cottage. No expense has been spared in the fittings of the rooms, and every provision is made for warmth

Miss Gertrude Willoughby of Fulmer Hall Slough.

A friend of Queen Victoria's grand-daughter, Princess Victoria and from whom the Queen accepted the gift of a blue Persian kitten in 1899.

'Miss Gertrude Willoughby is a great lover of Persian cats and keeps a large number at Fulmer Hall, Slough, where she has just built new and handsome catteries… and had the honour of presenting Her Majesty the Queen with a blue Persian kitten from Fulmer. She also presented Princess Victoria of Schleswig-Holstein with a kitten, and both are now pets of the palace'.

Lady's Realm magazine, 1900

and ventilation. There is a medicine chest which contains everything that is needful for prompt and efficacious treatment in case pussy becomes sick.

Then there is the garden cattery. I think this is the prettiest of all. It is covered with roses and ivy. There are three rooms with shelves and all other conveniences which can add to a cat's comfort and amusement. In the residences for the male cats, I have given them every attention possible. Each male has his separate sleeping apartment enclosed with wire and with a 'run' attached. Close at hand is a large square grass 'run' and in this each gentleman takes his daily but solitary exercise as no two males can be left together.'

Gertrude Willoughby was undoubtedly a distinguished and respected breeder, her cats were greatly praised by *The Windsor Magazine*, particularly her champion silver Chinchilla 'Zaida':

'One of the prettiest and most compact Persian chinchillas I have ever seen is Miss Gertrude Willoughby's champion 'Zaida'. She is a very young cat with a perfect form and a lovely coat. The 'Challenge Cup' fell to her last year, and this year all the honours of her class, with specials, medals etc. Miss Willoughby is one of the shining lights of the NCC and had the honour of conducting H.R.H. the Princess of Wales, with Princess Victoria and suite, round the Cat Tent at the last Botanic Show and presenting Her Royal Highness with a charming bouquet on behalf of 'The National Cat Club'.'

Although the *Windsor Magazine* was 'unable to show a picture', special mention was made of her beautiful Siamese, Fulmer Banjo:

'a lively pug-like specimen with a splendid fawn coat and tanned feet and ears. Miss Willoughby has a special liking for these curious and rare feline friends, although these animals are very difficult to rear and cultivate in our precarious climate.'

At the time it was generally agreed that Siamese were delicate and difficult to rear; there is no shortage of anecdotal evidence pointing to this fact and at the time our cold, wet climate was held mainly responsible.

A ROYAL HOBBY

As more cat shows opened up, the royal family took advantage of the opportunity to make a social occasion out of a conducted tour to view the celebrity felines. Edward, Prince of Wales was a cat enthusiast, so was his wife Princess Alexandra. Perhaps because most of these visits were informal, they received no press coverage. However, at the Crystal Palace show of 1896 the Prince presented two special prizes – autographed photographs of himself in expensive frames – to the owners of prizewinning cats: One to Mrs C Hill's 'Patrick Blue' the best long-haired; the other to 'Birkdale Ruffie' a sable tabby with black stripes who was the best of the 'roughhaired' class. Another distinguished cat, Madame Portier's 'Blue Boy' winner of the McLaren Morrison Indian Bowl as well as many other first and special prizes, was

Lady Decies' Silver Champion "Fulmer Zaida"

'Fulmer Zaida' Champion Silver Chinchilla.

Winner of the Challenge Cup and bred by Lady Decies (née Gertrude Willoughby).

Photograph by E. Landor

"BLUE BOY": BLUE PERSIAN.
Champion, 1897; winner of special, 1898. Owned by Madame Portier.

'Blue Boy' Champion Blue Persian. 1897.

Owned by Madame Portier and much admired by the Princess of Wales

elite breeders but equally admired. It was managed ostensibly, by their elder daughter, Princess Helena Victoria, ('Thora'), but it is clear that both her parents were involved. Prince Christian is said to have built some of the cat houses himself – a photograph of one remains in the royal archives; styled like a Swiss chalet, adorned with baskets of flowers and on top a crown with the monogram V.S.H.

Prince Christian himself owned at least one of the cats and his wife, described as 'a great patroness of cat shows', owned

Prince Maurice of Battenberg with a cat belonging to his cousin Princess Helena Victoria.

Photographed outside one of the pens at her Cumberland Lodge cattery c.1901–03. Royal Collection Trust
© Her Majesty Queen Elizabeth II, 2019

taken from his cage at the request of the Princess of Wales for an admiring stroke. There are several photographs of the Princess (later Queen) Alexandra pictured with cats in the Royal Collection. One dating from the 1870s, others of a pet Siamese taken on board the Royal Yacht in 1905–6. In 1901, soon after his accession, King Edward is said to have bought two pairs of Manx cats from a well-known breeder.

A ROYAL CATTERY

It is an interesting reflection that in spite of the formal etiquette of the time, a British royal princess could run a commercial cattery without any loss of dignity. In 1866 Princess Helena, Queen Victoria's third daughter, married Prince Christian of Schleswig-Holstein (thereafter assuming the title of Princess Christian). It was a condition of their marriage that the couple should live in England, because the Queen had come to rely on her daughter's everyday help. Prince Christian was the sporty 'outdoor' sort: a good shot, a skilled horseman, and an expert at forestry. He was also an animal lover having brought over with him a pair of his family's pet doves. Unfortunately, in company he was a notorious bore; and had the objectionable habit, as far as the Queen was concerned, of *smoking*. What to do with this capable but rather un-courtly son-in-law? The Queen solved the problem neatly by appointing him Ranger of Windsor Great Park. There he and his wife and subsequently their four children, settled in the 'grace and favour' residence Cumberland Lodge. There too, during the 1890s, they set up a cattery, smaller than some of the other

"PUCK III."

several more, including 'a very fine specimen of a blue [Persian]' for which she had paid 'a big price'. The Royal Photographic Collection preserves an album, probably put together by Princess Christian or Princess Helena Victoria, showing six of the family's cats. Although Princess Helena Victoria did not exhibit, she bought from, sold to or swapped with other leading breeders. She specialised in blue Persians and Chinchillas and was a patron of the Silver and Smoke Persian Society. One of her blues, 'Royal Bobs' which she sold to Mrs Collingwood, won champion status. She herself acquired from Lady Decies an outstanding white Persian, 'Powder Puff'. Cats can be capricious, as we cat lovers know and her Persian 'Imp' achieved the dubious distinction of lashing out at the Prince of

First Prize 'At the Cat Show'
From a picture postcard series by Louis Wain.

"IMP."

Cats Belonging to Princess Helena Victoria c.1900–02.
'That lovely Chinchilla' Puck III' & 'Imp' the cat who dared to scratch the hand of the Prince of Wales.

A unique portrayal of pedigree Blue Persian 'Kilpatrick' owned by Her Highness the Princess Victoria of Schleswig-Holstein.

National Cat Club Charity Card.

Wales when on a visit with his sister and his niece:

'Imp' is gifted with a most unhappy, irritable temper that renders him a very bad cat for show purposes. 'Imp' one time inflicted a severe scratch upon Prince Edward, who attempted to make friends with him by stroking his tail. Careless of the fact that the future occupant of the English throne was paying court to him, 'Imp' suddenly shot out a long, silky covered paw and drew blood from the hand of the Prince, who thereafter confined his attentions to the more peacefully disposed 'Ladybird' and that lovely Chinchilla 'Puck III'. (Frances Simpson)

OUR CATS – PUSS HAS A DEDICATED MAGAZINE

1890 saw the publication of *Fur and Feather* and from then on, articles on cats and cat shows featured regularly. But the first 'cats only' magazine did not appear until 1 November 1899, when the editorial column of *Our Cats* made its introduction:

'It is really remarkable that Puss has never yet had a "paper" all to herself, himself,

itself. Is it because the admiration for cats is too limited? Surely not. Their admirers, breeders and exhibitors form an enormous community, among whom are some of the wealthiest, most popular and socially influential men and women in the Kingdom. And is not the beloved and beautiful Princess of Wales herself a cat lover? What "Fancy" can boast a patron more distinguished, more popular than Her Grace of Bedford?'

REGIONAL CAT CLUBS GO THEIR OWN WAY

People eager to own and breed pedigree cats formed regional 'one variety' clubs: the Scottish in 1894, the Northern Counties, the Siamese and the Silver Smoke Persian 1900, the Manx and the Shorthaired 1901 and the Midland Counties 1902 – to name only some. Their aim was to increase membership by putting on

AT STUD

PERSIMMON II

Noted Brown Tabby Persian, sire of Champion Persimmon, with superb head, grand markings and colour, very healthy. Winner, and sire of Miss Whitney's noted " Tip Topper " and many other celebrated winners.

Fee, £1 1s.

Queens to be sent to Mrs. BIRD, Manitou, St. Peter's Road, St. Margaret's, Twickenham.

Advertisement for stud cats on offer in Cats for Profit and Pleasure by Frances Simpson, 1911.

Miss Frances Simpson's Brown Tabby "Champion Persimmon"

Brown tabby Persian 'Persimmon' owned by Frances Simpson.

Mrs. Sinkins' Smoke Champion "Teufel"

'Teufel', Mrs Sinkins' Smoke Champion who sired 'King Lobengula'.

and Starving Cats' (founded by Mrs Zoe Constance Morgan who aspired to identify with the aristocracy – see Chapter 6) and may have been on sale as a fund raiser:

'Funds urgently needed to meet increased expenditure of removing to more extensive premises at Regent's Park. The home is kept up by voluntary contributions. Please help. 17,087 cats have been received from January 1896 to June 1899 an average of 200 weekly.'

The patrons listed on the reverse are all members of the nobility: four Duchesses, one Duke, one Marquis, one Marchioness, nine Countesses and five Lords and Ladies. All have lent their name in support of the charity.

CELEBRITY STUD CATS

Cats for Profit and Pleasure was a useful little book for breeders and owners alike, full of handy hints and practical information on breeding, exhibiting, health care, diseases and management. In the advertisement section at the end of the book – which no doubt helped to reduce costs for the author – the stud list includes 'Persimmon II' sired by Champion 'Persimmon', a majestic brown tabby Persian.

Two ladies from Bath have also advertised their stud cats. Included on the list of desirable boys is their *'King Lobengula – a beautiful smoke Persian with orange eyes'* sired by Mrs Sinkins' 'Teufel', her smoke champion – a cat with a spectacular neck ruff – which Frances Simpson believed to be *'as nearly perfect a specimen as it is possible to find'*.

shows and giving out prizes; this did not in any way contribute towards raising the standards of competition or the improvement of breeds. They wanted autonomy; their own rules, standards and identity and they behaved like naughty children, forever challenging NCC authority. Louis Wain, the long suffering NCC Chairman of Committee accused the Silver Persian Society of being nothing more than *'an abnormal mushroom excrescence on the parent club, it has no place in establishing a breed of cat, in fact it has done nothing for the cat itself.'*

A card from a June 1899 cat show has a pink ribbon, probably intended to tie on to the cat's cage with the owner's details. It features an appeal for the 'London Institution for Lost

Frances Simpson Judging the 'Ring Class'.

From The Book of The Cat.

'THE RING'

Richmond Cat Show July 1902: A sunny summer day in the Old Deer Park at Richmond, where these elegantly dressed owners have gathered to show off their pedigree cats in the judging ring.

Although Frances Simpson describes the 'Ring Class' as an 'innovation' she clearly had mixed feelings about it and recommends its restriction to neuters only, who are large and more docile than studs. She continues *'I cannot say I find it very interesting to see a collection of toms, females, and neuters, long and short-haired, being dragged around by their anxious owners, whilst puzzled judges try hard to decide which of the motley and mixed assembly is most worthy of honours.'*

National Cat Club Show 1902: Writing in Cat Gossip magazine in March 1927, Editor and breeder Mr H C Brooke reminisces about an NCC Charity Cat Show given some 25 years earlier, when Lady Decies set up a ring-class with a five shilling fee:

'which nearly caused a fiasco as a savage fight took place between Mrs McLaren Morrison's Black Cherry and Mrs Stead's Black Champion Smoker Ranji. Ladies screamed, cats swore, Ranji escaped and hid under a piano and Dr Roper received a nasty bite. Those ring-classes! How well we remember our Red Indian Short Hair clearing the ring on one occasion.'

THE 'CAT CLUB' – A NEW VENTURE

In 1898 Lady Marcus Beresford the largest and wealthiest of the cat breeders left the National Cat Club to form a rival group – The Cat Club – with shows at the Royal Aquarium. She financed it so generously with her own money that, according to Frances Simpson writing in 1902 it was *'able to offer at its shows an absolutely unequalled list of prizes'*. In the early 1900s however, the number of competitors at major events began to fall off, due to fears of the spread of feline enteritis. The Cat Club became financially unviable and foundered in 1904. However, their motto *'beauty lives by kindness'* was adopted and began to appear on medals awarded at some provincial shows.

CAT SHOW MEDALS:

Top and middle row, left to right, obverse above, reverse below:

• The Cat Club London, St Stephen's Hall Westminster 1900 • Cruft's Show London, Westminster Hall 1894 • The National Cat Club, Clifton Show 1894 •

Bottom Row, obverse only, left to right:

• Northern Counties 1910. venue unknown. • Brighton Aquarium Show 1885 • Silver and Smoke Persian Society, Brighton 1903 • Southern Counties. c1900s.

(From the collection of Missi and Christopher Eimer with their kind permission)

THE NEW GOVERNING COUNCIL OF THE CAT FANCY IS BORN

While the Cat Establishment was growing and sprouting new branches, it was slowly rotting at the roots. There was constant in-fighting, personal conflict and even accusations of persecution between committee members – both the ladies and the gentlemen.

The scourge of feline enteritis – as it was now recognised – was spread by cross infection, leading to fewer entries in popular show events. Breeders feared possible contamination and began to advertise in specialist magazines instead. By 1901 the number of entries to the Crystal Palace show had fallen dramatically. Lady Marcus Beresford's

Miss Mary Gresham's Persian kitten 'Lambkin no. 2'.

Illustration by Harrison Weir

own Cat Club was also in serious trouble at her Aquarium venue and as a last resort, she suggested a merger with the NCC. However, nothing came of it and the Cat Club foundered in 1904. Quarrels between the NCC and its regional club offshoots rumbled on and by 1908, eight clubs had broken away to form the Cat Fanciers Association. It was agreed that the situation couldn't continue and a single governing body was urgently needed to replace the now unpopular parent National Cat Club. Finally, in 1910 at a meeting of all interested parties, a new authority was formed, to be called 'the Governing Council of the Cat Fancy'.

In July 1913 *Our Cats* magazine ceased trading, abruptly and without warning.

It was not until 1936 that another 'cats only' publication – *Cats and Kittens* would go on sale. Even this was to have a chequered history.

'DOGS, DOGS, DOGS'

Following the First World War, cat shows resumed on a smaller scale in the 1920s but for the next thirty-five years or so pedigree dogs gained the ascendancy over cats as fashion accessories. In an essay written in the late 1920s, the journalist Edward Lucas dreams that he is petitioned by a Siamese cat who speaks on behalf of cats in general:

'To-day it's dogs, dogs, dogs everywhere. Cats are hardly mentioned.'

'Couldn't you', she said, 'do something for us with your pen?'

'How do you mean?'

'Put us into one of your articles? … You see, we're tired of hearing the praise of dogs. Everyone has a dog nowadays, and every dog is perfect, and papers and books are full of them. You've written about them yourself often enough – too often – but when did you last write about cats?'

Not for a long time.' I said.

(From the anthology The Genius of the Hearth published 1932)

In a letter published in *The Daily Express* 16 December 1941 a reader is of the opinion that, contrary to popular notion, it is men rather than women – in the police, on railways, in canteens and fire stations – who are the true cat devotees.

'Ask any modern woman whether she likes cats, and almost invariably she will reply, 'No, I much prefer dogs or horses.' In truth she has little love for or knowledge of either animal, and only owns a dog because it is a fashionable or mannish custom. It would be a sign of weakness for her to fondle a cat.'

Chapter 4

Love and Kitties

Puss in Books, Picture Postcards and Greetings Cards

Advances in colour printing in the 1860s are to your advantage; from now on we shall be seeing much more of you Puss, if only on paper. Puss in Boots, Dick Whittington, Dame Wiggins of Lee and Her Seven Wonderful Cats; all books loved by generations of fortunate children. But books are expensive. The arrival of chromolithographic printing presses soon began to replace traditional hand colouring. For the first time books can be speedily produced at affordable prices.

When the new-fangled Christmas greetings cards arrive the robin redbreast is your rival for top choice, nevertheless you find your own niche market. In 1879 sales of cards move out of the sepulchral aura of the Victorian bookseller and stationer to a position in toy-shops, tobacconists and chain stores followed by a big growth in sales. In the early 20th century, picture postcard frenzy grips the public and you gain a 'fan club' of your own.

*****

When cats first 'took up the pen' to champion their cause with stories aimed at a nursery readership, books were hand coloured by teams of children or young women on a production line system.

The Three Little Kittens c.1890.

The kittens have found their mittens but they are far from home; unsure of their way through a forest of foliage and scared by something they think is hiding in the undergrowth. There is nothing of this in the accompanying text. The anonymous artist has used his imagination to create a haunting picture – vividly realised in this fine chromolithographic print by Thomas Nelson and Sons.

Using the black printed outline to guide them, each worker applied one colour to a page which was then passed along for the next application. Such slow, laborious work kept prices high and

books were sold mainly to the middle and professional classes who were able to afford such luxuries. Popular comic picture story books such as *Dame Wiggins of Lee and her Seven Wonderful Cats, Dame Trott and her Cat* and *Old Mother Hubbard* went into numerous reprints; favourites both of parents and children alike. Trading was competitive and as early as 1819 John Harris, publisher of *Old Mother Hubbard*, reduced his books to one shilling for a plain copy and one shilling and sixpence for colour, only to be undercut by rivals such as Dean & Munday who offered a colour book at only one shilling.

THE NEW COLOURFUL WORLD OF CHROMOLITHOGRAPHY

Steam driven printing presses arrived in the mid 1860s and were gradually installed by larger companies, enabling speedier colour production at moderate prices. Bright, cheerful poster advertisements began to decorate the streets, known as 'the poor man's picture gallery'.

The Three Little Kittens was something of a phenomenon among later 19th century children's stories; attributed to American writer Eliza Follen it first appeared in

The Three Little Kittens c.1890.

A fold-out booklet for small children, embossed and die-cut.

Published by Raphael Tuck c.1890.

1853 in *Nursery Songs for Good Children.* Probably remembered today, if at all, by its opening lines:

Three little kittens they lost their mittens,
And they began to cry,
"Oh mother dear, we sadly fear
That we have lost our mittens."
"What! lost your mittens, you
naughty kittens!
Then you shall have no pie."

American novelist Robert Michael Ballantyne brought out his own version in 1856, changing the last line to *'But I smell a rat close by'.* The cats chase the rat into a cave, their tails twirling in the darkness as they disappear, never to be

The Three Little Kittens by Maria Hoyer. From Miss Pussycats Party. The Grand Ball in Honour of the Prince of Taels.

Published in chromolithography by Ernest Nister c.1890.

seen again. Not a satisfying ending. After this, '*three kittens*' in various versions, took on a life of their own. There were at least 26 separate editions by different publishers in Britain and the United States up to 1900 as well as sequels and variations in prose and verse. One of the more inventive is by Maria Hoyer, where the three kittens are teenagers and their mittens are stolen by a spiteful dog. Without them, the kittens can't attend a grand ball to be held in honour of King Whiskerandos and his heir, the Prince of Taels who, it is rumoured is looking for a wife. The story is narrated by the kitten considered the plainest of the three – and of course she is the one who wins the Prince's hand.

Children's Christmas Annuals in picture book style were brought out for the gift trade by a number of publishers, notably Raphael Tuck and Ernest Nister who specialised in 'Catland' life and humour. Handsomely designed and printed, they included contributions from the most talented but not necessarily the best-known writers and illustrators of the day. A typical example: Ernest Nister's *Isn't It Funny* 1893 has drawings by Beatrix Potter, G H Thompson, W Foster and a short story by Edith Nesbitt, later to make her name with *The Railway Children* and other novels.

In 1886 Sir John Millais completed his famous oil painting 'Bubbles'. An angelic looking small boy gazes – as if towards Heaven – at a gossamer-like soap bubble. The original picture was purchased from the artist by the makers of Pears soap who

'The Mewsical Party' (above) and 'The Dancing Lesson' (below) by 'Catland' illustrator G H Thompson,

from Isn't It Funny

'Stealing Jam',

also by illustrator G H Thompson

added their own trademark to the tablet of soap displayed in the foreground.

ALL IN THE BEST POSSIBLE TASTE

In 1818 Thomas Bowdler published his own censored edition of Shakespeare's plays:

'It has been my study to exclude from this publication whatever is unfit to read aloud by a gentleman to a company of ladies... expressions which are of such a nature as to raise a blush on the cheek of modesty.'

Would the introduction of Victorian political correctness mean closer public scrutiny for anything considered offensive?

Regarding children's literature there was much debate but up to the 1840s the content of story books remained more or less unchanged. By no means were they all well written or illustrated, but what the most successful titles had in common was the knack of gripping and holding their reader's attention. Children are not squeamish and authors and artists of the day seem to have gone out of their way to describe and show the most lurid incidents. In a children's edition of *Blue Beard* published by John Harris in 1808 and quaintly subtitled *The Fatal Effects of Curiosity and Disobedience,* the severed heads of the six over-inquisitive wives are shown lined up in a row on a table. Evil – human or supernatural – is at the heart of the Brothers Grimm's *German Popular Stories* but as their first English translator, Edgar Taylor explained, his objective was *'the entertainment of young people'.*

'Bubbles'.

Oil painting by Sir John Millais

The 'Bubbles' kitten.

A parody, unsigned but probably the work of artist William Foster for a children's annual published by Ernest Nister in 1893.

'Killing the Chickens', from Pussy's Road to Ruin.

First published in English translation in 1840. One of twelve hand-coloured wood engravings.

PUSSY'S ROAD TO RUIN

Like others of its kind, *Pussy's Road to Ruin* is meant as a moral tale; but the impression it leaves is of gratuitous cruelty. 'Pussy', an innocent kitten, is persuaded by the sinister Grimalkin to join him in a series of vicious acts – the slaughter of a tame jackdaw, a brood of chickens and a caged canary – each attack vividly illustrated. Finally detected, Pussy is imprisoned forever in her owner's cellar, while Grimalkin is never seen again. *Pussy's Road to Ruin* went through ten editions in as many years and must rate as one of the most popular children's stories of its time.

Heinrich Hoffman's *Struwwelpeter* (scruffy Peter) is generally regarded as the most extreme example of its genre; sub titled *'Pretty pictures and funny stories for little children'*. A collection of gruesome verses caution against the awful consequences of naughtiness – which Hoffman said was intended as a parody. Amusing to adults perhaps, but for a small child, more likely to cause nightmares.

Cats make a guest appearance in *Struwwelpeter* in 'The Dreadful Story of Little Harriet and the Matches'. Little Harriet's two distraught pet cats Minz and Maunz take the moral high ground and beg her not to play with fire. They weep a pool of tears when she finally incinerates herself. There is a touching pathos in her remaining *'little scarlet shoes'*.

'So she was burnt with all her clothes,
And arms and hands, and eyes, and nose;
Till she had nothing more to lose
Except her little scarlet shoes;
And nothing else but these was found
Among her ashes on the ground.

'The Dreadful Story about Harriet and the Matches'

*from Heinrich Hoffman's Struuwelpeter
published 1848*

And when the good cats sat beside
The smoking ashes, how they cried!
'Me-ow, me-oo, me-ow, me-oo,
What will Mamma and Nursey do?
Their tears ran down their cheeks so fast
They made a little pond at last.'

'UNFAIR TO THE FAIRIES'

Perhaps Mr Bowdler's censorship of Shakespeare did have an effect. By the mid-1840s there were misgivings about the content of many children's books; were they appropriate for immature minds and could they even be harmful to children? Criticism came from various sources including authors and educationists all eager to have their say on the matter. The celebrated American author Samuel Griswold Goodrich who published one hundred and seventy volumes – many of them for juveniles, under the name of Peter Parley – joined in along with his English supporters. The function of children's literature they said, *'is to instruct'*. Their aim was to fill small heads as full of facts as possible. This was later ridiculed as *'Astronomy for babies and Botany made a parlour pastime'*. Others considered that a child's first reading should be a way of instilling religious instruction. But they too got carried away when artist Richard Doyle's charming *Fairyland* pictures came under their fire: *'Elves and goblins are no part of God's creation'* and airborne fairies *'easily confused with angels in a small child's mind'*. George Cruikshank, one of the leading illustrators of the day who in later life became teetotal, brought out a

version of Cinderella in 1853 in which the King proclaims: *'There shall be no more fountains of wine on my son's wedding day'*: to which Charles Dickens made a witty retort in his essay, *'Unfair to the Fairies'*, condemning the moralisation of children's books.

Another influential contributor to the debate was publisher and public figure Henry Cole, known for having produced the first Christmas card. Cole launched his own series of children's picture books under the name *'Felix Summerley's Home Treasury'* in 1844. He also complained of a lack of suitable reading matter for his own children – the books were either dull and instructional or travesties of traditional stories. Cole was a shrewd business man although his views may have been biased towards his own tastes; he was heavily committed to art book publishing for juveniles.

'The Home Treasury Series took itself seriously', wrote Gleeson White (*Children's Books and their Illustrators*. 1900). *'Its purpose was art with a capital A.'* Cole was certainly aspiring, if only to sell more books; he enlisted the talents of the most famous Royal Academicians of the period including H H Mulready and John Linnell. Others such as Harrison Weir had a good track record in children's illustration. Gleeson White remarked that:

'all [Cole's] books were marked with the new spirit which was working in many minds at the time and manifested itself most conspicuously through the Pre-Raphaelites and their allies.'

Each book enjoyed a quality of presentation never before attempted in children's fiction. Their sale was aimed at parents – rather than the children – who may have coveted them more for show on a library shelf than as much-loved titles for grubby little hands to pore over. With the conversion to chromo-lithography as the chosen print option, hand-colouring fell out of use. Old Dame Wiggins of Lee and Her Seven Wonderful Cats were forgotten, along with other fantasy figures such as the benevolent Old Mother Bunch who fed buns to the crowd from her broomstick at the Great Exhibition in 1851.

'Old Mother Bunch.' Witchcraft meets Victorian Technology.

Cats look on as Old Mother Bunch distributes buns from her broomstick to visitors at the Great Exhibition in 1851. A light-hearted take on press reports of the remarkable quantities of currant buns consumed during the event. The railway engines were full scale locomotives displayed by a number of British companies.

Hand-coloured print, © Victoria and Albert Museum. London

ANIMALS WITH CHARACTER

Today, Beatrix Potter's books are as popular as ever; her brush has never lost its magic. In 1901 after numerous rejections from publishers she self-published her first modest little book in black and white, *The Tale of Peter Rabbit*. It was successful enough to persuade Warne's to publish it commercially the following year. When Warne's asked her how much did she think they should charge for the book, she said that '*she would rather make two or three little books costing a shilling each than one large book costing six shillings because she thinks little rabbits cannot afford to spend six shillings on one book*'.

Although *The Tale of Peter Rabbit* is perhaps her best known story, during her main creative period, 1901 to 1914, rabbits appear in only four stories while cats play leading roles in six. Two more, *The Sly Old Cat* 1906 and *Kitty in Boots* 1914–15 remained unpublished. She recalled an interview with publisher Charles Faulkner in which she expressed very firmly her dislike of '*little men with cats' heads*' and '*animals in trousers*',

considered by Faulkner to reflect popular taste at the time. That was not the last on the subject of trousers.

TOM'S TROUSERS

In the Tale of Tom Kitten, Tabitha Twitchitt, the matronly mother cat is expecting fine company to tea so she washes and dresses her kittens in their best clothes before they go out into the garden. Unfortunately, Tom had put on a little weight, his clothes were too tight and '*he was quite unable to jump when walking on his hind legs in trousers*'. (Was this Beatrix's little joke?) The kittens romp around in the garden and contrive somehow to lose all their clothes.

Tom's trousers became a bone of contention between Beatrix and Warne's, who queried the phrase '*all Tom's clothes came off*'. Couldn't she change it to '*nearly*

The Tale of Tom Kitten.

Tom's trouser buttons are bursting off and his mother sews them back on again.

Illustration from The Tale of Tom Kitten by Beatrix Potter © Frederick Warne & Co., 1907, 2002.

all?' Even at the height of Victorian prudery, no one had ever questioned an artist's freedom to picture animals as they are in nature. Warne's concern may have been that children might identify with the lovable creatures in the story and decide to run around naked themselves.

CELEBRITY CATS OF SAWREY

Several of Beatrix Potter's animal characters were suggested by villager's pets at Sawrey in the Lake District where she lived at nearby Hill Top Farm. Tabitha Twitchitt belonged to the blacksmith's wife, and Ribby, in *The Pie and The Patty Pan*, was Tabitha's cousin. Tom kitten, Tabitha's notional son – borrowed from a stonemason working on her house – was also the model for Miss Moppit in her story for very young readers; at only a few months old his sex hardly mattered. Ginger, in *Ginger and Pickles*, was a '*bright yellow cat with short hair belonging to Miss Bunckle, the schoolmistress'*. In his real life, Ginger had fathered at least one litter of kittens at Hill Top Farm.

It was at Hill Top that, for the first time, she began to keep cats of her own – the house was infested with rats. In September 1906 she notes in her diary: '*Someone asked me this morning if I was still wanting a tiger?! A startling question, but they call barred cats – what I should call tabby, 'tigers' up here.*' The following month, Mrs Cannon, the wife of the tenant farmer who managed her property '*calmly announced that I should get 4 or 5 cats. Imagine my feelings, but I daresay they will live in the outbuildings.*' Two years later the cats had multiplied but by then she was reconciled to them. '*I say their kittens are all to be kept for a little while till we see which is the cleverer. There is one little grey kitten that is very sharp and fluffs itself out, and scratches great big Kep [her Collie sheepdog].*'

Ginger and Pickles was set in Sawrey, and when the book came out in 1909 the villagers were agog: '*They are all quite jealous of each other's houses and cats getting into a book.*' Ginger and Pickles was her fifteenth book in seven years, her financial independence was assured and her interest in farming and land owning took over her life.

LOUIS WAIN – A CHAMPION FOR POOR PUSS

Although Louis Wain, brought fun and laughter to millions of adults and children alike, he did not enjoy a happy personal life. In the 1880s he was employed as a black and white newspaper artist, a fairly common calling back then, so he considered it a breakthrough when the publishers Macmillan & Co. commissioned him to produce six whole-page cat-themed illustrations for *Madame Tabby's Establishment* published 1886.

Louis' father had been a commercial traveller in the textile industry and evidently made a good living. But when he died in 1880 he left Louis, who had just qualified at the West London School of Art, to support the family. His mother suffered from a paralysing form of gentility; although they were hard up, she could not manage without a governess for her five small daughters. This proved counterproductive. Louis married the governess against his mother's wishes – causing a family rift which did not alter the fact that they all still depended entirely on his earnings.

CAT NAMED PETER

Soon after their marriage, Louis and his wife Emily were given a black and white shorthaired kitten they named Peter. Sadly, at the age of only 28, Emily had

Bath Time. From Pa Cats Ma Cats and their Kittens. Published by Raphael Tuck 1902.

'I always have my bath outside the tub when mother isn't here. Then I don't get wet you see and there isn't so much danger of taking cold'.

Illustration by Louis Wain.

terminal cancer; the kitten was a great comfort to her and a distraction in her distress. *'It was Peter'*, Wain said, *'who first suggested to my mind my fanciful cat creations. As I sat watching his antics one evening, I did a small study of kittens which was accepted by the Lady's Pictorial.'* Peter made more appearances; he can be seen peeping out of a travelling basket at the Crystal Palace cat show in a set of drawings for the *Illustrated London News* in October 1884. He later figures in several drawings done for Charles Morley's fictional biography, *Peter, cat o' one tail* – a spoof detective story of a cat lost and found. When Peter went down sick with flu like symptoms there was concern for his welfare. He is featured on the back row of *'Madame Tabby's Academy'* with his head wrapped in a towel, initially published as a sepia print in 1888 and subsequently issued as a picture postcard.

In an interview with Louis Wain in 1895 when Peter was thirteen, he was still:

'Distinctly handsome, but the wear and tear of public life have left their mark. Now the old cat dozes over the fire – his every wish gratified – a King amongst cats.'

Peter lived on until the March of 1898 and Wain told an interviewer:

'...he died in my hands, a boy kitten again, talking and answering me as of old. It was a few minutes lived in the past between us again, with all its memories alive.'

CATLAND

In Wain's world, cats always did human things in human situations; a gentle poke of fun at some of the absurdities of Edwardian life. Catland was the subject of many of his illustrations and picture postcards. The name was first coined in the 1850s, years before anthropomorphic cats came tumbling off Wain's creative brush. Anticipated among others by George Cruikshank Jnr [great nephew of his famous namesake], in drawings such as *'Tabby's Tea Fight'* (1876) where fashionably dressed cats sip tea served with cakes by feline housemaids.

On a postcard franked in 1903 the sender relates that she saw some Louis Wain cards in a shop display but when she returned to buy them they had all been sold. The incident shows the popularity of Wain's Catland concept; a world where cats play croquet and golf, go to

'Madame Tabby's Academy'

Picture postcard 1901. Louis Wain's cat Peter is top row centre with his head wrapped in a towel because he has a head-cold.

the races, get drunk, attend boring tea parties and smack their naughty kittens. People loved the humour and through some sort of osmosis in the public mind, the oddities of his cats were transferred to their creator – which he seemed to relish and play up to. At a party at his home at Westcliffe-on-Sea, he asked for milk in preference to wine which he drank out of a saucer. In London he was lionised; so well known that he was waylaid by fellow theatregoers who demanded cat sketches on their programmes. Once, arriving by cab at a smart London restaurant he was greeted by a chorus of meows from a crowd of street urchins who even dodged the doorman to follow him into the dining room and perform cat antics at his table.

It could be said that Louis Wain lived nearly as many lives as the cats he drew. He made a huge contribution towards raising the profile of cats from their lowly status using his best weapon – humour, always a crowd pleaser. Gifted with unique artistic talents he was a witty cartoonist, prolific picture postcard artist, illustrator of many children's books and magazines, as well as publishing his own Louis Wain Annuals. In his other role as President of the National Cat Club he showed himself both capable and diplomatic – skills needed to preside over an organisation consisting mainly of spoilt and quarrelsome society ladies. His one unfortunate weakness; he was hopeless with money. He never made any of his work copyright but sold it on, allowing others to reprint and copy it over and over again. His forays into hare-brained business ventures were disastrous and his losses considerable.

When his sister Caroline, who was very close to him, died in the 1917 influenza epidemic he felt her loss deeply. By the early 1920s he was showing signs of mental illness, such as had claimed one of his sisters. In 1924 he was certified insane and spent the rest of his life in mental institutions, penniless but for donations from friends and admirers, and even a fund set up for his benefit. By his death in 1939 he was almost forgotten by a generation that had turned to new types of humour and subject. In spite of that, his fame lives on today; his work eagerly sought by collectors and he left us with his personal tribute to his beloved cat Peter:

'He became my principal model and pioneer of my success. He helped me wipe out, once and for all, the contempt in which the cat has been held in this country.'

THE ARRIVAL OF THE POSTCARD AND PICTURE POSTCARD

The postcard in its simplest form, just a space for the message on one side and the address on the reverse was introduced as a convenient business aid, available only at Post Office counters. It was seized upon by a grateful public who found letter writing a wearisome task when a quick, cheap postcard would do. This popular innovation was quickly followed by the picture postcard; no longer the monopoly of the Post Office but on sale everywhere, giving rise to the picture postcard collecting craze. Most families kept at least one album filled with every subject imaginable. By 1906 the number of postally franked picture postcards had peaked at a staggering 264.3 million. Workers now had regular holidays as well as annual day trips to the seaside and foreign travel had opened up for the well to do. So, whether comfortably off travelling abroad or counting the shillings in an English seaside boarding house, a postcard home was a 'must' – and so the choice of a cat was often 'on the cards'.

MIXED BATHING

Bexhill-on-Sea was the first English resort to allow mixed bathing in 1902, with other resorts following suit. Artist Violet Roberts pictures just such a scene where a terrified lady cat emerges from a bathing hut wearing only a large bathing cap. Lady cats always wear large bathing caps; gentlemen cats wear a happy smile. A Violet Roberts' cat – they are mostly female – is a happy-go-lucky creature who goes donkey riding on the beach and is often to be seen wandering the seaside promenade in her big hat hoping to find a man. It was said that Violet sent her art work to her brother who was also an artist – in the trenches during the First World War – for his appraisal.

'I Am Quite Upset'.

Known as 'write away cards' these were sold with different slogans as an aid to those who sit chewing the end of their pencil for inspiration on what to write home to Granny.

Early Picture postcard by Louis Wain. c.1905

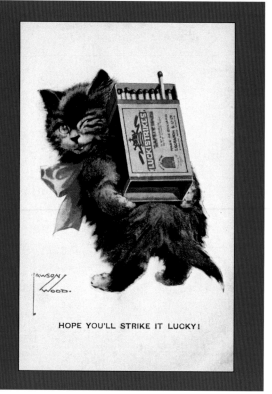

'I'm telling the tale at Pinner'.
Picture postcard postmarked 1913.

'This is my last day at Settrington', black humour that would not be acceptable today.
Picture postcard postmarked 1912.

'Hope you'll strike it lucky'.
Picture postcard. c.1920–30.

Mixed Bathing.
Picture postcard by Violet Roberts. c.1902.

From Newquay.
'You "AUTO" come here. It's ripping'.
Picture postcard c.1920.

Cats of all kinds, not only the 'lucky' black variety, were used as promotional gimmicks for holiday resorts large or small, all over the country. Some, classed as 'postal novelties' opened to reveal a strip of local views hidden under a flap, as in the Newquay example below where it is concealed under the car door.

Card designs were sold to wholesalers and the place names overprinted later on receipt of orders. Humour always sells well and in '*I'm telling the tale at Pinner*' two old cats gossip together; the sporran style muff with three mice hanging from it is a nice touch.

Lucky black cats were used for every kind of card and in '*This is my last day at Settrington*' an unlucky black cat supplies some black humour. No cat could drown in the sea at Settrington, which is in north Yorkshire and nowhere near the coast! Many years later, artist Lawson Wood's irresistible fluffy black kitten is a good luck token in harder economic times.

CATS REFLECT VICTORIAN FAMILY LIFE

Although Helena Maguire (1860–1909) was also a book and magazine illustrator, she is best remembered for her whimsical cats and kittens first published in the 1880s and '90s and later re-issued as picture postcards. Her work frequently featured on greetings cards of the period and also to advertise department stores and domestic products in the UK and on the continent. (See Chapter 8: 'Purr-suasion').

Maguire cats encapsulate Victorian family life from a child's view, recollecting events they would have shared: Winter snowballing and tobogganing; mixing the Christmas pudding, licking the spoon and bearing it triumphantly to the table. Packing their luggage and carrying it from the railway station at the start of a holiday; strolling in the sun along the promenade, making sandcastles, or out in a rowing boat. Finally, off to sleep, in a big brass bed.

Her cats are always furrily naked, apart from a ribbon or a bow and perhaps an accessory such as a parasol, a handbag, a hat or a walking stick. At a grand event, a party or a ball, lady cats wear necklaces of flowers or carry bouquets, and they and their male escorts are always gravely polite.

In later years, Frank Staff, musing on Edwardian postcards (in *The Picture Postcard and its Origins*), was intrigued by the spectacle of '*every sort of cat imaginable, posed in baskets, in flower pots, in teacups, under parasols, wearing sunbonnets, and having tea parties.*' His list covers only a fraction of the subjects to be found by any collector of cat-themed early postcards. They covered every activity: cats went cycling, motoring, flying, ballooning… and still found time to chat on the telephone.

Picture postcards by Helena Maguire, dating from the early 1900s:

Top – '*A family stroll along the promenade*'.

Bottom – '*All tucked up in the big brass bed*'.

Edwardian life was centred far more than today on home and family. Courtship, marriage, and their often less-than-idyllic consequences, provided ready material for postcard artists. In fact, a good deal of Edwardian postcard humour turned on toil and woe or the sheer tedium of everyday life; weekly washing endlessly boiling, scrubbing, wringing, drying and ironing the family's clothes, a visit to the dentist and the unbearable singer at a charity concert.

'Family washday'

Disaster strikes when the kittens tip over the basket of clean washing. No wonder they are contrite; the mother cat's anger seems to have taken on a Wagnerian dimension to match her inflatable underwear.

Picture postcard by German artist Arthur Thiele.

'Shopping'
One of a series, some adapted as Christmas greetings cards.

The anxious parents are out Christmas shopping when there is a problem with junior, does he want to 'spend a penny?' Although Boulanger's work is keenly collected, very little is known about this enchanting French artist.

Picture postcard by Maurice Boulanger, 1906.

'At the Concert'. Picture postcard by Arthur Thiele, 1910.

How she wishes she had stayed at home. These unwelcome events seem to have been part of Edwardian life.

'Poor Pa's Troubles' Picture postcard by Tom Browne. 1906.

Washing day. Pa has his lunch on the stairs. And poor puss is hoping for a few crumbs.

'The misery and discomfort of washday' as described in a contemporary issue of Girl's Own Paper: 'the scolding wife, the truant husband, crying neglected children, meals ill prepared, or not at all, the sloppy kitchen deserted by the cat'

The Cycle Race. Picture postcard by Louis Wain. 1904.

Edwardian cats loved cycling and here Louis Wain shows us again his great flair for chaos. Among the competitors there are three lady cats, each wearing knickerbockers, allowing more freedom of movement than contemporary ankle length skirts. The chain-drives of the bikes are cased-in to prevent mud and oil splashes.

A Family Outing. Picture postcard by N Parker. c.1911.

A continental card overprinted as a New Year greeting. There are kittens spilling out everywhere as father takes the family for a drive. It would certainly not be approved by health and safety regulations today.

'Hello, How's That Poor Dog Next Door?'

A lovely cat image from this much-admired artist, who gives us a rare sighting of an antique telephone. The first telephone exchange – in London – opened in 1879. The Times was of the opinion that the telephone *'is not an affair of the millions. It is a convenience for the well-to-do and a trade appliance'*

Picture postcard by William Ellam. Postmarked 1907.

'Half day trip to the man in the moon. Good bye earth.'

Picture postcard designed and photographed by E Landor. c.1904.

The card is addressed to a young lady in Nottingham. A message on the reverse from a fellow collector reads *'Just another for the Pussie dept. Hope your collection will improve'.*

'The bold duckling'.

Picture postcard by T Sperlich. Postmarked 11.1905.

'Challenging all comers'.

Picture postcard by B Cobbe. c.1906.

EVERY PICTURE TELLS A STORY – THE NARRATIVE ARTISTS

Picture postcard publishers found themselves in a happy situation with growing demand for every kind of

'What Can It Be?'

Picture postcard by Leon Huber. Postmarked 1906.

'Kittens on the keys'.

Picture postcard by C Reichert. Postmarked 1904.

postcard topic, particularly cats. The early 1900s brought along a number of accomplished British and continental artists who specialised in animal subjects. Pretty kittens – on their own or with other farm animals – were often featured getting up to some sort of mischief or enacting a mock confrontation.

THEATRE CATS AND ACTRESSES

Picture postcards of actresses, some cuddling cats, made attractive promotional handouts. These 'Stage

Musical comedy diva Isabel Jay and Mac, the lucky black stage door cat at Daly's Theatre. Having been well groomed, Mac is wearing a silver bell on his collar for the photo session. Picture postcard. Postmarked 1905.

Phyllis Dare and her fluffy Persian friend. Picture postcard. Postmarked 1906.

Phyllis Dare started as a child actress at the age of nine. Much loved by theatregoers everywhere, she introduced the tango to London audiences in the 1912 show Sunshine Girl.

Celebrity' series postcards were routinely slipped into popular magazines by newsagents to stimulate sales of other similar weekly 'penny' romance style publications.

Isabel Jay's biographer John Cannon writes: 'Although Isabel Jay was given a cat during the 1901 run of Ib and Little Christina at the Savoy Theatre, the one she is holding is 'Mac' the stage door cat at Daly's Theatre where he was probably employed to control rats and mice.'

CATS DEMAND THE VOTE

'We Demand the Vote'.

Picture postcard postmarked 1909.

A cat wearing a shawl in the colours of the suffragette movement and a shabby hat could imply a downmarket image with an intention to ridicule. The slogan at the bottom reads 'An advocate for women's rights'.

The suffragette movement was at first thought to be limited to a few upper middle class women eccentrics who smashed shop windows and knocked off policemen's helmets. Events took a more ominous turn when fanatics stepped up their campaign with arson and homemade bombs.

Whether these cats were viewed as deviants or heroines is not always easy to determine. Cartoonists are notoriously

The Suffragettes. 'Soft Persuasion'. Picture postcard by William Ellam, 1908.

A frail female cat protester is seen suffering at the hands of a bullying police constable. Ellam gives a sympathetic view of the suffragette theme where 'persuasion' was often anything but soft.

The Suffragette. 'Down With Tom Cats'.

A topical allusion to the by-election campaign of 1907, urging voters to keep the Liberal candidate out. The Liberal government was even less sympathetic to the cause than the Tories. Picture postcard by William Ellam

quick to exploit the humour of any situation but artist William Ellam appears to have been on their side.

CATS OF THE FIRST WORLD WAR

'Just Joined Up'.

Picture postcard by Vera Patterson.

'Carry On! With Good Luck to US all'.

Picture postcard.

A black cat sounds the bugle when the United States declared war on Germany in 1917.

With the outbreak of the First World War, the London offices of German print firms were closed down and staff repatriated. Raphael Tuck, which had been English domiciled since the 1870s and enjoyed Royal patronage survived; but Ernest Nister's was wound up in 1917. Although paper shortages restricted output, in some ways the war revitalised the postcard industry by introducing a wide range of new subjects to engage public interest. There was a big sale at the time for lucky charms, amulets and pictures of lucky black cats to send to those fighting in the trenches.

A LINE FROM THE TRENCHES

Lucky black cats on a card by French artist L.Pettier carries a poignant message still implicit today:

Dearest Love, You will be pleased to know that I am out of the stunt alright but poor Bobby Hills has gone West so I will write later, from your own Sweetheart, Will.

From early in the war there were food shortages but the government was reluctant to introduce rationing. Instead, there were rules and regulations as well as a food controller. Teams of local officials were appointed to prosecute hoarders and prevent inequalities in distribution. Zeppelin raids began in 1915 and continued until, in 1917, eleven were caught in a gale on their return flight and most were lost.

'You did startle me; I thought you were a Zeppelin'.

Off-beat humour on the Zeppelin horror. A cat looks up at a large caterpillar it mistook for a German zeppelin airship.

Picture postcard dated 1915.

Four long years of war and scarcely any food left. In July 1918 ration books were issued. A lucky black cat reads from the

'I Hope U Miss Me!'

News that the Germans had stepped up their U boat warfare against allied shipping was not a joking matter. In the month this card was posted 866,610 tons of Allied and neutral shipping were sunk.

Picture postcard. Postmarked April 1917.

'The Luck of the Black Cat'. Picture postcard. Postmarked November 1914.

A caption reads: 'Goodbye Daddy, kiss my Kitty for Luck'. It appears that a little girl has brought either her pet cat or her lucky black toy cat to see her daddy off to the front line.

poster that mice are to be rationed. Artist Louis Wain adds a little rhyming message to say 'do cheer up'. Things must have been really bad:

In December 1900 *Girls' Realm* magazine editorial gave an inspired summing up of the golden age of picture postcards, where cats played an important role:

'The picture postcard is a sign of the times. It belongs to a period peopled by a hurried

'A Food Controller'.

Picture postcard postmarked June 1918

'Mice To Be Rationed', by Louis Wain.

Picture postcard postmarked November 1918.

Wear a smile and a bright smile too, And ever keep up your pluck, For this black cat I'm sending you. Is sure to bring good luck

'I Don't Like These Food Hoarders'

Picture postcard postmarked 1918, by artist Donald McGill, much loved virtuoso of the saucy postcard.

'Lucky the Food Controller Hasn't Prohibited Game'.

Picture postcard. c.1918. A hungry cat makes a meal of the pet canary.

generation which has not many minutes to spare for writing to friends. It helps us to keep in touch with those we have left behind and gives us a glimpse of the places that for the time being form the background of our lives. I can imagine a future generation building up with their help all the life of today, …our children, our pets, our famous old people, our wild and garden flowers, our life of sport, and our life of stress and strain, our National holidays, our Pageants, and traces of our political life…'

Christmas greetings card.

Small calling card size 50 x 80 mm.

'Pussy and I have brought these flowers

And wish you merry Christmas hours'.

A Christmas card designed specifically for children c.1870, from the 'Pussy and I' series.

CHRISTMAS CARD CATS

Cats were not the first on the Christmas card scene: robins beat them to it. Punch magazine ran a column each November dedicated to the big Christmas card phenomenon with a review of the latest designs. In 1869 Mr Punch complained (tongue in cheek, no doubt) that he was *'weary of robins, can't they find some other form of felicitation? I hate these robins.'*

Cats began to appear in the 1870s, no doubt assisted by the spectacular success of the early cat shows both in London and the provinces which substantially increased the number of cats kept as pets. There was probably a sound reason why the publishing trade was slow to pick up on this trend; cat subjects might be of limited appeal for all recipients in a family. Nevertheless publishers responded to this new niche market by producing cards for juveniles. Pictures of favourite pets were soon exchanged between siblings while aunts and grand-mamas found them convenient when searching for 'something suitable' for the little ones.

SIZE MATTERS

Many early greetings cards were of the small, flat calling card format. Although the flat single card in various sizes remained throughout the century, novelty was always the name of the game and many intricately folded designs were published. The folder type card with silk cord and tassels arrived in the 1880s.

Although the greetings card market was expanding rapidly, fancy goods publishers

Greetings card.

The word 'Happiness' is printed below the picture of three small girls playing with a family of kittens. This example is dated 1880 and may be continental in origin. It follows the style of the more expensive and elaborate designs of the time; deeply embossed with intricate gold decoration and lace. The floral reliefs are fixed on afterwards to add a final flourish.

needed to be innovative in order to sell to a fickle public always out to buy something new and diverting. Novelty die-cut shapes could be applied to most subjects and proved lasting favourites.

Greetings cards in the form of paper fans were very popular with the Victorians; elaborate and exquisitely printed examples are highly collectable today. These were often sent as valentine offerings but below we have a die-cut example of a New Year card showing a line-up of cats.

Christmas greetings card, c.1870. 'Ice Cream'.

Small calling card size 85 x 55 mm.

A mother cat and her family of kittens discover the delights of a bowl of ice cream. A small Christmas card

Christmas Greetings novelty card. c.1880.

A very small envelope stamped 'A Merry Christmas' has a demure black kitten peeping out and the wording 'With (pussy's) love'. This is a card designed for Puss to send to a special friend, his owner or another pussy perhaps.

AND THE WINNER IS...

In 1878, Mr Punch, who nine years earlier had been complaining about

Christmas Greetings novelty card. 1880–89.

An endearing kitten waves to us from its crib which bears the message 'With Loving Christmas Greetings' printed in gold lettering.

'A Merry Christmas to you'.

Her own 'catland' version of Christmas from artist Helena Maguire. c.1890.

Christmas Greetings novelty card. 1880–89.

Another imaginative die-cut card intended for a fond relative to send. Message printed on the lid of the hat-box: ' A loving Christmas to my darling'.

Another clever idea; a fan shaped 'Happy New Year' card, 1880–89.

A Christmas card from the 1870s.

'Pussy and I drink a merry Christmas to you.' A card from the 'Pussy and I' series where pet cats are encouraged to be part of the family.

the monotony of Christmas cards, had changed his tune. The designs had *'grown in quality'* and were now *'so pretty, that it seems a shame to grumble at them'*. The present problem was their overwhelming quantity. For publishers to meet the demand and keep ahead of their competitors required an army of illustrators. Between 1880 and 1882 several large publishers including Raphael Tuck, launched design competitions to spot new talent and attract established artists to their fold. Entries to be judged by a panel of three Royal Academicians and the best put on display at prestigious London galleries. The total prize money ranged from £500 to £5,000, enough to attract the best-known artists of the day. One was Horatio Henry Couldery; his many paintings of cats or more often kittens had earned him the title *'Kitten Couldery'*. This went back as far as 1861 when he first exhibited at the Royal Academy's summer shows. His entry in 1875, *A Fascinating Tail*, earned him the much-quoted appraisal by the eminent critic John Ruskin who was a little skittish at Couldery's expense, or perhaps – kittenish:

'Quite the most skilful piece of minute and Dureresque painting in the exhibition – (it cannot be rightly seen without a lens); and in its sympathy with kitten nature, down to the most appalling depth thereof, and its taste and sensitiveness to the finest gradations of kitten meditation and motion – unsurpassable'.

(A Fascinating Tail realised £6,500 hammer price at Christies' auction room in September 2007).

Kittens in a hat. By H H Couldery. A winning Christmas card design entry in 1881.

Couldery always chose the shorthaired variety of cat as his model

'An Unexpected Visitor'.

Another H H Couldery entry for the Hildesheimer and Faulkner 1881 design competition, where it won a £75 prize. Three kittens frolicking in a lady's flower bedecked hat confront a ladybird which has crawled out of a rose.

Henry Horatio Couldery won a £50 prize in Hildesheimer and Faulkner's competition of 1881 for the above design. It was reproduced as a Christmas card and the signatures of the three judges, Royal Academicians John Everett Millais, G A Storey and Marcus Stone were reproduced on the reverse. Chromolithographs were hastily prepared in order to catch the Christmas trade at fine art stationers. A further dozen or so of Couldery's designs were published up to 1884 and he illustrated at least one nursery book entitled *Two Kittens*. Couldery was a superb cat and still life artist; some of his best work is kept in the Glanmore National Historic Site archive, Ontario Canada.

Of the 925 entrants to Raphael Tuck's 1880 prize competition more than half were women, hopeful perhaps of following in the footsteps of Kate Greenaway who, beginning as a poorly paid greetings card designer for Marcus Ward in the late 1860s, became one of the most highly regarded illustrators of children's books.

A Christmas card which is probably the work of Alice Havers, a popular designer and first prize winner of the 1882 Hildesheimer and Faukner greetings card design competition.

CATS SELL CALENDARS

Frances Simpson writing in 1902 (The Book of the Cat) was struck by the increase of late years in 'catty' Christmas souvenirs: 'We have cat almanacks, cat calendars and Christmas cards – thus giving proof of love and admiration for pussy.'

The calendar published by Ernest Nister in 1896 is a splendid example of 'Catland' humour and attractive colour. The subject is opening day at the 'Royal Cats Academy'. The artist is probably William Foster – son of the celebrated Myles Birket Foster – who was a prolific illustrator of juvenilia during the 1890s

'Furry Friends'.

Raphael Tuck calendar for 1908.

A handsomely produced calendar elaborately colour printed, embossed and die-cut. Definitely top end of the market

K.G *Not before published.*

Kate Greenaway.

Self-portrait with her cat.

The Girl's Own Paper 1902.

An accident-prone tail. Ernest Nister Calender for 1896.

A Kitten in an Edwardian driving glove

Washday.

Kittens at the washtub and working the clothes mangle.

and early 1900s. Two of the 'paintings' on the rear wall are borrowed from earlier Nister publications: a parody of Millais's *Bubbles* and on the right, partly hidden, a scene of a cat family at breakfast from a children's stand-up booklet. Bottom left, a gentleman cat is gazing intently at a picture while standing on the tail of the lady cat nearby.

SCRAP ALBUM CATS

For those Victorians fortunate enough to have time on their hands, agreeable ways to fill it were always welcome. Although we have come to regard reliefs,

A sheet of reliefs featuring cats' faces.

A kitten in a basket of daisies and forget-me-nots. Large relief, size 15x22cm.

A sheet of cats from the Gigantic Relief no 947 Artistic series by Raphael Tuck and Sons.

Reprinted by kind permission of Ms Joan Hoverstadt.

Kittens sing from the same hymn sheet.

or 'scraps' as we know them, as juvenilia, these pieces of colourful ephemera with their engaging social history were often collected by young women and fixed into albums – probably on rainy days long ago. The range of sizes and subjects of these fascinating pieces of ephemera is remarkable. Small embossed and die-cut prints with ready-gummed backs, published in 'broadsheet' format (approximately 24 x 19 cm) numbered from one to several to the sheet. Reliefs reflect Victorian life and cats were frequently featured.

Purpose-printed scrap sheets were leading lines in the catalogues of British based publishers of greetings cards and other ephemera, and 'cart-loads' were imported in from Germany. Pricewise, the German printers and publishers had the edge. In the 1850s they could produce full colour scrap sheets at one-sixteenth the cost of their British counterparts. Later, cut-throat competition forced prices down still further – at least sixty percent by the 1880s. *'Our collection of Penny Reliefs has been largely augmented this season'* proclaimed Raphael Tuck in its sales drive.

THE VALENTINE CARD

The St Valentine's Day tradition of exchanging gifts and tokens goes back several hundred years. The Victorians claimed this annual ritual as their own and the exotic flowering of the valentine card began a journey which lasted over several decades. As the years slipped by into the second half of the 19th century the valentine became more elaborate, with more lace, more embossing, more fine gilt dust sprinkled over intricately sculpted paper. The finishing touch, plenty of small 'scraps' printed in jewel like colours; these were attached by tiny folded paper springs for a three-dimensional effect often with a verse or declaration of love hidden beneath – unseen yet right under the nose of Papa! These extra embellishments pushed up costs; familiar to us nowadays as 'value added'.

For young Edwardians these offerings were not only too expensive to buy, but times had changed and it was no longer seen as 'cool' to send declarations of heartfelt love as had their parents or grand-parents. No longer fashionable, the valentine declined into a sad parody of its former self.

Fortunately for us, these amazing examples of Victorian printing skill and ingenuity were – like the Christmas card – often treasured by their recipients. Tidied carefully away into desk drawers or placed in albums, for future generations to admire and cherish.

Cats on Valentine Cards

With the exception of a devoted minority of adoring feline fanciers, cats were regarded by many in the first half of the 19th century as scratchy, anti-social animals given to howling and fighting all night. So it comes as no surprise to find that they first appeared on comic satirical cards often intended to be highly offensive to the recipient. Although some were no doubt sent tongue in cheek, others were meant to settle old scores or choke off unwanted suitors. To make matters worse, the unfortunate people who received these insults were required

Valentine card. 'May love be thine and thou be mine'. c.1840–50.

A partly hand-coloured valentine card designed to be sent to children from parents, reflects the growing acceptance of cats as nursery pets. It is rare to find a valentine card of this date showing the image of a cat.

Valentine card. A Sly Old Cat, 1840–50.

Was this Hate Mail?: That Bedlam dress will ne'er disguise, Your nature from discerning eyes,
For plainly may be seen, through that,
A selfish, sly and vicious cat.

to pay the postage; some complained, and a sympathetic Post Office obligingly refunded their money. With the introduction of the penny post in 1840 however, the rules were changed and the sender paid as we do today.

A mean looking cat wearing absurdly large headgear topped with a mouse. The verse refers to '*That Bedlam dress*' implying that only a lunatic would wear such a bizarre hair and dress style. The entire head is moveable and by means of a small lever at the end, can be made to nod backwards and forwards. Although St Valentine is not mentioned, the card would have arrived on the day. This was the kind of unsolicited mail that people complained about, often known as 'the vinegar valentine'. Lace paper production increased with improved techniques and was commonly used on greetings cards. On the valentine it remained for several decades as a symbol of bridal chastity.

'The Day of Love'.

An eight page valentine style gift booklet of the Edwardian period. Although unsigned, it is probably the work of Helena Maguire in her 'catland' style.

'To Greet My Valentine'.

A mobile novelty die-cut valentine card from the USA c.1919. A fun-loving cat holds a moveable fan fastened with a small metal rivet.

A late 19th century valentine. 'Faithfully Yours'.

The lace paper panel is fixed on with springs made of folded paper to form a three-dimensional effect for the cat to look through. The floral background is heavily embossed, with two small scraps added as a finishing touch.

Cats ensure they post early for Christmas!'

Chapter 5

'Mr Katzmit'

The London Cats'-Meat Men... and Some Women

One of your nine lives will be spent living *in Victorian London of the 1860s Puss, in an impoverished area of squalid houses each with a single outside water tap and a communal backyard. Typhus and cholera known as 'the fever' is endemic and rats come up from the sewers to hunt the streets for garbage to feed on.*

Your owners are migrants from the countryside who have come to London looking for jobs and they work every day except Sunday. You are needed to protect the home from the constant threat of destructive vermin; and in return, every working day, you earn your special reward - a delicious slice of horsemeat delivered to your door 'with your name on it'.

* * * * *

HOW THE CATS'- MEAT MAN DELIVERED

In Victorian London there were many cats who listened daily for his familiar cry: *'meeet, meeet, cassan-deeargs-meeeat!'* A welcome sound guaranteed to put a skip in their step - dinner was about to arrive through the letter box! A slice of horse-meat served on a skewer: puss ate the meat and the skewer remained as proof of delivery. Puss's

A London cats' meat-man (purveyor of horse flesh) in a street in Bethnal Green in 1902.

Although totally forgotten today, for well over a hundred years the cats and dogs of London waited for his visit. The decorations are to celebrate the coronation of Edward VII on the 9th of August.

© *Museum of London*

heroes, the London cats'-meat men - they never spread to any other city - were not shopkeepers but itinerant hawkers or 'carriers' as they styled

themselves. They made their rounds by appointment only, going from door to door delivering slices of cooked horse-meat for cats and dogs whose owners were out at work all day.

Although this may not accord with the traditional view of Victorian London, the City was growing rapidly; undergoing social and economic changes with migrants displaced from the countryside flocking to the capital to find work. The trade in cat and dogs meat increased in step with the growth of these labouring classes; the carriers' chief customers for half a century. For them, keeping a cat was a necessity. With overcrowding, poor sanitation, inadequate sewers and epidemics of Typhus and Cholera commonplace, cats were needed to combat the hordes of invading rodents which destroyed not only food but clothing, furnishings and even shoe leather. To keep puss fit and active, horse flesh was the most satisfactory answer, it was cheap and in plentiful supply - traffic was all horse drawn at the time - and (unlike fish) for the carnivorous cat, provided ideal nourishment.

Cats' meat carriers were by no means alone in their calling. The streets of

Victorian London were thronged with itinerant hawkers, pedlars and costermongers all selling food and household goods of every kind from nutmeg graters to house slippers; all out to catch a sale from the passing crowds by 'crying up' their goods against the opposition. In Henry Mayhew's seminal work on Victorian street life, *London Labour and the London Poor*, he estimated as many as 30,000 sellers were working the London streets, men, women and children included - whole families were involved, of these, over 1000 were cat and dog meat vendors. Mayhew, a journalist and editor, was also an active campaigner committed to improving the appalling conditions in work-places and factories of the time. In his interviews with the London street sellers, much was noted down in his own shorthand. These personal interviews breathe life into 1850s London and as we read, we hear the chatter of cockney street folk as it tumbles off the page:

'Vy, Sir' said one dealer to me. 'Can you tell me 'ow many peoples in London?' On my reply 'upwards of two million': 'I don't know nothing vatever about millions, but I think there's a cat to every ten people, aye, and more than that, so you can reckon. I must know, for they all know me and I sarves about 200 cats and 70 dogs. Mine is a middlin' trade but some does far better. Some cats have a hap'orth a day, werry few can afford a penn'orth, but times is inferior'.

The carriers bought direct from the knackers' yard, open daily between 5 a.m. and noon. The meat was cheap partly due to the Englishman's traditional distaste for eating it and also because everyone knew of the horrendous conditions and 'scenes of cruelty' at the yard where the horses were slaughtered; their carcasses cut up, boiled and sold on. Some of the animals brought in were diseased, others were dead - their flesh putrifying, but in the interests of a quick turnover, the yard owner often failed to boil the meat long enough to sterilize it thoroughly. The turnover was enormous. In the 1850's according to Mayhew, the twelve London knackers' yards, had a throughput of 750 carcasses a week between them. One yard alone supplied a hundred carriers and the total number of carriers '*a thousand at least*'. Carriers then cut up the cooked meat themselves to their own requirements before making their rounds to sell on to the householder at two and a half pence per 1lb., smaller pieces on skewers at a farthing, a half-penny, and one penny each. One meat seller claimed that he walked 30 to 40 miles in a day to reach all his customers, the best were the districts housing tradesmen, mechanics and labourers. The coachmen in the mews at the back of the squares were also very good buyers. Old maids, although plentiful as customers, tried to beat down the price as well as being bad payers. The dealers said they always had bad debts outstanding.

Clues regarding diets of cats in the average mid Victorian middle class household are not easy to come by. Letters published in the reader advice columns of magazines such as *The Queen* reveal that they were generally fed scraps from the owner's table mixed in with vegetables and gravy and supplemented with that old favourite of felines, a saucer of milk. Offal such as liver was included and lights, which are

'Cat's & Dog's Meat' from *Itinerant Traders of London* by William Marshall Craig.

A lady trader stands beside the fine classical architecture of Bethlem Hospital founded by Henry VIII for the cure of lunatics.

London Metropolitan Archives, City of London

BUY A MAT, OR A HAIR BROOM!

lungs and have very little nourishment value. It is understandable that for many comfortably placed households a regular call from the cats'- meat man would also be of benefit in feeding other pets, Fido liked it too!

In the early 1850s Henry Mayhew reckoned there were 300,000 cats in central London, equal to the number of occupied houses: not that every family kept one, but that many lodgers as well as householders did so. Thirty years or so later Andrew Tuer (*Old London Street Cries*) put the London cat population at 350,000 and Frances Simpson in 1903 at 750,000 or four times the number of dogs. These figures only include domesticated animals. There was an incalculable number of ferals and semi-ferals, often starving and diseased.

Today, street criers are the preserve of historians; probably the best known is the muffin man who rang a hand-bell to attract custom and is the subject of a children's nursery rhyme. *'The history of cries is a history of social changes'* wrote Charles Hindley in 1881 as he lamented the passing of the working traders such as *'Old chairs to mend', 'A brass or iron pot to mend'* and *'Any work for John Cooper?'* The muffin-man's bell long ago silenced by act of parliament. Remarkably, the cry of the cats'-meat man lived on for 50 years into the next century; he stands alone as the unlikely inspiration for artists, poets, satirists, sociologists, religious homilies and comic songs.

An early sighting may be that of watercolourist Paul Sandby's *'The Purveyor of Offals'* one of *'Twelve London Cries Drawn from Life'* 1759. The sale of attractive prints to the public flourished then, as it does today. Pictures of street vendors were always popular, often depicted as handsome, young and fashionably dressed; for added appeal to the buyer. Sandby declared his motive was not to romanticise his subjects as others had done, but to show them as they really were: dirty, grimy, ragged and villainous. Professor Sean Shesgreen, a leading authority on London street criers, suggests that *The Purveyor of Offals* was a fore-runner of the cats'-meat trade. By 1804 it seems trade was brisk and we see pictured a woman cats'-meat seller in a tourist guide with the lengthy title: *Itinerant Traders of London in their Ordinary Costumes with Notices of the Remarkable Places in the Background.* Smartly dressed, with her barrow all neatly laid out, she lends a decorative foreground to a famous London building. Just the sort of thing Paul Sandby would have sneered at.

It is from Craig that we hear the first of many accounts of the legions of hungry cats that followed in the wake of the carrier *'surrounded by a crowd of animals'* and that she sold:

'horse flesh, bullocks livers and tripe cuttings carried to every part of the town. The two former are sold at twopence per pound and the latter tied up in bunches of one penny each'.

Craig's observation that the trade was *'engrossed by women'* is not entirely consistent with early 19th century illustrations which suggest that the trade was more evenly split between men and women. As time went on women lost their market share, they were looked down on, caricatured and treated with contempt - as we shall see.

THE CAT'S-MEAT MAN.

CATS MEAT.

recruits usually began in a modest way with a basket 'rising to a barrow'. An article by the Reverend W. Baird

In Sam Syntax's *'Cries of London'* Sam, the cat's- meat man makes a delivery to a well-heeled family in an inner city street. 'Jane' is probably a family servant who is charged with purchasing the cats' meat. The neat panniers of Sam's donkey distinguish him as a more superior trader than his peers who make shift with hand-carts, wheelbarrows or baskets.

SETTING UP THE TOOLS OF THE TRADE

What led men - and a lesser number of women - to set up as cats-meat carriers? Some, for various reasons, had failed in their previous vocation. *'My father was a baker'* one carrier told Mayhew:

'but through the enlargement of the heart he was obliged to give up working at the trade. This made him take to the cats' and dogs' meat trade, and he brought me up to it'.

One inducement was the small starting capital needed. The only essential tools of the trade were weights and measures, a knife and steel for sharpening, and a receptacle to deliver the meat - a basket (or a barrow). Altogether, these could be bought for £2 new or as little as four shillings second hand. New

in the Alverstoke Hampshire, Parish Magazine of July 1865 gives an insight into the cats-meat trade. Baird's own intimate knowledge of London's East End society is enlightening:

'There is probably no branch of the street trade, in which there are so many different degrees of success as in this. We find men who earn a very fair livelihood in this way, and who do their best to maintain a respectable appearance. There are others however, whose sole worldly possession is the miserable basket in which they carry their merchandise'.

So even for a humble cats'-meat trader, business acumen was vital. A few traders used a dog drawn cart up to 1839 when a Police Act banned the use of dog-carts from the London Metropolitan area, then about 15 miles. Dogs were cheap to house and feed and whereas donkeys and ponies paid road tolls, dogs did not.

Victorians loved humour and *Tynt's Streetology* was a popular magazine that aimed to amuse its readers. It seems that street people - impoverished folk who could scarcely scrape a living - were regarded as figures of fun. 'Paunch', see opposite, is the seller of 'mousers' grub'. He is an 'idler' who sits in his small heavily loaded cart - while his dog does all the work. Cats meat-men had a name for being drunkards so the local public house is shown on his itinerary. He is the cats'-meat swell, or 'toff' of Peter Street, where he lives, which is also his office or premises where he keeps the horse meat victuals for the cats. He holds up a half-penny skewer of meat threaded kebab style, the traditional way the meat was served to customers, ready for puss to eat.

Again, Henry Mayhew gives us some fascinating anecdotes which have the genuine ring of tap-room chatter. The carriers, he says, *'meet up at the Donkey Market in Smithfield every Friday afternoon where they retire to a public house to spend the evening'*. He may well have been present on one or two of these occasions:

'There was one black lady who used as much as 16 pennyworth every day. She used to get out on the roof of her house and throw it out to the cats on the tiles. She brought so many cats round about the neighbourhood that parties in the vicinity complained... between ten and eleven in the morning the noise and cries of the hundreds of stray cats attracted to the spot was terrible to hear. The riot and confusion and fighting was beyond description.'

An even more generous feline benefactress described to Mayhew as *'a mad woman in Islington'* bought as much as:

'14 lbs. of meat a day. The party who supplied her had his money often at £2 and £3 at a time (large sums for a carrier). Every stray cat that came she would take in and support. The stench was so great that she was obliged to be ejected.'

Yet crazy as they were thought to be and sadly inadequate their efforts, these must be amongst the earliest testimonies to un-self-serving kindness to luckless cats on the part of people themselves deprived.

THE CATS'-MEAT WOMEN

Early 19th century illustrations suggest that the cats' meat trade was evenly divided between men and women; but as time went on it is clear that women lost their market share. There seems no obvious reason why a sturdy wench

Cats'-Meat Nan. 'The Lady as Cries Cats' Meat'.
From Charles Hindley's *History of the Street Cries of London.* 1884.

Accompanying satirical verses for Cats'- Meat Nan:

Old Maids, your custom I invites,
Fork out, and don't be shabby,
And don't begrudge a bit of lights,
Or liver for your tabby.

Here's famous meat, all lean, no fat -
No better in Great Britain;
Come buy a penn'orth for your cat
A happ'orth for your kitten.

Come, all my barrow for a bob!
Some charity diskiver;
For faith it ar'nt an easy job
To live by selling liver.

could not hold her own with a man, yet Mayhew was assured *very few women do well at it*. Perhaps they were at a disadvantage when it came to 'chatting up' housewives and maidservants. We must also remember that all Mayhew's informants were men, and rivalry led to hostility between the sexes. Most of what we know about the women carriers in the 1830s and '40s comes from doggerel verses, published as ballads, presumably all male composed and prejudiced, hardly to be relied on at face value. The least the women were charged with was incompetence. One is so engrossed in 'crying up' her wares that she fails to spot a hungry dog plundering her barrow - *which caused a deal of sport* to the bystanders. Another loses control of the dog pulling her cart when he chases after a cat. A third, 'Catsmeat Nan' is immediately placed as 'downmarket' because she sells to *old maids*. Having *bawled til I am sick* she wants to see some cash *I never give no tick* - this could also have been another reason why she was uncompetitive. She ends up offering her whole barrowload for a *bob* (a shilling). Nan's meat includes offal such as liver and lights which sellers generally included in their range in the early part of the 19th century.

It is interesting too, that her meat *all lean, no fat* was apparently considered then as now, preferable for cats.

Then there was 'Kitty Flare' caricatured as hideously ugly, lecherous, sly and full of jokes - who cuckolds her husband Bob, with 'Jim Crow, the

dancing black man':

'The busy nurse came down with speed
And unto Bob she did discover
That Kitty dear was brought to bed,
And all her care and trouble over;
Oh such a bargain for you Bob,
Such a curious little fellow
With face coal black and curly nob,
The very picture of Othello.'

From a scurrilous Broadsheet Ballad circa 1833-43 published by Birt's of Seven Dials in the East End of London.

The Reverend Baird writing a generation later strikes a more humane note, again from his personal experience of London's East End, where there were women:

'whose decrepitude prevents them from gaining any other occupation, but who can just manage to crawl along from house to house with their scanty baskets of horse flesh'.

But even as the Reverend Baird's sad scenario was taking place, some traders were making a good living aided by a growing population, which between the censuses of 1831 and 1861 grew from 1.907 to 3.227 million. A tendency towards gentrification was emerging amongst the carriers; one was rumoured to have savings of £1000. Another, Mayhew visited at his home and found it:

'more comfortably situated than any of the poorer classes that I have yet seen. He lived in the front room of a second floor [apartment] in a respectable quarter of town and his lodgings were the perfection of comfort and cleanliness. I found his family preparing for supper. In a large morocco leather easy chair sat the cats' meat carrier himself; his blue apron and shiny hat had disappeared, and he wore a 'dress' coat; and a black satin waistcoat instead. His wife, who was a remarkably pretty woman and of very attractive manners, wore a 'Dolly Varden' cap placed jauntily at the back of her head, and a drab maroon dress. The room was cosily carpeted and in one corner stood a mahogany crib in which one of the children was asleep. The cleanliness and wholesomeness of the apartment were striking.'

Dolly Varden, famous for lending her name to a hat is a character from Charles Dickens's *Barnaby Rudge*, the implication here is of a woman who cares about her appearance and is a credit to her husband; the entire family seem to have stepped out of a Dickens novel. Cats'-meat traders were well known as snappy dressers: shiny top hats, black plush waistcoats, trim blue apron over corduroy trousers and distinctively, two or three blue-and-white handkerchiefs knotted round their necks.

As their clientele became more genteel, so did the cat's-meat men's pretensions. By 1885, one at least - J. W. Evans - had begun to advertise in the newspapers.

Mr Evans of Drury Lane even claims to be purveyor to the Royal Family. Although such claims were not so closely monitored then as they are today, this may not have been farfetched. There were pet cats in the Royal household long before this date, as well as Royal Mousers in the stables. Another to lay claim to royal patronage was 'Mr. Katzmit,' author Charles Morley's fictional character set in his garret-room around 1890. Morley portrays the carrier's life style in telling detail, based on his own factual observation:

'Presently we found ourselves in a narrow byway composed of dirty houses which had seen much better days. We mounted a break-neck set of stairs, which twisted and turned until they led you into a low little room, in which a great fire was blazing, and the heat of which reminded one of

the tropics, except for the strong odour of fried onions. In the centre of the room was a square table without a cover, over which an old man of sixty was standing. He was slicing up a huge dark-looking piece of meat, and wielded a sharp blade with

Dinner Arrives.

A housemaid takes delivery of the cats' meat for her employer's pets in a genteel London suburb.

From a chromo-lithographically printed and embossed relief, c1885.

wonderful dexterity, dividing the slices with amazing equality, putting down the knife every minute, and slipping the slices on to a wooden skewer. He shared his abode with a pet shop proprietor who kept a small menagerie, and a lady who earned a living through her troupe of performing white mice, and who was 'a bit queer':

'That's 'im: Mr.Katzmit, PUSSY

BUTCHER to the Rile Family and Aristocracy' whispered Mr Chaffinch, pointing respectfully to the old man. 'A wonderful old fellow. Don't mind if he doesn't notice you. He's a bit proud since he became a Rile tradesman and mixed with the nobility. Ha! He knows a lot about cats, he does.'

'Mr Katzmit,' Morley enquired, 'Will you tell me how you got your position as purveyor to the Court?'

'I had a brother sir, as was a Rile sweep, and swep the the Rile chimbleys, and a sister who was a Rile landry, and lung up the Rile linin, and a cousin as cleaned Rile windows - the family 'as been connected with Rilety as long as I can remember.'

Whether Mr Katzmit was speaking the truth or not I cannot say. I can say, however, that his cart bears the Royal Arms.'

As the middle classes took to keeping cats as nursery pets, the carriers began to infiltrate the leafier outer suburbs. The writer of a letter to the Illustrated London News could choose between two competing cats'-meat men:

'As the hour for the visit approaches, the cats are sure to be waiting at the door, and set up their sweet voices as soon as they hear that of the vendor of the food. They take not the slightest notice of a rival practitioner who perambulates the streets at nearly the same time. On Sundays, when no visit

"ME-E-EAT!"

'M-E-E-EAT!'

A very happy tabby cat carries off his slice on a skewer.

Dawn of Day magazine. May 1888.

Dan The Cat's Meat Man, Sheet Music.

Words composed by E.A.Sheppard and Charles Collins. Sung by Fred Earle.

takes place, they never appear to expect the workday ceremony.'

In the 1880s an anonymous contributor to Charles Hindley's *London Street Cries* describes the local cats'-meat man's daily visits to another outer suburb:

'Every morning as true as the clock - the quiet of "Our Village Green" is broken by a peculiar and suggestive cry. We do not hear it yet ourselves, but Pincher, our black and tan terrier dog, and Smut, our black and white cat, have both caught the well known accents, and each with natural characteristics, - one wagging his tail, the other with a stiff perpendicular dorsal appendage - sidles towards the door, demanding as plainly as possible to be let out. Yes, it is our "Dandy Cats' and Dogs' Meat Man," with his "Ca'me-e-et - dogs' me yet - ca' or de-arge - me - yet!!!" that fills the morning air, and arouses exactly seven dogs of various kinds and exactly thirty-one responsive feline voices - there is a cat to every house on "Our Village Green"- and causes thirty-one aspiring cats' tails to point

1st Stanza:

Down in our locality they call me Dan,
Everybody knows me as the 'Cat's Meat man'
Walking about with my basket full of meat
Up and down the street.
People say I'm a friend to all the cats,
And they make a fuss of me, they do!
And the poor old 'moggies' soon as I pass by,
They wave their tails and all begin to mew...

3rd Stanza:

All the cats I serve are always wearing smiles,
Always advertising me upon the tiles.
The Tom cats, say when their sweethearts want a treat,
'Come along to Dan and try a skewer full of meat!'
Black cats, white cats, and "ginger" ones as well,
when they're praising up my meat don't fail.
But the Manx cats never say a word for me
Cause they don't know the way to tell the tale!

Top: Picture postcard 'Popular Play
"The Lights of London".

Bottom: Picture postcard by Tom Browne,
'How Happy I Could be With Either'.

Will Puss choose the milkman or the cats'-meat man?

*'How Happy I could be with either - were t'other dear
charmer away'*

from the 18th century Beggar's Opera, a pastiche of
popular contemporary songs centred on two ladies
who fight over their chosen man.

to the zenith. We don't know how it is, but the Cats' Meat Man is the most unerring and punctual of all those peripatetic functionaries who undertake to cater for the public. The baker, the butcher, the grocer, the butterman, the fishmonger, and the coster, occasionally forget your necessities, or omit to call for your orders - the Cats' Meat Man never!'

The letter brings to life an everyday domestic scene in a comfortable Victorian household where everything is delivered and supermarkets are not yet invented. Of particular interest is the writer's ability to convey the cry of the cats'-meat-man on to the written page, these descriptions are now our only link to a unique and forgotten sound from long ago.

Perhaps because they were thought of as trusty and reliable compared with some other door-to-door tradesmen, the cats'-meat men seem to have found favour with middle class householders. In 1888 they were even the topic of a homily in the religious magazine *'Dawn of Day'*, clearly meant to be read and acted on by women unduly preoccupied by their daily chores. The message: the family cat can sense the approach of the carrier when he is still a street away and rushes out to greet him; whereas the women, engrossed in gossiping and ironing their washing, are scarcely aware when he knocks on their door. Just as many poor sinners are deaf to the word of the Lord. Well done you cats!

Music Hall entertainment had a knack of embracing every aspect of daily life however hum-drum. Dan, The Cat's Meat Man sheet music was published in 1913. 'This song may be sung in public without Fee or Licence, except at Theatres and Music Halls, which rights are reserved. For Pantomime permissions apply to Francis Day & Hunter.'

Picture postcards of the time portrayed the cats-meat man as friendly and genial and this seems to reflect the way he was regarded. Among any group of people numbering a thousand or more there are 'baddies' as well as 'goodies'. But clearly he was seen as 'on the side of the angels.' Many years later a correspondent to *Cats and Kittens* magazine, January 1953, recalled those times, and the kindness to cats of the carrier who had delivered regularly to his own family's pet:

'Often there would be another cat, not a paying customer, but with tail erect, rubbing against his legs. And always he found a titbit for the stranger, a small one if it was obviously from a good home, where it was fed, a larger one if it was a stray. I do not know if he was typical of the hundreds of cats'-meat men who walked the streets… but he was certainly in his rough and ready way, a cat lover, it gave him genuine pleasure to see his customers pleased.'

It may have helped that some carriers, at least, were more prosperous than ever before through their involvement with the several London based charities which had sprung up in the 1890s dedicated to the welfare of cats and dogs. Horseflesh was the cheapest way to feed large numbers of animals and for the carriers delivering in bulk it meant they could afford to cut their prices to the customer.

This may explain the cordial relations which existed between the carriers and the National Cat Club, whose members often supported these same animal charities. Before the turn of the century the NCC had begun to treat the cats' meat men to a generous annual dinner party at Christmas or New Year at one or other London restaurant or hotel.

One event described guests being welcomed with an address by an NCC representative, and a leading cats-meat man responded (there was no organised trade association). The menu included Brown Windsor soup, roast beef and two veg., with a choice of pie or suet pudding with custard - washed down with beer. It sounds rather formal and the gentlemen of the NCC ate separately from their guests - but 'a good time was had by all'.

PUSSY'S BEST FRIENDS CELEBRATE

On a grander scale and less patronisingly class-conscious, was the dinner held in January 1901 at the City of New York restaurant in the Strand; jointly sponsored by the National Cat Club and *Our Cats* magazine, and organised by the Club's Chairman of Committee, Louis Wain. With Wain on board, an element of fun was bound to pop up somewhere and we are not disappointed. Two hundred and fifty cats' meat men sat down to eat, but another four hundred and fifty who

The Cat's–Meat Man.
From The Little People's Book of Fun, published by Ernest Nister. 1903

had applied for tickets had to be turned down; the room could hold no more. This was a famous occasion; later recalled by Frances Simpson in *The Book of The Cat* with further reminiscences from contributors to *Cat Gossip* magazine March 1927. It seems the event got off to a chaotic start, a moment captured for us by Wain himself in an article for *Boy's Own Paper*. On his arrival at the door: 'a mass of small boys who were present set up a dismal caterwauling in my honour the moment the cab drew up. I walked through a perfect pandemonium of cat calls, meows, and unearthly yells. But it was all in the best of temper. I was a popular hero that night. Even when I had seated myself at the table, one of these urchins who, by some means known only to small boys, had managed to escape the vigilance of the doorkeeper, came upon all fours, arching his back and purring round my chair. It all added to the joviality of the occasion, and I can assure you that my friends enjoyed the fare we provided and which, I need hardly say, was not cat's meat!'

A letter from the Princess of Wales was read, wishing the dinner success. The menu included Mock Turtle soup, roast beef or boiled mutton (merrily greeted by the men with their familiar calls of "Meat! Cat's Me-e-e-at!"), cauliflower, sprouts (handed round by the Duchess of Bedford), and baked potatoes. Then followed plum pudding and cheese and biscuits. In addition, each guest was given a tin of tobacco, worth two shillings and ninepence.

Following the meal both Louis Wain and the Duchess of Bedford - the then president of the National Cat Club - paid tribute to the cats' meat men for their humanity:

'I do not know' said the Duchess, 'that it necessarily follows that because you are a seller of cats' meat you are all fond of cats, but I have heard of your going out of your way to be kind to starving pussies. As the owner of what was once a stray cat* and afterwards fed I believe, by a cats' meat man, I have pleasure in wishing you all prosperity in the New Year.'

*The cat referred to by the Duchess had narrowly escaped being destroyed, before being rescued by a carrier and handed on to her. She named it 'Napoleon'.

As if a Duchess addressing a company of cats' meat carriers is not surprising enough, to end the proceedings there was a concert in which - an almost bizarre touch - the celebrated author, breeder, and show-judge Frances Simpson sang at the piano for assembled guests.

The irony was that horseflesh was falling out of favour with many of the National Cat Club's breeders and fanciers. Pedigree cats were expensive to rear and as prone as any other to infections for which there was then no known cure. Caution and care regarding what they were given to eat came under growing scrutiny. Critics claimed that the meat

went 'off' quickly in hot weather when it was often fly-blown and from diseased animals. Horseflesh was defended by such authorities as Harrison Weir and J. G. Gardner who wrote in favour, as long as it was fresh. However, Edith Carrington writing in 1890 (*The Cat, her place in Society and Treatment*) was adamant:

'The abomination called 'cats' meat sold about the streets should never be bought, though some cats like it better than anything else. It is generally horse flesh taken from diseased carcasses.'

The pro, or anti, horseflesh debate continued unabated between breeders and fanciers. 'Ordinary' cat owners were oblivious as long as the meat was cheap and easy to obtain. To judge from the number of illustrations in books, picture postcards, and other printed ephemera, the cats'-meat men seem to have attracted more favourable publicity in the early 1900s than ever before.

During the 1914–18 war they fade from view and those who remained in business must have been hard hit as food shortages pushed up the cost even of inferior grades of meat. After the war the trade revived and for another twenty years and more cats'-meat men were again a familiar part of the London street scene.

MEMORIES

In 1995 Cats Protection magazine *Cats* published correspondence about cats'-meat men during the inter-war years. One letter from Mr K. Noir, described

(in detail which Henry Mayhew would have applauded) the carrier who in the 1920s delivered to the north London street where he lived as a boy:

'Each weekday evening at about 5-30 he would come round the corner in dirty mac and greasy cap, pursued Pied Piper-like, by a horde of hungry cats'.

These however, 'were not the recipients of his wares, for he was not a hawker but came only by arrangement. A basket over one arm contained the orders of sliced horsemeat, impaled upon roughly cut sticks, similar to those used for toffee-apples. He need not knock on any door. The pussy's meal was simply shot through the letter-box and of course, the house cat was waiting on the doormat. He devoured his meal and the stick was left to reassure the mistress of the house that the goods had been delivered.' He charged a penny a day and called on Saturdays to collect his pay.'

WAR COMES AS TIMES CHANGE

During the 1930s the motor vehicle had largely replaced horses as a means of transport. Fewer horses were slaughtered, disposal of their carcasses was more strictly monitored and Veterinary certification was required before it could be sold as edible.

More dramatically, the outbreak of the Second World War in September 1939 was followed at once by a massive cull of domestic animals. Vets and charitable institutions were besieged by owners queuing to have their pets put down.

The records of the Royal Society for the Prevention of Cruelty to Animals and the People's Dispensary for Sick Animals agree that within days, between 400,000 and half a million dogs and cats, chiefly the latter were destroyed. The majority were taken to the PDSA's estate near Ilford, and buried in pits because local authorities' incinerators could not cope. This was a shameful episode, suggestive of mass panic and hysteria, which was concealed till after the war because it reflected badly on Londoners' morale. A further slaughter took place in August 1940 when enemy air raids began in earnest.

The American novelist Alice Grant Rosman, who lived in London during the first years of the 'blitz' writes of one of the shelters that had been set up, manned by voluntary workers to care for injured or destitute animals. She noted that the only tradesfolk to call there daily were *'the milkman and the cats-butcher (who delivers by perambulator)'*.

In March 1942 a correspondent to Cats Protection magazine recalled a scene that had stuck in her memory since the previous year:

'It was a bleak morning in April 1941 in a south London suburb which had been severely blitzed the previous night. The streets were littered with broken glass. Firemen were still playing their hoses on charred, smoking ruins, but the mean street where the cats' meat man had his shop had escaped, and here stood a queue of shabby, dusty people, mostly women, pale and haggard but cheery. They chatted as they slowly moved along to receive each half a pound of horse-flesh. Pussy must have his dinner - whatever happens.'

The shop was a last resort. The carrier was no longer able to sell door to door. After this, silence; or at least no later mention is found. In 1952 author Warren Tute sought out and interviewed a former carrier, Jim Meade, who had retired in the 1920s to keep a pub in Hannibal Street in the East End. A great cockney character, he was involved in local government and served on the boards of several hospitals:

'Used to be in the meat trade', he rapped out. 'People used to ask- what's your job? I used to say "dumb animals, food purveyor." Had four men working for me. Cat's meat. Used to serve it out on skewers a farthing a time.

One of the last of his kind. A cats'-meat man on his rounds, c1940-41 during the London Blitz.

Nine Lives, A Cat in London in Peace and War,
by Alice Grant Rosman.1941.

Chuck it down the gratings, flip it through the letter-boxes, up through the windows while the guv'nor was shaving. Good business. Look what I pay now, - eight bob a week for two pound of horsemeat for two cats and one dog, - terrible!'

Warren Tute and Felix Fonteyne

Cockney Cats. 1953.

Chapter 6

Health Matters

The Slow Move into the Twentieth Century

Because you always 'walk on the wild *side' Puss, it is assumed you can look after yourself and that a cat is not worth saving anyway. Throughout the 19th century your dietary needs are sadly neglected and once again you come last and least. Even veterinary surgeons are ignorant, having been trained mainly in the treatment of horses and farm animals. Although you are established as a popular pet, many of your tribe still wander the streets and quiet cemeteries starving and diseased, where death awaits at the hands of the vivisector and fur trader – or in the lethal chambers of the newly formed cat rescue charities. You will live through the horrors of two World Wars when food will be scarce and many thousands of pets are again routinely put down. Although the 20th century brings more hardship, it sees the start of a better life for your fellow cats and the foundation of your own charity, Cats Protection.*

*****

In *Household Words*, 18 April 1857, a weekly journal published and edited by Charles Dickens, he writes:

'At last the cat has been promoted to the literary honours which have so long been her due and so long been delayed. She has *had an entire book written about her, all to herself, by the Honourable Lady Cust.'*

PUSSY'S FIRST CARE BOOK

In her modest little volume *The Cat, its History and Diseases*, Lady Mary

Title Page of The Cat, its History and Diseases, 1st edition 1856, by Lady Mary Ann Cust.
Bodleian Libraries, University of Oxford
G. Pamph 2366 (9)

Ann Cust tried to answer some of the questions being asked by a growing cat ownership on how to care for their pets. She dedicated her book to Professor Owen, a member of the Royal Society. In the preface she remarks that while books had been written on the natural history of dogs, cows, pigs and other animals, she had looked in vain for a similar work on 'The Cat', an animal to which she herself is very partial. So she had '*determined to take up her pen on the subject, for the benefit of those who have some regard for the Cat; regretting to be obliged to concede, from such an omission, that the cat is not now considered worthy of notice, or its life worth preserving.*'

However, as we read on, it becomes clear that cats did, after all, have their devotees; and it was her aim to answer the questions of numerous friends '*who have appealed to me, saying, "my poor puss is so ill! and I cannot find any work upon cats. Do tell me what I must do?"*'

Lady Cust had once been Lady of the Bedchamber to the Duchess of Kent, Queen Victoria's mother, and she was among the few British breeders of thoroughbred Angora cats – most of which were still imported from France,

Spain and even direct from Persia. No doubt the friends she refers to were ladies who, like herself, owned longhaired cats. The first part of Lady Cust's book is merely a résumé of Moncrif's *Les Chats* which was not yet available in English translation. But the remainder is a pioneering attempt to address common problems such as administering medicine: wrap the animal in a cloth to stop it struggling and be sure to wear thick gloves. Hand rearing kittens deserted by their mother: feed cow's milk sweetened with brown sugar. Treating diarrhoea: mutton suet, dissolved in warm milk followed by a teaspoon of chalk mixture used for the same purpose in human beings; together with seven or eight drops of tincture of rhubarb and four or five of laudanum every few hours. Lady Cust's sound advice was no doubt gained by her practical experience in breeding cats.

She recognises feline enteritis ('distemper' as she and later Victorian writers call it) as a separate and *very dangerous*' disease for which there was no known antidote: the only recourse was to try to nurse the animal through with tiny amounts of *melted beef marrow*' or the like to help maintain its strength. She refers to an unidentified skin complaint causing incessant itching as well as the hair to fall off (possibly an early stage of ringworm). Treatment was flowers of sulphur mixed with fresh hog's lard. '*Fleas*', she adds, '*are very pernicious to cats, they make them thin*'; but she does not explain what to do about them. At this point she concludes

'I have now written all that would be interesting to know on the subject of cats.'

GRASS IS GOOD

Much of Lady Cust's homespun advice may have been known already, handed down by word of mouth, to those who cared to know. But in one vital respect she broke new ground:

'It is a curious fact that cats will never prosper without grass to eat! I have long observed and been convinced of this; and was ridiculed for my opinion when I asserted it, even by some members of the Zoological Society, who would not believe that grass was necessary to the feline tribe in general, or that they would even eat it, until they witnessed the veracity with which it was devoured after deprivation of it for even a few days.'

Lady Cust's book must have sold well: it was reprinted in 1857 and in a new edition in 1870 before it was superseded by William Gordon Stables' *Cats, their Points and Characteristics* in 1874. Although more entertaining, it added little to care and maintenance. In fact, the best sources of information – such as there were – came not from text books but from the agony columns of the up-market ladies magazines. *The Queen* in particular, ran a weekly feature, 'The Naturalist' where readers' queries regarding domestic pets could be answered by editorial staff or by fellow subscribers. From the late 1860s more and more of these enquiries centred on cats – mostly the long-haired varieties.

THE AGONY COLUMN

Many letters to 'The Naturalist' column were concerned with the grooming of longhaired cats. Brushing and combing was advised and owners were reassured that bathing in warm soapy water could do no harm. Unfortunately, some owners saw their cats in the same light as dirty linen and added washing soda to the bath water. This may explain some of the sorry stories of severe skin irritation – rashes, sores and swellings with animals tearing out their fur. There was a different problem for an anguished reader in August 1872:

'Can any subscriber tell me what to do for my Angora cats?' wailed Ethelred Florence: '*I have three in a London house, which possesses a small garden. They are fed on lights and milk, and take plenty of exercise, yet they seem to pine away most dreadfully, in fact, they are only bones and fur. I have two small dogs who look fit and well, I cannot understand why the poor pussies should look so miserable.*'

This letter produced a crop of suggestions from readers ranging from digestive disorders due to swallowing matted fur, intestinal worms from eating lights, to an unbalanced diet. But what was a *balanced* diet? No one really knew but Ethelred Florence was undoubtedly misguided regarding the food she was giving her pussies. Lights (lungs) have hardly any nutritional value for a cat and should only be fed occasionally, if at all. Milk is another problem; although it is seen as a traditional food and they love it, cats are lactose intolerant (unable to digest sugars

Picture Postcard dated 1913. 'A Knowing Cat'.
Milk straight from the cow

in milk once they are weaned), making it difficult to digest and often the cause of diarrhoea.

It seems milk for Puss direct from the cow was not an unusual occurrence in the dairy farming world and the practice must have continued for a very long time. In his book 'Cats' Company', Michael Joseph quotes a story which was sent to him:

'A cat who was attached to the farm belonging to my grandfather's house in the 1860s used regularly to accompany a cowman when he went milking. The cat would sit close to him in order to have a jet of milk directed into his mouth straight from the cow.'

Another reader of The Naturalist column in *The Queen* for 31 August 1872, who signed herself 'Archeress', had kept Persian cats for many years she said and had seen them in the same poor condition that Ethelred Florence had experienced. 'Stop feeding lights' she advised, and 'too much meat of any sort is bad for them. The left-over's from the dinner table are quite enough, supplemented with fish and poultry bones, plenty of cabbage and potatoes, as much milk as they like and (following Lady Cust's advice) access to fresh grass.'

In emphasising the importance of vegetables in the diet, 'Archeress' is advanced for her time but she gave bad advice over poultry bones which can be sharp and dangerous for the intestines. It is interesting to note that the concerns of all these apparently upper crust lady breeders were with regard to the new Persian longhairs. No one wrote in to agonise over the kitchen mouser.

Any debate about whether or not to feed cats kept only to kill vermin is firmly settled in Stephen's *Book of the Farm*, 1844. The advice given is valid today:

Cats… neglected of food… will not hunt. A regular fed cat makes the best hunter, because it hunts for sport, and not pressed by hunger will watch at the same spot for hours. Being strong from its daily wholesome food it feels courage to encountering any vermin and will kill numbers in the course of a day. A starved cat which hunts for food (not sport) eats the first prey it catches and gorging itself lies down to sleep. People who will not take the trouble to feed a cat daily and regularly must be troubled with vermin.

Turning from food to medication highlights the differences between then and now. In the 19th century flea infestations could be severe. Keating's, the well known insecticide manufacturers, marketed their 'Persian powder' which, it was claimed, 'if rubbed in among the roots of the hair, will destroy them (fleas) all in the course of an hour or two'. One reader who had found this treatment completely ineffective and her cat 'still swarming with fleas' resorted to washing it with carbolic soap. When this failed, the advice given by the editorial column was: 'The carbolic soap is not sufficiently strong – try carbolic acid.' Disastrous advice as carbolic acid is phenol based and extremely toxic to cats.

STARTING FOR THE LADIES' PLATE.

Starting For the Ladies' Plate. Title Page.
The Comic Offering 1831.

FLORENCE NIGHTINGALE'S GRIEF

Help was not forthcoming on these problems from the veterinary practitioners of the day who were trained mainly in the care of horses, cattle and other farm animals; small pets were not usually catered for or even understood. Florence Nightingale came upon veterinary ignorance to her cost and the lives of two of her beloved cats. On 11 December 1884 she writes to her brother-in law, Sir Harry Verney, who lived a few doors from her own house off Park Lane: *My beautiful cat died in the night and her kitten is dying – the result of a veterinary surgeon's "Wash"!! May I bury them in your garden?**

* There is no explanation as to why Florence asked this favour when she had a garden of her own.

A fortnight later she vents her anger in a letter to Professor Burdon Sanderson MD, whom she knew, and who had been instrumental in founding Brown's Hospital for Animals, a charitable institution which later became Battersea Dogs and Cats Home. She minces no words:

'-my unhappy experience of what you would call the Brute-like ignorance of Veterinary Surgeons in treating thorough-bred cats. Within the past month, a highly recommended Veterinary Surgeon so treated the last of a famous breed of real Persian cats – that they died – a mother and her kitten in 36 hours of torture. Both were in perfect health before. The cat had scratched a small wound on her neck, occasioned, as he said,

by 'parasites'. To destroy these 'parasites' he destroyed the cats, in spite of my warnings and entreaties to run no such risk, steeping both cat and kitten in a "Patent Dressing" which he said, he always used with success.'

There was more of this emotional outburst which is out of keeping with Florence Nightingale's normal gritty, down to earth approach. She was advised to prosecute the vet in question who ran a large practice near London tending all kinds of animals. *'I do not wish to injure him,'* she said, *'But I wish to save future animals from Veterinary Surgeons. It is not only for the sake of valuable pets but for the sake of all animals that I write.'*

The most devastating of all diseases, feline enteritis or 'distemper' as it was then known, came to a crisis point with prolonged outbreaks from around 1890 up to the early 1900s, at least in London and the south-east.

The Naturalist column in *The Queen* August 1872 gives us a classic description of how the cats: *'begin by being continually sick, with diarrhoea, and soon become unable to move and in a few hours are dead.'* The editor's reply was not comforting: *'Distemper is of the nature of typhoid in man, no medicine is of the slightest use.'* The writer was advised that the only hope of recovery was to try nursing the cat with a nourishing liquid diet such as beef tea or gravy running from a large joint of meat.

Once again Florence Nightingale's pets were hard hit. Her brother-in law, Sir Harry Verney, offered to find her replacements and she wrote to thank him:

'There are this year five little graves of my five beautiful kittens, and a sixth of my dear old Pet, in your garden at South Street,' she writes, *'But I feel as if I had no heart to begin again [breeding them]. So I think I will not write for either kitten, as I am strongly tempted after you had taken so much trouble.'*

DEATH STALKS THE CAT SHOWS

Cat shows were a ready source of cross-infection and relations between competitors – rarely amicable – were not improved by allegations that cats had been 'poisoned' by their rival catteries. For poisonings to be taken for granted as a normal hazard seems strange to us today, and from the evidence, not even logical. This was not the view of J G Gardner in 1890*:

'It seems impossible anyone could be so wicked as purposely to poison a beautiful unoffending creature, yet I fear there is little doubt.'

*Rev. J G Gardner. The Cat, being my Experience of 'Poor Puss'.

He had recently lost two kittens bought at the Crystal Palace show in 1889. Both were suffering from poison he said, although he had taken the precaution of going to the Palace himself to fetch them home. Gardner also refers to a complaint *'something very much like distemper'* (in dogs), which had affected several of his own kittens recently although none of these had ever been to a show. Strangely, he did not see a connection between the two. However, when reading the accounts of these 'poisonings' it becomes clear that none of the cats died in the show hall – it was invariably after they arrived home. It is more than likely that these mysterious deaths were due to enteritis. Unfortunately, whatever the cause, cat shows came to be regarded as a potential threat to valuable animals and by the early 1900s the numbers of competitors at major events began to decline.

ALAS POOR PUSS!

If sound advice and competent veterinary treatment were scarcely to be had for those who could well afford to pay for them, what chance was there for the less fortunate? Of all domesticated animals, the 'alley' cat was most neglected. '*There is no creature under the sun which is so systematically ill-used and carelessly treated as pussy*', writes Gordon Stables in 1874: and though he praises the work of the Royal Society for the Prevention of Cruelty to Animals in general, yet even in their case he claims: '*Alas! Poor pussy comes last and least.*' Maybe this was because the governing body of the RSPCA consisted entirely of upper class males who by tradition and social conditioning were contemptuously anti-cat. But in fairness, as late as 1884, a decade after Stables was writing, the Society had only about eighty paid inspectors nationwide while the numbers of cats in central London alone was conservatively estimated at 350,000.

HER MAJESTY URGES ACTION FOR POOR PUSS

By now however, cats had powerful lobbyists, including Queen Victoria herself. In August 1886 the queen writes to her private secretary, Sir Henry Ponsonby, complaining about the arbitrary way in which the police impounded and destroyed stray dogs, and suggesting that charitable institutions should be set up to look after them. Cats, she concludes, '*should likewise be well cared for in homes.*' In another letter of about the same date, addressed directly to the RSPCA, she urges the society to do something for cats, '*which are so generally misunderstood and grossly ill treated.*'

1887 was the fiftieth year of Queen Victoria's reign and the RSPCA hit on the idea to commemorate her Jubilee by striking a silver medal to be awarded, as from the Queen herself, to people who had performed outstanding services in the cause of animal welfare. It appears that the queen was advised on the design of the medal by her close personal friend, the Baroness Angela Burdett-Coutts who, like herself, was an ardent supporter of the society. The Baroness – who King Edward VII described as one of the most remarkable women of her time – had a love of dogs and cats. She had paid for a drinking fountain in Edinburgh to commemorate 'Greyfriars Bobby', a dog who was said to have followed his master to the grave, and to have revisited the spot daily until his own death in 1872.

When the design for the medal came to be examined by the Queen and the Baroness, there was something missing:

'*having been examined, revised and approved, the Queen detected the absence of a domestic cat among the group of animals which forms the obverse... and directed that a cat should be inserted*'.

So on this important occasion, Her Majesty did not forget Poor Puss who was squeezed in beside the back legs of the horse.

Silver medal awarded for outstanding service to the Royal Society for the Prevention of Cruelty to Animals. First struck in 1887 and since presented annually. By courtesy of the RSPCA.

CONVENIENCE FOOD FOR DOGS AND CATS

From the 1860s onwards, a profitable service industry had gradually emerged to supply the needs of the more privileged cats and dogs. It was the inspiration of James Spratt, the father of all modern processed pet foods, who arrived here from the United States in the late 1850s. The story is well known that on docking here he noticed dogs on the quayside scavenging discarded ship's biscuits and foresaw a demand for biscuits specially formulated for dogs. He was not the first inventor of dog biscuits, far from it. *The Domesday Book,* compiled in the late 11th century refers to '*mille panes canibus*' – loosely translated as '*thousands of cakes of dog bread*' – made in Cheltenham, Gloucestershire.

In the years following 1823, *The Sporting Magazine* carried a series of advertisements by a Mr S Smith for 'DOG BISCUITS' for Greyhounds, Pointers, Fox Hounds etc. Mr Smith distributed his product via the navigation system along the Thames as well as the Kennet and Avon, Grand Junction and connecting branch canals. Cats were an afterthought of course in a market aimed mainly to serve the hunting and shooting fraternity. However, as the century progressed, dogs began to be bred for their decorative qualities as domestic pets and there was a surge of interest in exotic long-haired breeds of cats. James Spratt saw a gap in the market and in November 1861 he obtained a British patent 'for the invention of "IMPROVEMENTS

SPRATT'S PATENT
CAT FOOD.

TRADE MARK.

It has long been considered that the food given to that useful domestic favourite, the CAT, is the sole cause of all the diseases it suffers from; nearly all Cats in towns are fed on boiled horseflesh, in many cases diseased and conveying disease.

This Food is introduced to entirely supersede the present unwholesome practice; it is made from pure fresh beef and other sound materials, not from horseflesh or other deleterious substances. It will be found the cheapest food to preserve the health and invigorate the constitution, prolong the existence, and extend the usefulness, gentleness, and cleanliness of the Cat.

Sold in 1d. Packets only. Each Packet contains sufficient to feed a Cat for two days. The wrapper of every Packet is the same in colour, and bears the Trade Mark as above, and the name of the Patentee, and no other Packet is genuine.

DIRECTIONS FOR USE.

Mix the food with a little milk or water, making it crumbly moist, not sloppy.

SPRATT'S PATENT MEAT FIBRINE DOG CAKES, 22s. per cwt., Carriage Paid.

SPRATT'S PATENT POULTRY FOOD, 22s. per cwt., Carriage Paid.

SPRATT'S PATENT GRANULATED PRAIRIE MEAT CRISSEL, 28s. per cwt., Carriage Paid.

Address—SPRATT'S PATENT,
HENRY STREET, BERMONDSEY STREET, TOOLEY STREET, S.E.

Spratts Patent Cat Food Advertisement.

An early attempt at convenience food marketed for cats; prominently displayed in Cats, their Points and Characteristics by W G Stables. Published 1874.

IN THE PREPARATION OF FOODS FOR HOGS, DOGS, CATS AND POULTRY, AND IN APPARATUS FOR THE SAME".'

In the advertisement for his product, Spratt does not pull his punches when trashing that of his competitors, notably the sellers of boiled horse flesh, which in his opinion, is from diseased carcasses.

His food was sold in one penny packets, sufficient for two days, so it was cheap and claimed to be '*made from beef and other sound materials.*' There was no need for cooking but simply mixed with a little milk or water '*to preserve the health and invigorate the constitution, prolong the life, and extend the usefulness, gentleness and cleanliness of the cat.*'

Other makers of ships' biscuits such as Wright's, Entwistle's and Spiller's also turned their hand to producing dry pet food with varying results. John Jennings in his *Domestic and Fancy Cats* of 1893 condemns most of them on the market:

'Some of it is simply rubbish; the chief effort being the extraction of cash that might be more advantageously spent on sound nutrients. The only exception that needs mention is 'Spratts Cat Food' which can at least be recommended to cat breeders without risk to their stock.'

Cat Foods.

164. Malted Food for Kittens	... ...	per doz. 1/- Tins		9/9
		per Tin		2/6
165. Pepsinated Meal for Cats	... ...	per doz. 1/- Tins		9/9
		3d. Tins, per Gross		27/0
166. Cat Food	... 4-oz. Packets... ...	per Gross		8/6
		7-lb. Bags		2/0

For Cat Baskets, *see* Appliance List.

☞ No prices marked on bags or packets.

Cat Foods.

Pack Shots from Spratt's Patents Wholesale Catalogue for 1906

J G Gardner on the other hand had touched on Spratts Cat Food without much enthusiasm: *'if you can get your cats to eat it, it would save a world of trouble.'* And as cat owners, we know how notoriously 'picky' cats can be. The National Cat Club by contrast, was fulsome in its praises. They were particularly impressed with the 'pepsinated' variety produced by Spratt's; a process whereby the food was partly pre-digested by enzymes:

'The N.C.C. pride themselves upon the food that is provided by Spratt's Patent [at their shows] and certainly nothing could be better for cats than the minced beef or mutton prepared with Spratts pepsinated meal, nor more calculated to allay any attack of indigestion caused by excitement or worry from the journey or new surroundings of a show.'

Popular though Spratt's convenience foods had become with the general public, discerning breeders were not convinced they were an acceptable option to the endless chores of choosing, preparing and cooking a varied diet. There was no quick fix and in 1902, Frances Simpson even suggests investing in a good mincer to help with the tasks of blending together meats with

Sherley's Lactol for Weaning and Rearing Kittens.

'A substitute for mother cat's milk – three times stronger than cow's milk.'

oatmeal, porridge, rice or macaroni. To keep pussy warm in winter; brown Hovis bread soaked in warm milk, or tinned sardines mashed up with breadcrumbs for a bulkier meal. As a special treat, a sheep's head stewed until the flesh falls off the bones and served in the broth. In summer, Nestle's or other brands of evaporated milk because they kept fresh for longer.

A F Sherley & Co. started trading in the 1870s and became the best known British manufacturers of cat medicines and health foods for nearly the next hundred years. Their little booklets on cat care, which sold for a few pence, went through many editions from before the First World War until the 1970s.

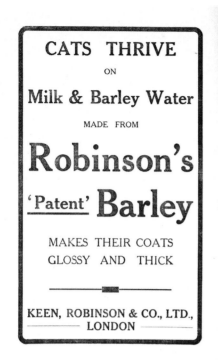

Robinson's Patent Barley. 'Makes Their Coats Glossy and Thick.'

Both Benger's and Mellin's Foods marketed for human invalids and babies were readily given to kittens in the belief that 'what is nourishing for infants must also be good for young kittens'. Pick-me-ups for sick and nursing cats included some still familiar names such as Bovril and Brand's Essence of Beef.

EARLY ANIMAL CHARITIES – The Self Starters

For over seventy years, from the 1820s to the 1890s the SPCA – Society for the Prevention of Cruelty to Animals, which later became the RSPCA – was the only nationally active animal charity in the United Kingdom. Within the domestic domain dogs were their main concern;

cats were an insoluble problem. Hundreds of thousands of homeless and diseased cats – and dogs – roamed London and other urban areas. Prosecution in cases of cruelty were mostly impossible to administer and the charity was severely understaffed.

By the early 1880s some independent local charity cat shelters were being set up nationwide, having been given impetus by the shortcomings of the RSPCA. The Royal London Institution for Lost and Starving Cats was founded by Mrs Zoe Constance Morgan who adopted royal status when Princess Alexandra signed up as Patron. An ostentatiously liveried horse drawn cart and uniformed attendants – and later a motor van – guaranteed a stylish send off to the lethal chamber for the unfortunate strays.

Frances Simpson in her *Book of The Cat* 1903, said the shelter had so far received 47,212 strays, averaging 300 weekly:

'Not a day passes without several wretched cats having to be destroyed at once on admission and 80% are destroyed within 24 hours.'

THE CART OF THE ROYAL LONDON INSTITUTION FOR LOST AND STARVING CATS.

The Cat Collection Cart of the Royal London Institution for Lost and Starving Cats.

The Institution was at the high end of cat rescue with a stylishly appointed horse drawn cart and uniformed attendants.

The Book of The Cat 1903.

And she estimated that in the period 1901–1902 there were as many as 750,000 cats in London of which 80,000 to 100,000 were destitute.

She goes on to discusses the plight of the domesticated puss turned out of its comfortable upper class home in smart areas of London when owners lock up and leave on long vacations. This was commonly known as the scandal of Belgravia:

'During the Summer months when households leave town for their holidays 'poor pussy' is forsaken and forgotten and no provision made for her. She is forced to take to the streets where she seeks in vain to stalk the wily London sparrow or pick up any scraps from the gutter.'

How many healthy pet cats with homes were picked up and destroyed by the rescue operators is a matter of speculation but some of these same independent cat shelters began to offer boarding facilities.

A MORAL DILEMMA

Not everyone agreed with the wholesale destruction of stray cats; Poor Puss had devotees – mostly women and generally thought to be mentally deranged – who went out on to the streets to feed starving strays. Some kept multiple cat families at their homes, a practice not popular with neighbours, as testified by the cats'-meat carriers who supplied them with horse meat. (See Chapter 5.)

KATE CORDING – A ZEALOT FOR HER CAUSE

Kate Cording set up her own rescue operation, the Feline Defence League, in 1902 at Fellowship Cottage, a three-storey house in Islington. Unlike the social climbing Mrs Morgan, Kate often used a pedal cycle with a shelf at the back for feline cargo, following a ban excluding animals on public transport. On Sundays she could hire a pony and trap at a discount. Dressed shabbily to avoid attention, she travelled extensively the alleyways and courts of slum areas where she was far from welcome. She and her team – some, working women themselves – faced hostility and insults, even physical attack. She was '*assaulted*

by roughs in Red Lion Square, Holborn, my hat torn from my head and my body banged about, all because I was carrying a cat in a basket.'

In her fund-raising book, *Waifs of A Great City*, a photograph captioned 'Cat Hunting To Date' shows Kate and her helper Miss Clegg dressed for their hunting expedition; they wear enormous hats, carry a large cat basket, lantern and

BRINGING STRAY CATS TO THE HOME.

[Photo by Bunnett, West Kensington.

Kate Cording and her young assistant bring back the strays to Fellowship Cottage c.1906.

From 'Waifs of a Great City – The Beggar Cats of London,' 1907

fishing net – and they look somewhat formidable. '*The life of these workers is one of constant contact with grey houses, mean streets, dirt, squalor and sordid surroundings. They work for starving cats in the heart of slumland.*'

Destruction for the cats was total. One or two were re-homed as pets to people she trusted; others, '*who, by reason of past sufferings or specially sad circumstances,*' earned the right to a permanent home at Fellowship Cottage. One of these, 'Netto', had been fished out of a grating with an angler's net, and 'Hoxton', '*an old half blind wreck of a once handsome cat*'. Yet another, named 'Caspar' is featured in Kate's publication, sitting beside his mistress as she works at her typewriter.

Kate Cording fought off her critics using reason and not a little rhetoric, her philosophy was:

'*The greatest possible good for the greatest possible number. Though I suffer more than anyone knows in taking life, I know that I slay in love and pity and as a stern matter of duty to save these creatures from starvation, neglect, and the vivisector's knife.*'

Kate Cording claimed that between September 1899 when she 'took up rescue' and October 1906, a total of 21,486 cats had passed through her hands. The exacting work broke her health and on her death in 1913 Fellowship Cottage was taken over by the RSPCA who, having always lent their support, also paid for her funeral.

Cats Protection charity estimate that there are nine million stray cats and half a million feral cats in the UK today.

*****

While local welfare groups such as Fellowship Cottage were pursuing dedicated work in their area, a new wave of 20th century charities arrived with much larger aspirations: Our Dumb Friends League (re-named The Blue Cross in 1954), the People's Dispensary for Sick Animals, and the Cats Protection League – now known as Cats Protection. Our Dumb Friends League (Blue Cross) devoted its limited resources to improving the lot of working horses and donkeys and opened an animal hospital in 1906 in Victoria, south-west London, where animals of owners too poor to pay received free nursing and veterinary treatment. In the First World War it set up ten hospitals for horses in France and three more for the 'war dogs' used as messengers and to draw gun carriages on the front line. At home, ODFL extended its remit to include small domestic animals, stray and starving dogs and particularly *the unpleasant and insanitary diseased cats which were not confined to slum districts but lurked in squares and quiet thoroughfares.'* The first shelters for cats and dogs opened around 1908 and at about that time the League took over the running of the Royal Institution for Starving Cats in Camden Town. By 1914 similar shelters were also in operation in nine other large towns and cities in

England and one of several committees appointed to regulate the League's activities dealt specifically with the *'Receiving Centres* for *Stray Cats'.* By 1918 the Dumb Friends League was handling 10,000 unwanted cats a year.

'I was visiting the slums in London,' recalls Maria Dickin in *The Cry of the Animal,*

Out-Patients Clinic for Small Animals.

The Royal Veterinary College 'Poor Persons Clinic', c.1895.

A line of anxious people await treatment for their pets at The Royal Veterinary College out-patients clinic held in the covered Practice Yard. Fresh straw has been strewn and a small boy pushes his pet in a home-made barrow to join the queue while a member of staff or senior student with an assistant examine a small dog 'patient' waiting on the benches.

Two top hatted gentlemen attend a dog on the operating table; left is veterinary surgeon Frederick Hobday with an assistant who is applying an anaesthetic – chloroform or ether – by means of rubber bellows through to a face mask.

Although no cats can be seen among the animals awaiting treatment, there would undoubtedly be some in the covered baskets such as the one on the knee of the lady at the right side of the picture.

The College performed a valuable service for pet owners attending their 'Poor Persons Clinic' at a time when veterinary treatment was largely focused on horses and farm animals.

[From The Royal Veterinary College Alumnus Association publication A Photographic record from the 1890s. Mary Evans Picture Library/Virginia Hobday.]

'trying to do what I could to help women and children, and as I walked the streets I was amazed and horrified to see the sufferings of the animals… many dogs and cats walking on three legs and dragging along an injured or broken limb; others nearly blind with mange or covered in sores. In the backyards I saw dogs and cats, as well as goats and rabbits, huddled up in corners, suffering from enteritis, pneumonia or other ailments.'

To try to relieve some of this suffering she determined to set up a clinic where animals would be treated free of charge. But this was 1917, one of the grimmest phases of the war and she was opposed and ridiculed. The poor had no sick or injured animals she was told – or if they had they would not take the trouble to bring them for treatment. Finding suitable premises was almost impossible. Eventually she got permission from a clergyman and great animal lover who was doing good work in destroying (diseased) stray cats. She had a cellar lit by a paraffin lamp, a three-legged chair, a wooden form, a box of simple remedies and a lethal chamber. But she was fortunate in gaining the services of a well-known animal practitioner, of much experience, who included Royalty among his clientele. A notice board was put up outside 'ALL ANIMALS TREATED. ALL TREATMENT FREE.' So began the People's Dispensary for Sick Animals, which within the next twenty years became and remains one of our largest animal charities, with an impressive presence overseas too.

CATS PROTECTION – AT LAST POOR PUSS COMES FIRST

Those of us who know and admire cats – and Cats Protection – carry in our minds an image of Mr Albert Steward who, in his spare time rode around the Slough area in the 1920s on his bicycle with panniers strapped either side, picking up destitute cats. The stuff of folklore perhaps – nevertheless it is true.

The idea of a Cats Protection League was first put forward by Miss Jessey Wade – founder of Cats Protection – at a meeting of pedigree breeders and fanciers at London's Caxton Hall on 16 May 1927. Mr Albert Steward was appointed General Secretary in 1933 – a post which he held with distinction for the next forty years – and a bank account was opened with an initial balance of only one pound ten shillings. On a meagre budget CPL was limited to what could be done most cheaply, simply and usefully. An elasticised safety collar costing only sixpence each and marked with the owner's address for the speedy return of a lost feline, was later modified to become the quick-release-clip collars sold today at a modest price.

In January 1931 the CPL launched a monthly newsletter The Cats' Mews-Sheet, inviting readers' letters, with reports from local branches. Short articles were included on topics such as the responsibilities of cat owners, cat health, lost and stray cats, and so on. These were supplemented by educational leaflets covering various topics: sexing a cat, looking after kittens, keeping a cat in at night and providing for it when you go on holiday. By this time the need for fresh grass was widely recognised and it was easy to grow indoors in pots or window boxes. The seed merchants Sutton and Sons sponsored packets of grass seed in answer to an appeal 'on behalf of the countless cats living in London and elsewhere who are deprived of grass.' Small packets of the right sort of seed were on offer 'gratis and post free to any reader who applies for it.' The Mews-Sheet of 1931 also reported 'in excess of 50,000 cats a year are taken from the London streets by one shelter alone.' The numbers are staggering but at that time neutering was not a viable option and did not begin until the early 1960s when Cats Protection saw some of their first cats neutered and by the end of the decade numbers had rapidly risen to thousands. Sizeable donations were rare, but in 1935 one generous supporter bequeathed a small late Georgian house, Prestbury Lodge in Slough, which became the

THE CAT

Vol. IV. No. 1   Monthly Price Twopence.   15th JANUARY, 1934.

Editor—JESSEY WADE

"Cats," said Sir Walter Scott, "are a very mysterious kind of folk"

"There is more passing in their minds than we are aware of"

Issued by the Cats' Protection League
42 DOLPHIN ROAD, SLOUGH, BUCKS

ANNUAL SUBSCRIPTION 2/6

Title page of The Cat, first issue, in enlarged format, which took over from The Cats' Mews Sheet on 15 January 1934.

(Photograph by permission of Cats Protection)

League's headquarters up to 1978. Cats Protection is the UK's leading feline welfare charity. It helps around 200,000 cats each year through its network of over 250 volunteer-run branches and 36 centres. They run nationwide rehoming and neutering programmes and seek to educate people of all ages about cats and their care. 'Our vision is a world where every cat is treated with kindness and an understanding of its needs.'

During the 1930s two factors added to the difficulties of all animal charities: the severe economic depression when millions lost their jobs and could barely feed themselves let alone their pets; and the massive slum clearance launched in central London and other inner-city areas. Our Dumb Friends League reported:

'tenants were moved into new blocks where pets were banned. When moving day came, many of them simply left their pets behind, either to starve in boarded up buildings or to scratch a living from the refuse left in the deserted streets.'

Local authorities were often indifferent and did not inform the charities in advance. Central government – always slow to act on matters concerning animal welfare – was deaf to repeated complaints from the charities. The 1938 Report of Our Dumb Friends League's Animal Shelters Branch reflects the anger and frustration:

'It is difficult to write year after year of the terrible sufferings inflicted on cats without repeating the same remarks – perhaps it is as well to do so – it is possible that by constant repetition, it may wake up the men and women who vote at Parliamentary elections to insist, that at long last, the status of cats should be increased. The League is tempted to wonder what would be the attitude of the authorities if it, and all other societies banded themselves together and refused to collect any further cats… the authorities would have to take some action and would have to legislate in order to protect the public from an increase in stray cats throughout the country.'

The theme of this seriously escalating problem was returned to a year later by Our Dumb Friends League:

'The public so often says that it does not see stray animals, therefore there can be no strays, but very few members of the public have ever been in a churchyard at night and groped among the grave-stones. Had they done so they would have found many cats, their bones sticking through what little flesh was left on their bodies. Yet these cats breed, with each newborn kitten there is another stray.

Should the Institute [for Lost and Starving Cats at Camden Town] close its doors, there would be at the end of one year, 100,000 stray cats over the area it covers, and at the end of two years, nearly half a million. That is the work that occupies much of its time and that the subscribers are asked to support.'

The published experiences of these early charity workers such as Maria Dickin, make for painful reading so it comes as a welcome relief to find a touching story of the self-sacrifice some poor people were prepared to make for their animals – in this case a dog and cat – looked upon as fellow members of their own family. A PDSA worker writes:

'I wish I could show you Brown Street, its poverty, grime and despairing sordidness; its

CATS' AND DOGS' AMBULANCE.

Cats' and Dogs' Ambulance.

A novel way to collect and transport stray cats and dogs. Pedal tricycles of similar design were widely used in the 1920s and '30s by 'Stop-me-and-Buy-one' men selling ice-cream to passers-by in busy streets.

Courtesy of the Blue Cross, formerly Our Dumb Friends League.

The PDSA clinic in a poor neighbourhood in the 1930s.

A working horse has joined the queue as well as a caged parrot. In front of the Vet in the white coat, a lady holds up what appears to be a kitten and a small boy (front) clutches his pet cat.

Courtesy of the People's Dispensary for Sick Animals.

narrowness, its noise, its terribly overcrowded little houses; its poor shops from which the merchandise overflows on to barrows and stalls all along the edge of the pavement, so that butchers, fish stalls, greengrocery, every article of clothing for both sexes and all ages... make a continual market and an indescribable din of hoarse voices... Now if you could see all this and hear all this you would understand that the people who live and work and shop in it, needs must – for they have not one sixpence to spare. And if this is their life, what of the animals?' Yet here, among the other hawkers stood the barrow of the cats' and dogs' meat man. 'It brings tears to the eyes to know that out of their shillings to be laid out so carefully on necessities, there is to be a "pennorth for Bob and a ha'porth for Nell".'

(See Maria Dickin. The Cry of the Animal.)

The years between the first and second World Wars saw major advances in the treatment of both human and animal diseases. Domestic pets were gaining a much larger share in the practice of the average vet while clients' expectations became more demanding. Veterinary colleges put more emphasis on surgical procedures and the use of anaesthetics, so for the first time it became relatively safe, for example to spay a female cat or painlessly neuter a tomcat. In the case of the deadliest killer, feline enteritis however, progress was slow. In 1936, injections of an antitoxin given in the weeks prior to a show were recommended, but it was to be another thirty-five years before a fully effective vaccine became available.

The range of 'home remedies' had remained the same since 1900 or before. The 1928 and 1938 updates of John Jennings' classic *Domestic and Fancy Cats*, first published in 1893, still listed Benger's Food and Brand's and Valentine's meat essences as *'pick-me-ups for pussies'*. In the opinion of breeder Evelyn Buckworth-Herne-Soame in 1933: *'It is true that they cost three shillings and sixpence a bottle, but one bottle will see a cat through a long illness.'* (See her book *Cats: Long-Haired and Short*.)

Much more information is available regarding the food on offer to ordinary domestic cats in the 20th century. In an informative article from *Your Cat* magazine in July 1995 Wyn Francis tells how she fed the cats of three families in Dover in the 1930s. All three neighbours formed a rota whereby each fed the cats

The PDSA Carries On.

London bombings in the Second World War. A PDSA mobile clinic is at work in a shattered street. There is a line-up of pet dogs but the three children appear to be concerned about their cat that is being examined inside the van. Another cat or kitten is held in the arms of a woman waiting in the queue.

Courtesy of the PDSA.

twice a week and on Sunday they were given the remains of the family dinner. There was plenty of fish available in Dover and a penn'orth of fish heads boiled up would more than suffice for four or five cats – *'and any other that happened to pass through the yard'*. These were the days before over-fishing and some grew to an enormous size, yielding a lot of flesh, easy enough to pick off, but smaller fish heads when boiled had to have all the bones removed (for the cats' safety) and it was, as she said *'a rather messy job'*. Chicken was expensive but rabbits were cheap and plentiful and a couple would feed both the family and the cats. Offal purchased from the butcher was her least favourite, lights (lungs) and melts

(spleen) – the smell of it cooking brought in all the cats of the neighbourhood. These were lucky cats indeed to be given regular fish meals. Although at the time most families were feeding their pets portions of their own leftover food, the market for commercial products was expanding.

By the 1930s the original primitive ingredients of dry packeted cat foods were modernised and had become very big business; advertised with half or whole page advertisements in national publications such as *Picture Post*, *The Radio Times* and in leading cat magazines. Spratt's Patent was still a market leader but with stiff competition from Spiller's.

In America, canned cat and dog foods first appeared in the 1920s – brands such as 'Speak For It' in Massachusetts, 'C-A-T' in California and 'Kanna' in Arizona and elsewhere. But in British households, dogs took precedence over cats in relative popularity. The first canned pet food to be marketed in the UK was 'Chappie' for dogs, made by the giant American food company Forrest Mars following its takeover of the small English company of Chapple Brothers.

GREAT EXPECTATIONS!

SPRATT'S Cat Food

SPRATT'S PATENT LIMITED, 58 MARK LANE, LONDON, E.C.3

Great Expectations!

Spratt's Patent Cat Food advertisement in Cats and Kittens magazine November 1937. 'No more messy meals to prepare for pussy. Spratt's Cat Food contains meat, fish and cod liver oil and is ready to serve'.

The first widely available brands of canned cat food were Red Heart and Kit-e-Kat. The former was launched around 1936 as a dog food and a couple of years later followed up its success with a cat formula. Kit-e-Kat, now the longest surviving British brand, also began life in the autumn of 1938 and a third candidate, 'Stamina' appeared just before the start of the Second World War.

FEEDING PUSS IN WARTIME

Cats Protection cautioned its members to be prepared to:

'lay in the foundations of a stock-pot', made up of cheap cuts of beef and rabbit meat.

'Keep All Your Rations – And Give me Kit-E-Kat!' Advertisement in The Cat magazine 15 November 1939.

Britain was at that time in the phase nicknamed 'the phoney war': military action had barely begun and food shortages were yet to come.

By permission of Cats Protection.

Not only the flesh itself but the liquor from the pot, soaked in stale bread or toast, or blended with boiled rice, lentils or pearl barley, to make a nourishing meal. There should be no difficulty, so the writer thought, in maintaining your stock-pot even when meat was rationed'.

This turned out to be wishful thinking. Another suggestion borrowed from a First World War recipe, was a sort of savoury pudding, consisting of scraps from the table, moistened with Marmite, and baked for an hour. *'If a meal for a cat cannot be secured from our own table,'* a vet had said, *'we are in a sorry plight.'* But sadly, so it was to be.

As the war went on, meat rations were

reduced to a few ounces a week per person. Canned foods were controlled under a 'points' system and amounted to little more than a pound in weight per month. Poultry remained un-rationed as did fish, other than by scarcity; but trawling in the open seas was limited by enemy action and there were long queues for what little fish there was. In general, controls bit sooner, more widely and deeply – and for longer than during the First World War.

As for our domestic pets, 1940 saw the demise of all proprietary products, depending as they did on meat, fish, cereals and milk derivatives – all requisitioned exclusively for human consumption. A directive from the Ministry of Food in 1941 made it illegal to feed milk to cats, except those employed in *'war work'*, i.e. in keeping down vermin in warehouses containing 250 or more tons of foodstuffs. Sherley's, the leading manufacturers of medication and dietary supplements for dogs and cats were forced to withdraw 'Lactol', a milk concentrate for weaning kittens, which had been amongst its best-selling lines for upwards of forty years. When it came to medical supplies, humans had

This R.S.P.C.A. ambulance driver had to dig for some hours before he unearthed "Ginger"

The RSPCA ambulance driver had to dig for several hours to find 'Ginger'.

From Animals Were There by Moss and Kirby.

priority again. A worker with Our Dumb Friends League recalls:

'drugs were scarce. We survived in the main on aspirin. We called them by important sounding names LPT and LBT, but all this meant was 'Little Pink Tablets or Little Blue Tablets.'

WARTIME PANIC

On the morning of 3 September 1939 when war was declared, a voluntary worker at Our Dumb Friends League's Hammersmith Branch made her way there by trolley bus:

'The air raid warning had gone off, which had upset people. By the time we arrived there was already a queue of at least 50

THE BLESSINGS OF PEACE
or
MR EVERYMAN'S IDEAL HOME

THE LAST TO LEAVE
(Fortunately, the R.S.P.C.A. Ambulance was round the corner)

A light-hearted view of a serious problem by E H Shepard, illustrator of the A A Milne Winnie the Pooh books.

Punch Magazine 24 November 1937.

'The Last to Leave'

The anxious face of poor puss at the window of a bombed-out building. The photographer obviously couldn't resist the shot, but readers were told not to worry: 'fortunately, the RSPCA Ambulance was just around the corner'.

Animals Were There,' Moss and Kirby, 1947.

people with their animals, as well as protesters, trying to dissuade them from having their animals put down. People were intending to leave London – they were concerned for the safety of their children and wanted to get out, but could not take their animals with them. Many were broken-hearted about it. This went on for quite a while and some lovely animals were put to sleep.

It was the younger people who left London; the attitude of the older ones was – "we've seen one war through and we'll stay to see this one out." Of course, lots of people did go off and leave their animals to fend for themselves.'

(See The Blue Cross at War 1939–45.
Carmen Smith.)

An advertisement for Red Heart tinned cat food in Our Cats magazine 1952 features an Abyssinian; a rare species in the 19th century and first seen at the Crystal Palace cat shows of the 1870s.

Kit-E-Kat advertisement.

'How I Love it Every Day!

Feed your cat this easy way!

Woman magazine 1952.

Kit-E-Kat advertisement:

'What's the excitement? – No need to ask it!

There's Kit-E-Kat In Mummy's basket!'

Punch magazine 1955.

There were reasons other than leaving London – or the big cities – which influenced people to have their dogs and cats destroyed and there were many more cats than dogs. Apart from bombing, the greatest single fear was of poison gas attack. All civilians were issued with a gas mask which was carried slung from a shoulder strap. To anyone familiar with feline psychology, a gas mask for cats might seem 'a no hoper'. Nevertheless, a 'French scientist' came up with just such a device – to which both the RSPCA and Cats Protection promptly gave the 'thumbs down'. Rather more practical were the gas-proof shelters for dogs and cats marketed by at least two companies, priced at £3.3s. and £6.15s. according to size. Another firm advertised 'Bromosed', a sedative for calming frightened animals which was listed on Cats Protection's *Useful Information* leaflet along with 'Gasorb', a compound of gas absorbing chemicals.

The bravery of the civil emergency services from 1940 to 1944 during sustained air attacks on British cities has been well documented. Often the danger was not only of fire and crumbling masonry but of time bombs with sophisticated fuses which had to be disarmed immediately and on the spot. Once the human casualties had been recovered, workers from the animal charities were allowed in, at their own risk, to do what they could to rescue the trapped, injured or traumatised domestic pets.

POST-WAR AUSTERITY and IS YOUR CAT GETTING ENOUGH?

Peace came, but austerity and rationing lingered on for several years and it was the need for a balanced diet that drove the cat food trade. With scant food scraps to feed to our pets post-war, the lack of necessary vitamins and protein could soon put health at risk. Pet food manufacturers offered a resolution to the problem and it was factored in at the heart of all convenience food products.

Kit-E-Kat, the market leader in canned food, returned early to the post-war momentum along with Wiles and Red Heart. Spratt's Patent, trading on the fame of a long-standing brand name, continued to push their handy packets of *'completely balanced all nourishing meals'*. Kit-zyme marketed food supplements and *'pick me ups'* to boost the appetite.

1952 advertisement for American brand Puss 'n Boots made by Coast Fisheries, a division of the Quaker Oats Company.

Although not on offer in Britain, it was popular in the USA and elsewhere including the Caribbean.

Whiskas advertisements issued a stern warning against 'vitamin hunger': *'Your cat may <u>look</u> healthy,'* they said, but *'a cat needs more than scraps inside him.'* Cat powders from Tibs were a handy extra to *'stir in to pussy's morning saucer of milk'*, thus adding vital vitamins and minerals often lacking in a poor diet.

Kit-E-Kat press advertisements aimed to reach a wide public through popular magazines; later backed with a television campaign made memorable by simple rhyming jingles.

Full of fish, full of meat,

Food that kittens love to eat.

Isn't it a pity that,

All kittens don't get Kit-E-Kat!

Food for cats had come a long way since James Spratt patented his biscuits for hogs, dogs, cats and poultry in 1861:

Chapter 7

Jobs for Cats

The Golden Age of 'Bureaucats'

You are inquisitive by nature Puss. *A characteristic you first developed in the wild as a means of self-preservation, always investigating for hidden danger. In this way you have inherited a taste for adventure; it is in your genes. You will hunt in high places, the War Office, the Admiralty, the British Museum, even the Indian Civil Service. Battles over your weekly pay are discussed at the highest level with questions raised in Parliament. As with many dedicated and efficient workers, your true value is not always appreciated. In your long years on the railways you will find many true friends among the rail fraternity which ends only with the demise of steam powered locomotion. You will not be the home loving type; you want to have fun.*

*****

Not every cat wants to be a fireside fixture. For generations some have chosen to follow their ambitions to earn a living. Others just want a bit more adventure in life; a career where they can meet people and find job satisfaction. Cats have always had an aggressive streak of independence which has defined their character and led them in to some unlikely locations: libraries and museums, on steam railways, in post offices, hospitals and as church and cathedral minders. Cats have moused in Government buildings everywhere including the Palace of Westminster and the British Civil Service at home and in India. In the late 20th century they found a niche in public relations where they are still usefully employed.

An illustration by cartoonist Larry for Behind the Lines.

Recollections of a GWR Goods Agent, by Christopher Burton.

Cats have a long tradition of service on the railways.

'I wouldn't be a War Office cat even for a very great deal!'

– Florence Nightingale

We might think it beneath the dignity of senior civil servants to correspond at length about their office cats. But in the more leisurely Victorian age it seems everyone had plenty of time and inclination. In 1860 the welfare of the official mouser at the War Office provoked some tart remarks from Florence Nightingale to Sir Sydney Herbert, Secretary of State for War, regarding the inefficiency and *'shilly-shallying'* of his staff:

'There are rats in the W.O. – also a cat. There are seventeen months' minutes (memos) to apply for 6d a week for her, 40 minutes to say that she ought to live on rats. Other minutes that she ought to have milk – but that 6d a week is too much.

Others again ask what she is to live on in the meantime. I am very anxious to know what is your decision. Whether you have given any as yet – whether you think fivepence three farthings would be too much? I incline to fivepence half-penny. [PS] This is fact not fiction. But I would not be a W.O. cat, even for a very great deal.'

Quite when cats were officially recognised by other government departments is lost in the mists of time. It is said there was a cat at the Treasury as far back as the reign of Henry VIII. There was certainly a cat at the Home Office by 1883, the Admiralty by 1902 and the Foreign Office and the Treasury not long after. By the early 20th century, there were cats in the pay of the British Civil Service in India.

WANTED
THREE GOOD MOUSERS

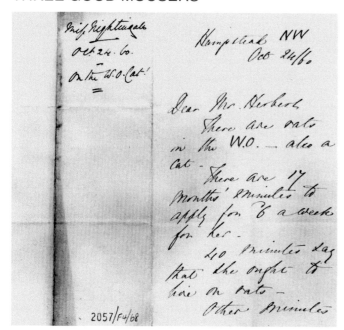

Florence Nightingale's letter to Sir Sydney Herbert, Secretary of State for War regarding an increase in the allowance to feed the War Office cat.

Food and Board Included

The Post Office archive is far the bulkiest single source to have been thoroughly researched and is the subject of Russell Ash's fascinating book *Dear Cat* (1986) to which the writer is indebted. Post offices not only handled paper work but were large repositories of foodstuffs, textiles and other vulnerable goods in transit. On 23 September 1868 the Controller of the London Money Order Office has a nasty shock when he finds that the mice have got the upper hand. He writes an urgent memo to the Secretary of the Post Office, asking his permission to recruit three cats:

'I beg to report that very serious destruction and mutilation of the paid Money Orders stored in the Registration Lockers of this Department has been brought about from mice: traps and other means have to no purpose been used for the riddance of these vermin. I have requested the resident porter to procure three cats for the purpose and for the support of which he will be reimbursed. I understand that one and a half pence per day is usually allowed at the [British] Museum and I propose that Tye (the porter) should be allowed two shillings per week for the keep and care of these cats which, if approved, can be defrayed by the surplus cash arising from money left at the windows of this department and unclaimed.'
(Post Office Archives.)

As with the War Office eight years before, parsimony was the order of the day. 'Three cats may be allowed on probation' came the stern reply, but:

'they must undertake a test examination and should, I think, be females. It is important that the cats be not overfed and I cannot allow more than 1/- a week for their support. They must depend on the mice for the remainder of their emoluments, and if mice be not reduced in number in six months a further portion of the allowance must be stopped. Can any statistics as far as to mice be furnished from time to time?'

The following May the Secretary, curious of the outcome writes again:

'How do the cats get on? Is it not time a report was made?'

To which the Controller replied:

'I am enabled to report that whether influenced by the Secretary's caution that they would, under certain contingencies have diminished rations, or by a laudable zeal for the Service and their own characters, cannot clearly be made out, but it is certain that the Cat System has answered extremely well.'

There was a snag; due to the Secretary's insistence on female cats, an 'increase in that portion of the establishment' had occurred. The powers-that-be still remained unconvinced that, on a combined salary of one shilling a week, the three cats at the Money Order Office were good value for money. The matter went as far as the Accountant General of the Post Office, who revived the idea of a periodic 'test examination' for the cats, enabling them to re-apply for their own jobs. He proposed appointing a 'Commission of Inspection' to oversee the whole exercise. Nothing further came of this and the porter in charge of the cats continued to provide a quarterly statement of account.

These early exchanges anticipate the Post Office's cat correspondence for nearly the next hundred years and their fondness for setting down the minutiae of everyday life is now our pleasure to read. Time after time the same questions were posed, disposed of and re-posed by succeeding generations of officialdom. Were the cats overpaid for their services? Wouldn't poison or traps be cheaper and more efficient? Why should the cats be paid at all when, as in the wild, they could subsist on what they caught? Alternatively, wouldn't scraps from the canteen suffice? Was it these very scraps left lying about which attracted mice in the first place? Weren't cats as big a threat as rats to mail consignments of meat or game? The Anti-Cats were usually high-ups, remote from the battle zone. The Pro-Cats their subordinates, manning the front line.

While cats at the British Museum and some other public buildings were allowed 10½d each per week in 1868 the Post Office cats got only 4d. Five years later, at the Money Order Office, the porter's wife who looked after them complained that this was not enough. Cat meat alone

cost a shilling a week and she 'expends about 8d a week from her private purse to provide them with milk'. As a result, the weekly allowance for all the growing number of Post Office cats was raised to 6d; and once fixed, it remained for the next forty years or so.

In May 1873 the Post Office Store on Southampton docks, where sacks of mail bound for Australia were kept, became rat infested. The Docks Authority held the Post Office to blame and insisted they installed a cat. The animal was to be the responsibility of the Foreign Mail Guard who wasn't perhaps too keen on the extra work so he came up with some ingenious excuses to increase the maintenance. The Surveyor in Southampton conveys the objections of the Guard in his memo to the Secretary of the Post Office:

'Mr. Wadman, the Guard whose duty it will be to look after the cat, argues that such a sum as 6d or 9d per week would be quite insufficient. He says no nourishment whatever can be derived (by cats) from rats which reside in the store room as they feed on nothing but the hessian mailbags: besides, he very properly points out, that the wear and tear of shoe leather in going to and fro will cost at least one fourth of the proposed allowance, and whatever small balance there may be left over will not be sufficient to compensate him for the loss of dignity in carrying the cats' food through the streets in Her Majesty's uniform.'

This tactic was partly successful; after further negotiation a special rate of a shilling a week was approved. Meanwhile the rats did themselves no favours by

misbehaving in the most outrageous way. Regular reports came in of calamitous events – a rat jumped on to the shoulder of a cleaner when she was on a staircase and a night shift worker put her hand on a rat in the dark as it was having a kip in her handbag

ONLY THE MICE NOT ON RATION

Picture Postcard dated July 1909 and captioned '"Simmy" the famous Post Office Cat, Lee' [Devon]. Inscribed on the reverse:

'Will tell you about this dear old pussy when we come home'. Unfortunately we shall never know the story of this handsome Persian type cat who was enough of a celebrity to be featured on his own picture postcard.

An allowance of six old pence a week was probably never enough to keep a cat in food and milk and was often topped up by the voluntary contributions of kindly members of staff. But as food prices rose in the first World War the shortfall grew much worse. In January 1916 the Superintendent of the London Engineering District wrote to his superior regarding the big increase in the price of milk and asking permission to increase the weekly allowance for the cats. The rate was then raised to 7d per week: the extra 1d was regarded as a 'war bonus.' But the introduction of meat rationing in 1917 left the cats worse off than before. In May 1918 the Camden Road office complained to the Postmaster General that their cat allowance barely covered the cost of milk; on top of this they had to spend another shilling to one shilling and three pence a week on lights (the cheapest sort of offal). The Postmaster was unimpressed, saying lights were *'known to be expensive'* he asked them to suggest some alternative and why not *'dilute the milk?'* The postal staff at Camden Road were evidently fond of their cat and no doubt, not overpaid themselves. There is a hint of desperation in their reply:

'There seems to be no other food; ordinary cat's meat [i.e. horse flesh] is now 8d per pound and more expensive than lights. The cat having always been used to milk alone, will not drink milk and water. 7d a week has never been sufficient to keep a cat, had there not been a fair amount of food left over from the dinner table to help. Since meat rationing nothing is left and all food for the cat has to be purchased.'

In 1915 food shortages had prompted the question, were all of the twelve cats then employed in the London postal districts really necessary? This led to an exchange of letters between various high-ranking officials: but the opinion at grass roots, was that they

were necessary and a report by the Office of Works on rodents in Government buildings concluded that poison and rat traps were inefficient.

HELLO SAILOR!

Cats serving in the Royal Navy, whether on ship or on shore, always had a better deal than those in the Post Office. Ever

HMS "Barfleur" 1905–6 and HMS "Renown".

Picture Postcard, 1906. A formidable looking ship's cat poses in the barrel of a big gun.

since 1902, cats in the Admiralty building in London had been paid a shilling a week and no less a person than the First Lord of the Admiralty had acknowledged the *'beneficial effect on their efficiency and morale'*. Since then, inflation had doubled the cost of what could once have been bought for a shilling, and in 1921 the head of the Admiralty's London book bindery appealed on behalf of his departmental cat:

'Is it possible to allow a little extra for the cat? 13/- a quarter does not go very far now, in fact it does not pay for the milk she has. I get 2d a day, this only equals 1d. on what we used to get…'

'PUSS'S DINNER IS NOT SERVED MY LORD'

Once again, a trifling request concerning a cat was viewed as a matter for serious and prolonged consideration; the simple little memo progressed via no less than ten high-ranking officers before landing on the desk of the First Lord. Along the line of command various questions were raised. Was this the same cat as that originally appointed in 1902? Was it a naval rating, a civil servant, or an unpensionable employee? As in the Post Office, opinion was split between Pro- and Anti-Cat. One official thought the allowance should be doubled to two shillings a week. Another that:

'.. the use of this weapon for the destruction of rodents is rapidly becoming obsolete owing to the progress

being made in chemical warfare. In view therefore of the serious need for economy, and the high prices obtaining in the fur trade, it is for consideration whether this type of destroyer should not be placed on the disposal list.'

The First Lord demurred:

'In these times, when it is incumbent on all good citizens to practice frugality and to share any necessary privations, it would be detrimental to the Admiralty and repugnant to its feelings, to confer a bonus on its own cat – unless some special and temporary circumstance, such as an increase in family can be adduced in support of the present claim.'

However, he finally manages to pass the buck 'in a matter which is primarily one of Navy Victualling' so the decision rested with the Fourth Sea Lord – not with him. 'All I insist on is that whatever the decision, it must not involve a supplementary estimate or any discussion in Parliament.' Heaven forbid – how the daily newspapers would have laughed!

The Fourth Lord's response was prompt and terse; the bindery cat was not his responsibility either, 'as no one at the Admiralty buildings is on navy rations'. Such a good excuse! Eventually, after the momentous issue had lingered on for some while a compromise was reached between the Financial Secretary and the First Lord. The bindery cat was awarded an extra 6d a week since 'considerations of humanity preclude any further delay'.

CATS OF THE RAJ – THE BRITISH CIVIL SERVICE IN

INDIA

'It seems a shame
When the English claim
The earth, that they give rise
To such hilarity – and mirth.'

– Noel Coward. Mad Dogs and Englishmen.

The National Army Museum preserves a directive dated May 1921 from the Finance Department of the Government of Central Provinces in India. It is addressed to the Lord Bishop of Nagpur and almost every other conceivable dignitary, informing them that the Government is raising 'the maximum allowance for the feed of cats from one to two rupees a month [i.e. from one shilling and sixpence to three shillings.] 'And that Government is pleased to sanction the continuance of the enhanced rate until further orders'. Others on the circulated list included:

The Judicial Commissioner and all Commissioners of Divisions.

The Political Agent, Central Provinces.

Commissioner of Settlements and Director of Land Record.

Chief Engineers Buildings and Roads and Irrigation Departments.

All District and Sessions Judges.

All Deputy Commissioners.

The Venerable The Archdeacon.

Chief Conservator of Forests.

Inspector General of Civil Hospitals.

Director of Public Instruction.

Inspector General of Police.

Inspector General of Prisons.

All Superintending Engineers.

The Inspector General of Registration.

The Sanitary Commissioner.

The Director of Agriculture.

The Director of Industries.

The Registrar, Co-operative Societies and Excise Commissioner.

It is remarkable that many cats may have worked in these far away corners of the British Empire where their natural predatory skills were relied on to keep the British Civil Service in India working efficiently.

Another reminder of this whimsical lost world comes from Girl's Own magazine for May 1907 along with how to make lampshades and recipes for jam which, it seems were serious occupations for female teenagers at the time:

'A government clerk in India, who was in charge of certain official documents, had obtained permission to keep a couple of cats to deal with the rats, who did much damage to his papers, the larger cat receiving rather better rations than the other. One day head office at Calcutta received this despatch: "I have the honour to inform you that the senior cat is absent without leave. What shall I do?"

After waiting a few days and receiving no

Directive regarding increase of allowances for cats employed in the British Civil Service in India, 1921.

National Army Museum

reply he wrote as follows: *"In re. absent cat. I propose to promote the junior cat, and in the meantime to take into government service a probationary cat on full rations."'* These decisions are never easy but it is nice to know that both cats were allowed their full rations.

*****

Back in Westminster, poor Rufus the senior cat at the Treasury was suffering because his wages were still stuck on one shilling and twopence a week in 1924. Colleagues were concerned; Rufus appeared half starved and even lost interest in hunting. As usual, the question of Rufus's pay rise ascended several layers of grudging officialdom until it was taken up by Dame Maude Lawrence, the head of women's branch of the Civil Service who referred it to Philip Snowden, the Chancellor of the Exchequer. As a member of the first British Labour Government, Mr Snowden no doubt saw it as a flagrant example of a non-union employee exploited by his grasping bosses. Rufus was given a fifty per cent rise forthwith.

The reader may well suspect that a good deal of official 'cat correspondence' must have been written tongue-in-cheek. Otherwise the miniscule cost of keeping a cat – or even two or three – compared with the multi-million pounds yearly expenditure by government departments, the Post Office and the armed forces, hints at bureaucratic lunacy. But, as Florence Nightingale commented earlier regarding the War Office *'this is fact, not fiction'.* Post Office headquarters regularly circularised the branches, asking whether they still drew a cat allowance and if so, whether it was still essential. One branch postmaster in the 1920s, quoted in *The Post Office Magazine*, replied to such a questionnaire:

'A cat is still necessary, and a statement is enclosed showing the number, colour, and approximate age of official mice captured in the past twelve months. It is considered that the exceptional energy, initiative and good judgement displayed by this member of staff calls for special recognition, and it is recommended that the weekly allowance be increased by twenty per cent.'

By the early 1950s the pay of Post Office cats had once again lagged behind the cost of living. In January 1952 the Incoming Parcels Office at Leamington complained that the current one shilling a week was far from enough – *'the fish and milk costs at least a shilling a day'* – resulting in this particular cat's pay rising dramatically to three shillings and sixpence a week. About the same date the national newspapers got wind of the Post Office's alleged starvation of their cats; while the anomalies in their pay structure for equal work in different parts of the United Kingdom led to representations on behalf of those felt hard done by.

PUSS
A SERVANT OF THE STATE

In March 1953 the matter was raised in the House of Commons by an Irish MP:

'Could the government explain why the official cats in Northern Ireland receive less than their counterparts in London?' The

Assistant Postmaster General Sir David Gammons no less, felt called upon to respond:
'There is, I am afraid, a certain amount of industrial chaos in the Post Office cat world. Allowances vary in different places, possibly according to the alleged efficiency of the animals and other factors. It has proved impossible to organise any scheme for payment by results or output bonus. These servants of the State are, moreover, frequently unreliable, capricious in their duties, and liable to prolonged absenteeism…'

He denied any discrimination against Irish cats, or as between tom cats and she cats. *'Head Postmasters have full discretion to give a maternity grant.'*

In 1954–5 the whole issue of cat allowances was reviewed and a new rate of one shilling and sixpence a week was confirmed in the Head Postmasters' Manual. From then on, authority to pay the cats' wages was delegated to local head postmasters and telephone managers; with the result that the flow of correspondence, which had lasted for nearly ninety years, was silenced. The official one shilling and sixpence a week was still quite unrealistic – with a pint of milk costing 7½d and tinned food at 9d for a small can. The wage was raised again to three shillings and sixpence and successively during the '60s, '70s and '80s. Blackie, cat of the London Post Office headquarters became the first cat to earn £2 a week, which led to his appearance on BBC's 'Nationwide' television programme in 1983.

THOSE MAGNIFICENT MOUSERS

Many a worthy bureaucat has lived and died in anonymity, his or her name and devoted service unrecorded. Some achieved fleeting celebrity, often less for their efficiency than for some newsworthy eccentricity. A famous few are still remembered from long ago in cat anthologies. It is related that traditionally, every official mouser at the Home Office was named Peter (or Peta), and that one of them had a spell on sabbatical at the Foreign Office, where apparently, they were in greater need. But this overlooks Emily, a 1920s Cinderella; who, rescued when starving by a kindly charlady, rose to be the favourite of the then Home Secretary, and always attended conferences in his office. Tabs in the War Office, also a cat of the 1920s, was renowned for his agility; he is said to have extracted a large mouse from the trouser leg of an officer in Military Intelligence without awakening him. Brutus of the National Gallery, who flourished in the 1930s was the only cat allowed on the terrace, and had a special pass to admit him. In 1952 author Warren Tute had the bright idea of interviewing and photographing a number of distinguished cats in central London. Where better to start he thought, than the Bank of England? The Bank frostily denied that they owned any such animal, though suspicion rested that they did but were too stuck up to admit it.

Minnie of the Stock Exchange agreed to co-operate provided her picture did not appear in any publication detrimental to the Stock Exchange. At HM Customs and Excise the last of a celebrated line had just passed away, *full of dignity to the end'*. His successor, a six month old tyro, was still learning the job. Whisky, of Lloyds the insurers, had come to them from a nearby cafe, where the customers had objected to him sitting on the cakes. At Lloyds his arrival had proved a boon because, as one employee explained, the *'huge rats'* in the basement used to *'put out their tongues at you'*. But within days all that was left of them was their tails, which Whisky didn't relish.

Tibs, the official cat at Post Office headquarters in St Martin-le-Grand from 1950–64, was still only two when Warren Tute interviewed him, but already *'larger and fiercer'* than most; with a haughty reserve becoming to one who had inherited his position through his mother, Fluffy, and his grandmother, Minnie, before him. He declined to be photographed with the top-hatted doorman, or in a chair which Sir Rowland Hill – founder of the penny post – had sat on. But he allowed one shot only of him on top of an 1856 pillar box.

Very sensibly, Tibs lived in the refreshment room, was adored by the staff, made an appearance at a 'Cats and Film Stars' party and grew to be 23 pounds (10½ kilos) in weight. This posed a problem when in 1957 he developed an abscess behind his ear and required veterinary treatment. As an official report explained; *'the cat is such an enormous animal that it would not have*

been accepted on public transport and taxi fares would have been incurred – if taxis could have been obtained'. So the People's Dispensary for Sick Animals stepped in and collected Tibs in their van. While he was away having his operation the Post Office Personnel Department issued bulletins on his progress and on his return to duty the staff donated £50 to the PDSA in appreciation. A touch overweight he may have been, but Tibs was no slouch. During his fourteen years in office never a rodent was seen in the building. When he died, the office cleaner who looked after him remarked *'there will never be another Tibs'*; and his obituary was published in the *Post Office Magazine* in January 1965 under the heading *'Tibs the Great is no more'*.

MIKE – the cat who assisted in keeping the main gate of the British Museum from February 1909 to January 1929

Probably the best known and documented of all these bureaucats was Mike of the British Museum. Mike was one of a long line of British Museum cats, beginning early in the 19th century with a couple belonging to the then Keeper of Manuscripts, Sir Frederick Madden. When one of these favourite cats – named Mouton – died, he was stuffed to preserve his memory. Sir Frederick's cats were probably his personal pets but by 1900 the British Museum had the services of a professional mouser. Black Jack worked the Museum Reading Room, where he could warm himself in cold weather under the reading lamps

and the kindly scholars used to let him in and out of the door. But he was banished after an unfortunate mishap when he was accidentally locked in there one Sunday and whiled away the time by sharpening his claws on the bound volumes of old newspapers. After this he disappeared for a while, probably hidden until the rumpus blew over, by his friends on the staff. Among these was Sir Wallis Budge, Keeper of the Egyptology Department as well as custodian of the ancient Egyptian cat mummies. Black Jack no doubt regarded him as the patron saint of all cats past and present. So what more natural than to turn to him when he had a problem?

One morning Black Jack turned up carrying a large 'Something' in his mouth, which he dropped at Sir Wallis's feet and solemnly walked away. The 'Something' revealed itself as a tabby kitten. The staff named him Mike, and he was added to the payroll of resident Museum cats. As he grew up he became the scourge of vagrant dogs and the flocks of pigeons that dared to trespass on the Museum forecourt. The dogs fled in terror as he swelled himself up to twice his normal size and hurled himself at them. He palled-up with the gatekeeper, and spent much of his time with him in his little stone Lodge. This was more to his liking than the main museum buildings, because he was free to come and go, night and day, whenever he pleased. The gatekeeper provided a special shelf for him to sleep on, in a corner away from the draughts, and the waitresses brought him food and milk from the refreshment room. Alternatively, he might dine out of an evening in the apartments of one or other of the resident museum staff, where he was a welcome guest. He preferred sole to whiting, we are told, and whiting to haddock, and sardines to herrings. But for cod he had no taste at all.

Every week-day morning at 9am, when the main gate was opened, Mike was in attendance; along with the policeman and the uniformed official wearing a gold banded top-hat who rejoiced in the title of King's Messenger. Not that Mike cared at all for the many thousands of visitors who passed him by over the years. In fact if anyone stopped to admire him he would spring smartly out of their way on to the pediment of the Lodge door. He particularly resented ladies poking him with their umbrellas; and as for being cuddled, *'many a fair hand has had its glove ripped open by a swift stroke of Mike's claws'* as Sir Wallis Budge recalled.

Sir Wallis was Mike's lifelong friend and patron; and after the cat's death on 15 January 1929 at the age of twenty one, his biographer and memorialist. Though Mike had sought few friends, he had made many at home and abroad. London newspapers published his obituaries and he inspired two valedictory poems; one by his admirer Dr Arundell Esdaile, includes the lines:

I scorned the public as it came and went,
To blandishment and fish indifferent,
But sat for nineteen years and kept the gate,
In every hair an Officer of State.

The other by F C W Hiley, a former keeper at the museum, concludes:

Old Mike! Farewell! We all regret you,
Although you would not let us pet you,
Of cats the wisest, oldest, best cat,
This be your motto – Requiescat!

*****

THE RAILWAY CATS – DEDICATED LIVES

The railways were once the largest corporate employers of cats in Britain. The archives of the major companies, up to their nationalisation in 1948, are deposited in the Public Record Office and the study of these to find references to their feline employees would be a formidable undertaking. However, articles in the railway companies' 'in house' magazines and the personal testimonies of employees spanning over fifty years have proved fertile ground.

As one correspondent puts it, cats were as much a tradition on the steam railways as semaphores and lamp-men:

'There is puss, the proud and favoured habitué of the station refreshment rooms, who often vaunts a coloured ribbon – down to the lowly but well fed comrade of the shunters, usually found occupying the daylight hours in a box, or on an old coat behind a red hot stove in winter'.

Cats were also employed in parcels and goods depots to protect perishable freight in transit; in the locomotive sheds where lamp-oil and lubricants, enticing to rodents, were stored; in the sidings to prevent them infesting empty carriages; and still more vitally, in signal boxes where rats not only gnawed the telegraph wires that interconnected stations and the cables that operated the signals but their nests could foul the levers on the old mechanical systems. Would passengers, we wonder, have felt more, or less, secure, had they known that their safety depended partly on the vigilance of the signal box cats?

Railway companies actively encouraged their local officials to employ cats. An official cat allowance paid out of petty cash was usually available and seems to have been less stingy and less stringently monitored than in the Post Office. As to numbers of paws on the ground, as far back as 1888 at the goods depot of the Midland Railway at Trent (according to W M Ackworth, *The Railways of England*), there were:

'Eight cats who are borne on the strength of the establishment, and for whom a sufficient allowance of milk and cats'-meat is duly provided. And when we say that the cats have under their charge, according to the season of the year, from one to three or four thousand empty corn sacks, it will be admitted that the Company cannot have many servants who better earn their wages. The holes in the sacks, which are eaten by the rats which are not eaten by the cats, are darned by twelve women, who are employed by the Company.'

But job security came at the risk of injury or even sudden death. For cats, the railways were fraught with danger. *'One of the refreshment rooms at Preston has a tailless cat, upon whose stately beauty passengers often pass comment, under the impression that puss is a Manx cat. But she*

Tabby kittens learning their trade.

Picture Postcard dated 1900.

lost her tail when it was cut off by an express train passing through the station.' A black cat working at Huddersfield station also appeared one day with its tail missing, it was thought it had been sheared off between points' blades. In Oxford in the late 1970s the resident cat was observed to place its paws on the rails before crossing, to alert it to any vibrations from an oncoming train. On electrified lines it was remarked that whereas dogs and other creatures were usually killed by stepping on a live rail, it seemed cats never were. The only conclusion was that cats were able to sense the danger and jump clear of it.

An article which appeared in the LNER Company magazine in 1931 recommended that apprenticeship was best begun as a kitten *'so that their training inculcates the railway atmosphere'.* And in practice, railway cats often inherited their posts from railway mothers. But of course there was also an influx of strays seeking their fortunes. One that arrived at Temple Meads station, Bristol, in 1971 and presided over the goods yard for several years, was known to have travelled down overnight in a container wagon from Dundee.

In the 1980s another job-seeking stray having failed to obtain an appointment at Liskeard on the Cornish main line, boarded an empty carriage and descended at Looe. *'A good career choice'* wrote our informant, *'as Looe is awash with fish, not to mention Cornish cream.'*

Some, even among the well fed official cats, felt an urge to wander – to foray into the wider railway world. One was Albert of Wrenthorpe station, West Yorkshire who *'has caused anxiety on many occasions. He has visited nearly every depot in the West Riding, and some so frequently that he is "known" and promptly returned the following day.'*

L.M.S. Magazine 1931.

Cats were not routinely neutered as they are today, but no doubt Albert enjoyed his little excursions, safe in the knowledge that his good friends would see him home.

'In the watches of the night he is always fresh and bright;

Every now and then he has a cup of tea,

With perhaps a drop of Scotch while he's keeping on the watch,

Only stopping here and there to catch a flea.'

From Skimbleshanks: The Railway Cat,

by T S Eliot, Old Possum's Book of Practical Cats.

No accounts of real life cats manning passenger trains in an official capacity have come to light; but they may exist – even if only in an unofficial capacity because more likely than not, T S Eliot's *Skimbleshanks* was based on observation. Skimbleshanks, readers may recall, oversees the London to Edinburgh night mail – responsible for all aboard, passengers and staff alike. If he should be late turning up for duty, there would be consternation on the platform, for without his nod the guard can't blow the whistle to depart.

Eliot was 'eying the world' as Skimbleshanks would, who was quite a character, somewhat manipulative, unflappable and with a firm belief in his own importance. It may have been just such feline quirks that endeared so many station cats to railwaymen and the travelling public. Old Bill for example, the booking office cat at Armley on the LNER in Yorkshire in the 1930s, *'a great favourite with staff and public alike'* in spite of his prickly personality:

'He was the terror of hundreds of mill girls, especially those who teased him, as he had an uncanny faculty of picking them out as they passed the barrier, and many torn stockings were the result of the vendetta against the culprits.'

LNER Magazine 1933.

There are many memorial plaques inscribed to the memory of railway favourites to be found. On a wall at Fishguard and Goodwick station in South Wales is a plaque dated 2 August 1931, and inscribed: 'IN MEMORY OF THE STATION CAT. SADLY MISSED BY GOODWICK STATION STAFF.'

'Here lies our dear old station cat.
She killed some mice and many a rat.
Her days are gone, she did her best,
And now in peace she's laid to rest.'

When Selwyn, cat of the historic Diggle signal box on the Manchester to Leeds line, died in 1998 after twenty two years' service, the staff were so touched by his loss that they held a collection for Cats Protection in his memory.

In 1975, another much loved cat, Thomas of Mirfield on the Leeds – Huddersfield line needed an operation to have one eye removed when he was injured. Although Thomas was on the establishment, British Rail was perhaps understandably reluctant to pick up the tab for the high cost of vet's fees. But staff were determined that Thomas should have his operation. Thomas's story was reported in the Huddersfield Daily Examiner and subsequently followed up by the national press. Donations flooded in from all over the country – far more than enough to pay the bill.

YOU CAN'T TOUCH ME I'M PART OF THE UNION

In the early 1950s, railway trade union intervention was needed on behalf of a feline member facing redundancy. *'I well remember'* writes a former railwayman: *'There was a staff consultation meeting concerning the withdrawal of freight facilities from Midhurst in Sussex. The*

Thomas of Mirfield.

Thomas the station cat had wandered in to Mirfield in Yorkshire as a half-starved stray and was taken on as an official employee. He is pictured here with his boss Ken Jones, the station Superintendent for Dewsbury area, who kindly provided the photograph.

trade union side put a question "What is the future for the cat in the warehouse?" The chairman of the meeting asked the station master if there was indeed a cat. Answer. "Yes." The chairman asked if any monies were officially being paid out for the cat's keep. Answer again, "Yes". At this point the trade union representative stated that he was not prepared to agree to the withdrawal of facilities until a proper home was found for the cat. The following meeting confirmed this provision had been met and a date for the closure was agreed.' (Hugh Compton, Woking. Letter in response to author's enquiry in *Railway and Canal Historical Society Bulletin*, March 1998.)

Another former employee, Charles Meacher from Yorkshire, with fifty years' service on the LNER and British Rail recalls:

'Inevitably there were many kittens, and workers would give them a home with their families. I remember when leaving duty one winter's day I stopped to talk to a well wrapped-up colleague. We said our "cheerio's" and just then a wee kitten looked out from my friend's overcoat front and meaowed his own "cheerio!"'

By 1968 steam locomotion had been replaced by diesel and electric power.

*****

A RAILWAY CAT

She envies no man's hearth place – freedom's best,
And the long run of sheds, where sacks of seed,
Oil cake, guano, Spratt's Food, and the rest,
In hempen mountains stand, – and rat folk breed.

These are her happy hunting grounds! – How fleet
Amidst the bulging piles, – beneath the beams,
Hung o'er with dust thick cobwebs, – soundless feet
Fly scampering by; anon an engine screams.

The Railway Cat! What recks she of the noise
Of shunting engines – shrieking steam – and loads
Of groaning, grunting wagons, men and boys:
Is she not queen of all the iron roads?

She purrs, and swinging slow from paw to paw,
Dreams — where the charcoal brazier casts a glow,
Of moonlight raids, warm blood and sated maw;
Dreams that the poor tame house-cat cannot know.

Roaming at will amongst the silvered sacks,
The moon bathed silence stirred by velvet wings
Of bat-folk in the rafters, – while through cracks
In walls and floor, a little night wind sings.

She envies no man's hearth-place! Being wise,
And craving freedom for her wild cat-soul,
What smouldering fires do gleam in those green eyes,
What scorn of aught that savours of control!

M A Northcote.
From the Siamese Cat Club Cat Gossip magazine, 23 February 1927,
by courtesy of Julia Craig-McFeely.

Chapter 8

Purr-suasion

The Power of Cats in Advertising 1830 - 2000

For over 140 years Puss, you have proved your power to motivate people to buy. Your appearance in a multitude of diverse advertisements allows us a unique insight into the social melting pot of the late 19th and 20th centuries through their shopping habits. We find an ever-changing society and begin to understand why advertisers used your image to reach out to their target customers.

*****

AN EARLY ADVERTISEMENT
Poor Puss Makes an Entrance

By no means a grand entrance – but an important one. The first series of press advertisements to feature a cat began to appear in the years before Queen Victoria came to the throne. Our Puss is not seen here as a fireside pet; his back is arched, he glares aggressively at his own reflection in a polished boot. One of a series of advertisements for Warren's Boot Blacking – or 'shoe polish' as we now know it – that appeared in *Bell's Life in London*, a sporting magazine for gentlemen published from 1822.

A False Alarm.

A quarrelsome Cat, of a foe in pursuit,
One morning encounter'd a *reflecting* Boot
From 30, the Strand, and erecting her back,
Commenc'd on the *Jet* a most furious attack,
   Her shadow an enemy seeming ;
And hideously squalling, she placed on the rack
   The family, of jeopardy deeming ;
But known when the cause of the tumult, not lacking
   Was laughter,—the incident teeming
With proof of the merits of WARREN's JET BLACKING !

This Easy-shining & Brilliant BLACKING,

PREPARED BY

Robert Warren,

30, Strand, London ;
AND SOLD IN EVERY TOWN IN THE KINGDOM.

LIQUID, in Bottles, and PASTE BLACKING, in Pots, at
6*d.*—12*d.* and 18*d.* each.

[*Turn over.*

The Earliest Known National Advertisement to Feature a Cat.

Bodleian Libraries, University of Oxford,

John Johnson Collection: Boots and Shoes 1 (27c)

The advert was also produced as a series of trade cards, each carrying a household hint offering 'Warrens' Useful Knowledge' on the reverse. Nevertheless it is the slow-burning start of a fascinating feline journey into the world of advertising.

Up to the early 19th century, the pictorial images in newspaper advertisements – if any at all – were small, stylised wood-cuts. By the 1820s, some enterprising promoters were breaking the mould. Illustrations grew larger, taking on a more central role to convey the sales message and some signs of humour and imagination began to emerge. In 1853 Parliament finally lifted the grossly unfair tax on newspaper advertisements and advertising began to blossom.

It appears that even a leading illustrator like George Cruikshank was not too proud to turn his hand to advertisements; some for lotteries and more famously, for Warren's Boot Blacking, which are said to have made the maker a fortune. Cruikshank's first-time portrayal of a cat was addressed to the men-about-town hunting and shooting fraternity. *Bell's Life in London* started out as an anti-establishment newspaper with radical views, but from 1830 onwards it devoted increasing coverage to the turf as well as boxing and field sports, to become a regular fixture amongst the middle and upper classes. The tenor of some of the other advertisements gives a broad hint as to their lifestyle: '*Grouse Shooting to Let'*, '*Gentlemen's Elastic Belts,*' – providing support for the corpulent – brands of champagne and patent medicines to treat gonorrhoea. The blacking advertisement ran regularly in *Bell's Life,* thus Robert Warren was said to have been the first to advertise a product nationally. When the young Charles Dickens applied for a post with the *Morning Chronicle* his uncle, Henry Barrow, stated in his reference of recommendation that Dickens had penned 'puff' verses for Warren's Blacking Company.

What emerges unexpectedly from Warren's advertisements is not just indifference or dislike of cats, but fear. In the verses shown above, a family are sufficiently scared by the hideous squalling of the cats, that they fancy themselves '*in jeopardy'*. In another variant verse, '*all inmates were forced from the house to retreat'* on the approach of two dozen marauding cats. However strange it may seem today, there is some evidence that colonies of feral cats could present a real danger, especially in inner city areas; perhaps driven by hunger. In her personal Journal, Beatrix Potter gives examples of attacks by cats on people, including herself, in central London in

the 1880s. Charles Dickens mentions two '*tigerish and fearsome cats from a neighbouring mill'* which continually invaded a house he rented in Boulogne in 1856:

'It is impossible to shut them out, and they hide themselves in the most horrific manner, hanging themselves up behind draperies like bats, and tumbling out in the dead of night with frightful caterwaulings.'

From a commercial point of view however, there is not much mileage to be had from savage cats and the Warren's advertisements stand alone in time and content. It was only when cats became popular middle-class household pets that advertisers began to explore their promotional potential.

Although Puss made an early advertising debut, the Warren's Blacking display series of the 1830s–'40s which started the cat advertisement ball rolling, signifies nothing more than the lack of sentiment for animals at that time. No more is seen of cats in the market place until the 1870s when a sudden synergy sprang up between vendors and cats, prompted by the arrival of cheap mass-produced colour printing and the first cat show in 1871 which led to an increase in cats as house pets.

The colourful late Victorian trade card was a direct descendent from that of the 18th century tradesman's card or letterhead. Often imaginatively designed and finely engraved, these pictured the shop frontage; perhaps a glimpse of the interior to show the stock-in-trade, whether grocer, barber, butcher or wine merchant. Trade cards served retailers

well enough when their clientele were confined to one locality, which also worked well for the Victorian shopkeeper. Women were the main purchasers of household goods, whether a housewife or maid-servant patronising the local shop or the lady of the house ordering goods to be delivered; all seemed susceptible to the kittenish charms of Poor Puss. His image made the fortunes of numerous manufacturers and saw Globe Polish through many campaigns, with Brasso following suit. Both companies used fluffy kittens as their brand image although every cat found its own niche.

PUSS AT HOME – The Victorian and Edwardian Consumer

Cats made themselves very much at home within their special niche in late Victorian and Edwardian society. Not only were they family felines but promoters of a wide range of domestic products, confirming the close daily life that existed between cats and their human owners. With charm and grace, puss took on his new role as 'commercial traveller'.

Trade cards were the ascending stars from 1870 onwards; companies chose images of popular appeal and together with the latest developments in colour printing these proved a huge success at a time when press advertisements were looking uniformly grey. Colourful cards were often produced in sets for overprinting with the trader's name, address and product information, to be handed out free to shoppers at the point of sale; an acceptable reminder and memento of their local shop. These decorative little items were often regarded as great family treasures and held a place of honour on many a kitchen shelf or mantelpiece. Cats were routinely featured with dogs and children. The continental Liebig Meat Extract Company (who produced meat essences extracted for use in cooking, later to become Fray Bentos) would be a forgotten name today but for the superb quality of chromolithographic print on its trade cards. As many as thirteen colour workings were often used in their production; not only making them highly collectable but ensuring a good survival rate ever since 1872.

Scotts was another large commercial company keen to exploit the huge popularity of these high-quality colour printed cards. Pleasing subjects, whether beautiful paintings of mother and child or animal and fish studies were snapped up by their customers.

Cod liver oil – a dreaded dosage of the

Scott's Emulsion Trade Card c.1890. Pure Cod Liver Oil.

A pretty picture to keep and a reminder of the benefits of Scott's Emulsion.

19th century nursery – was then a brown oily liquid with a strong fishy flavour and nauseous after taste.

Cod liver oil is rich in vitamin D, vital in the treatment of rickets and soft bones, then commonly found amongst the children of poor urban dwellers lacking sunlight; the properties found in cod liver oil are still valued today.

Scotts marketed it as an emulsion by blending in hypophosphites of lime and soda; substances often included in medicines of the time in the belief that they healed damaged nervous tissue. Scotts claimed that its oil was:

'almost as palatable as milk, so that children and invalids take it readily.' It was claimed to restore the health of 'wasted, sickly children to strength and vigour, and makes them fat, strong, plump and dimpled, like the picture on the card. Don't fail to try it if your child has ricketts, or any form of wasting, and see wonderful results.'

PUSS AMONG THE QUACKS

The social history of the cat followed much the same course in the United States as in the United Kingdom and their trade cards were if anything even more prolific, colourful and innovative. Here Dr Isaac Thompson aims to sell his Eye Water to a well-heeled clientele. *Cassells Family Magazine* gives guidance on fashionable wear for small girls in 1882: *'very low-waisted dresses and jackets of a plain colour.'* The fashionably dressed little girl seen here is trying out the Eye Water on the family cat who is also stylishly turned out in a smart grey

Dr Isaac Thompson's Celebrated Eye Water.

An American Trade card of the 1880s. 'For All Complaints of the Eyes. Its Merits Stand Unrivalled.'

striped tabby coat and unlike most felines in such situations, appears remarkably calm.

Dr Thompson gives no details regarding the content of his Eye Water, so we can only assume it was a general 'cure-all' for application to minor eye ailments. His main concern is to warn the public against crafty imitators and his ranting style is typical of the day when such potions and lotions were sold at country fairs and in market places:

'Each bottle is stamped with my proprietary stamp. None other genuine.

THE GENUINE EYE WATER

is enfolded in an engraved envelope on which is the likeness of the Original inventor, Dr. Isaac Thompson, with a fac-simile of his signature. This well-known and efficient remedy has acquired a world-wide reputation, having been before the public for over eighty five years. Its reputation has been sustained by merits of the medicine. Price 25 cents per bottle.'

Electrical devices of the pseudo-scientific kind were advertised to an enthralled public eager to know more of the many health benefits on offer from this new form of energy; half magic, half science. Unfortunately, they were often in the devious hands of quack doctors waiting to take every opportunity to exploit the gullible. Many ailments curable today, had then to be suffered; the desperate public were buying 'hope'.

There were such items as Pulvermacher's Electric Belt; when strapped around the appropriate part of the male anatomy, generated an electric current within the body guaranteed to cure a range of conditions including impotency and failing libido. An Electric Corset marketed by the Harness Company to develop ladies' bosoms, described as *'the very thing for ladies'*; it not only *'aids healthy chest development'* but is a guaranteed cure for such ailments as *'weak back, organic diseases, sleeplessness and rheumatic affections'*. Two ladies of voluptuous proportions are pictured and from their corset area, spectacular flashes of lightning zig-zag in and out of small batteries fixed either side of the hip. Harness also competed against

Pulvermacher with its own Electropathic Belts, said to generate an electric current within the body to cure *'hysteria, nervousness, sleeplessness, sciatica, lumbago and torpid liver'*. In fact they contained only zinc and copper plates which were of no practical value. Everyone had gadgets: there were electric hairbrushes and combs and an electric Eye-Battery for failing sight; even Charles Dickens used an electric Voltaic Band for his gouty foot.

PUSS NEVER LOSES THE THREAD

Advertisement for Dr Thomas's Eclectric Oil 1907.

An innocent looking grey tabby in a pack shot pose is combined with the alleged powers of electricity – the 'magical fluid' – a guaranteed cure for all human ailments and disabilities.

Machines A Coudre. An advertisement for sewing machines.

Although this is a French trade card c.1880, cat images like this often appeared both sides of the Channel where the same art work was used for a range of products.

A cats' hairdressing salon is one of the wilder flights of artistic fancy taken in order to get a product noticed. Strangely, this card is not advertising the services of a salon as might be expected, but sewing machines and accessories.

Throughout the nineteenth century, advertisements in books were frequently used as a means of reaching the consumer, and *Pussey's Wedding*, a book for children, doubles as an advertising vehicle for a group of exclusive London Stores. Cats often featured in Singer advertisements, possibly because they had good domestic credentials, were quiet and useful, and could purr or 'sing'. Everything Miss

Pussey's Wedding.

Illustrated by G. Cruikshank Jnr. Read, Brooks & Co. London 1874.

©The British Library Board. 12837 p52.

Tortoise-shell orders for her new home is from the sponsors of this book which will also hopefully, be read as a bed-time story for children by well-to-do Mamas. Although George Cruikshank must have had a slight problem with illustrating a tortoise-shell cat that had most of her fur covered in fashionable Victorian clothes, he obviously did his best.

The Bride Working at her 'Singer' Machine

That young Tom will Miss Tortoise-shell wed,
There is now no reason to doubt,
For the villa is taken; – Messrs Rose, Wood & Co.
Have orders to furnish throughout.

The usual presents were made to the bride
The most useful – a 'Singer' machine;
She's a singer by taste, and sings at her work
She's the happiest kitten I've seen!

Singer Sewing Machines, at Prices to Suit all Purses.

From a promotional picture postcard, 1904.

The Standard Rotary Shuttle Sewing Machine Co. Cleveland Ohio.

An 1890s trade card advertising Standard's best Rotary Sewing Machine, 'The Nation's Pride', with the stars and stripes flying overhead. A pretty child and cute kittens make this an irresistible picture for the scrap album.

Isaac Merritt Singer, the son of German immigrants to the United States, arrived in Boston in 1850 when he was trying, unsuccessfully, to market a machine he had invented for the printing trade. It was there, by good fortune, that he met Orson Phelps, another aspiring engineer who was having his own problems with his venture into the sewing machine market. Knowing nothing about sewing machines, Singer nevertheless rose to the challenge. He made several adjustments to improve the design as well as adding a floor treadle which left the operator's hands free.

The Famous Corticelli Spool Silk Cat Logo. Life Magazine 1902

The cat that made Corticelli brand a market leader. Corticelli Cat has the characteristics of a longhair but pedigree is not an issue here; his fluffy charm and charismatic personality persuaded millions of American housewives to open their purse and buy.

Italy was famous for fashionable high-quality silks so it was a shrewd business move when the American manufacturers, the Nanotuck Silk Company, chose an exotic sounding Italian name – Corticelli – as well as a cat to lead their brand

Corticelli Trade Card.

The Unequalled Spool Silk.

image. These enchanting kittens played and frolicked endearingly in women's magazine advertisements in every home in the USA. Women loved them and to prove it, bought all the Corticelli products in phenomenal quantities. The Corticelli Silk Company became very large and very rich.

In 1802 James Coats, a weaver from Paisley, invented a twisting yarn to be used for ladies mourning wear, up till

Trade cards. J & P Coats Six Cord Thread 1887.

Coats chose shorthaired cats and kittens familiar to families who kept a female 'mouser' at their kitchen fireside.

then imported in from China at high cost. His business had been hit hard when the Paisley shawl went out of fashion but with his looms busy once more the company expanded. They installed their own mills in the United

States in the 1870s and '80s and went on to enjoy worldwide sales. Corticelli adopted the kitten as its muse (or mews) in 1900, but the J & P Coats' kittens evidently pre-date it by at least thirteen years: on the trade card shown, with a kitten bearing a shoulder bag marked 'US MAIL', the kitten in the foreground is busily writing in the hope, no doubt, of catching the post. The kitten's letter is dated December 1887.

Although these three J & P Coats trade cards provide no explanation, a piece of the Coats story can be seen in each one: the kittens being taught the economics of life and perhaps how a good thread can help; the kitten with the US mail bag that shows the company's success in exporting to the United States; and kittens studying a globe of the world and learning of the world-wide sales the company enjoys.

THE SHOCKING HISTORY OF HOW PUSS PEDDLED ILLICIT GIN

By 1736 drunkenness had become a serious social problem. Cheap Dutch gin was the culprit, imported since the reign of William and Mary at the expense of French wine and brandy. For many it offered the quickest way to get comatose. In order to curb sales on what had become the elixir of the masses, draconian legislation was implemented. The imposition of an annual fifty pound licence fee put many out of business. What hit hardest, particularly for the poor, were the new rules restricting 'over the counter' sales at pubs and other outlets where no less than a two gallon quantity could be purchased. No more penny nips or 'drunk for a penny, dead drunk for tuppence'. The new legislation amounted to prohibition and was so unpopular that it caused riots on the streets. It was not an easy law to enforce, and excise officers relied largely on paid informers, members of the public prepared to snoop on lawbreaking landlords in order to earn a little cash in exchange for their information.

THE CAT AT THE WINDOW –

Captain Bradstreet's Novel 'Cat' Gin Dispenser

One such informer was Captain Dudley Bradstreet, who soon came to realise that he had chosen a dangerous career. Informers were often attacked; one was stoned to death by an angry mob, two more murdered a short time later. So he decided to play 'gamekeeper turned poacher' and having read up the small print of the legislation, spotted a loophole which he could conveniently exploit. In order to enable officers to enter premises, the informer must supply the name as well as the address of the person said to be breaking the law. We can almost hear Captain Bradstreet's voice, telling us that through a trusted friend:

'I rented a house in Blue Anchor Alley, got it well secured… and purchased in Moorfields the Sign of a Cat and had it nailed to a street window; I then caused a leaden pipe, the small end out about an inch, to be placed under the paw of the cat; the end that was within had a funnel on it.'

UNDER THE PAW OF THE 'INCHANTED CAT'

With his ingenious plan in place and quantities of gin stored ready for use the message was put on the grapevine and he sent out:

'a person to inform a few of the Mob that Gin would be sold by the cat at my window next Day, provided they put the money in its Mouth, from whence there was a Hole that conveyed it to me.'

Next morning the cunning Captain waited:

'nearly three hours before anybody called… at last I heard the Chink of Money, and a comfortable voice says "Puss, give me two Pennorth of Gin." I instantly put my Mouth to the Tube and bid them receive it from the pipe under her paw, then measured and poured it into the funnel.'

In just a month Bradstreet had made £22.00, a considerable sum at the time. But very soon Blue Anchor Alley became impassable with the noisy crowds that arrived daily *'to see the Inchanted Cat, for so Puss was called'*. Naturally, neighbours complained, demanding to have the Cat-man removed. But when an angry mob arrived at the door bringing with them such officials as *'Justices, Parish Officers and Constables'* there was no way they could gain admittance. Captain Bradstreet concludes:

'My scheme of a Puss now becoming common, was practised by many others, which greatly diminished my business, and made me drop it, and turn my head to something else.'

And somehow, we can't help wishing him luck.

(See The Life and Uncommon Adventures of Captain Dudley Bradstreet, 1754; also Mother's Ruin by John Watney)

If things seem dark and gloomy,
Take my advice to-day,
A little of what you fancy
Will clear the clouds away.

Picture Postcard by popular comic cat artist Reg Maurice, post marked 29th October 1929.

It seems a drop of gin could still raise the spirits in spite of the economic gloom. Pussy's chosen tipple is 'Old Tom' which remained a popular brand in the inter-war years and is still marketed today.

Poster for *Old Tom Gin* showing the famous 'cat and the barrel' alliance c.1890.

Old Tom gin has a proud history, no jumped up fancy French bred cats to be seen here; only true British tabby shorthairs are good enough to represent the brand.

James Mellor & Sons Liverpool.

W Wilders' 1910 Poster for Cream Gin.

Traditional tabby cats with striking tiger markings stare out through lucky horse-shoes in a unique trade mark.

OLD TOM GIN – A Little of What You Fancy

Old Tom Gin, featuring the famous cat and barrel trade mark, led the market amongst its many competitors. The origin of the name is uncertain but is said to have been named after Thomas Chamberlain of Hodges Distillery where it was first produced sometime in the 1720s. Boord & Co, the London distillers joined cat and barrel together as an item to promote their cream gin around 1849. Cream gins were sweetened and blended with herbs and spices for a more distinctive flavour and aroma, and given romantic names such as 'Cream of the Valley'; 'the Celebrated Buttercream' and 'Out and Out' (an 'out' was a dram measure). Numerous companies have produced 'Old Tom' which in the United States became a brand nickname for sweetened cream gin.

NEWSPAPERS ARE SET FREE OF TAX

The duties on newspapers had first been imposed as a reprisal against anti-government propaganda in an attempt to gain control by limiting their circulation. By the mid-19th century this was seen, quite rightly as an impost on information. The duty on advertisements had already been scrapped in 1853 and the tax on newsprint followed two years later. This was life changing for the industry. Newspapers and magazines extended their pages and many new titles appeared, while advertisements grew dramatically in size, variety and visual quality. The upsurge in advertising came at a time when cats were in the ascendancy; when they overtook dogs as the more popular or at least more publicised domestic pet. The first cat shows of the early 1870s also contributed to raising their profile.

Pears was a popular brand, having won no fewer than fifteen prize medals for its soap, which was claimed to be *absolutely pure, free from excess alkali and artificial colouring*. A well-dressed mother is pictured bathing her contented baby as he strokes two fashionably fluffy kittens. All framed within artistic lettering, an abundant swathe of roses and a butterfly. There is a recommendation from Mr J L Milton, Senior Surgeon at St John's Hospital for the Skin, London, who bestows his generous praise: *after fifteen years of careful trial*.

Pears Soap advertisement.

Aimed at the luxury goods market, 'a speciality for Infants'.

Illustrated London News 24th April 1886.

Swan Soap advertisement.

'The Floating Soap'.

Punch magazine, 31 January 1900.

Swan Soap was made by Lever Brothers at their Port Sunlight factory. A white swan – chosen as a symbol of purity and elegance – is joined here by another of equal status; a luxuriously coated, white longhaired cat, now a status symbol in the homes of the upwardly mobile. The advertisement boasts of *Swan White Floating Soap, consequently is always in sight*. Puss has a front seat to watch the fun as the children turn a bar of Swan soap into a boat to see if it will sail.

Icilma Castille Soap.

One of a series of small advertisements to sell Icilma soap as a luxury product with the help of a white thoroughbred Persian. Icilma soap was made using 'Icilma water', the remarkable oxygenised natural spring water 'only found 900ft below ground in Algeria'.

Illustrated London News, 10 May 1902.

Tulip Soap Card. 'Are You Ready?'

Tulip toilet soap was a popular brand bought by Edwardians. Another irresistible trade card by animal artist Helena Maguire, who preferred to use the shorthaired cat as her model.

The Sphere 1902.

A fashionable long-haired thoroughbred represents a brand leader.

Half page advertisement for Odol Toothpaste.

As with the sale of soap, toothpaste was also aggressively marketed as a luxury product accompanied by the obligatory thoroughbred cat. Half and full page advertisements competed in leading newspapers and journals. Musical comedy stars and actresses gave their personal endorsements. The venerated Victorian actor Sir Henry Irving was quoted: *'I find Odol excellent'* and his leading lady Ellen Terry had: *'just ordered some more and shall use it constantly.'* Women were the main purchasers of many household products, so the appeal of a cutely be-ribboned kitten as the representative of Odol brand toothpaste would have been entirely appropriate, carrying a subliminal message of luxury, purity, cleanliness and good breeding. The advertisement has the merit of simple poster design and was probably used for that purpose. The kitten image is bold and eye-catching, his attention focused on the brief product caption – all can be scanned by the eye in seconds – message received.

Kalodont Cream was endorsed by the Dowager Crown Princess Stephanie of Austria, widow of Prince Rudolf, heir to the Imperial Austro-Hungarian throne. Rudolf died in a suicide pact with his seventeen year old mistress at Mayerling in 1889.

Princess Stephanie was by no means the first continental royal to lend her name to a commercial product; viewed by the more impoverished crowned heads as a convenient way to make a little extra cash. Czars, Grand Dukes and Duchesses all gave testimonials. Most willing were the German Princelings. Queen Victoria would certainly not have been amused at such mercenary conduct; for her, 'By Royal Appointment' was an honour freely bestowed.

WASH-DAY 'BLUES' AND HOUSEHOLD CHORES

Although Thom looks a happy cat as he makes light work of the family wash, in reality, wash day was never welcome, particularly for the women of the household. If it was a large property, with well-off owners, then it was the task of women servants to endure the drudgery. First, many heavy buckets of water had to be filled and carried to the copper boiler to be heated. There was the soaking, scrubbing, rinsing, ironing, starching and

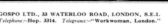

Gospo the British Cleanser.

White Cat cake soap, powders and cleansers. 1910–20. White Persians make an attractive pin-up picture.

Thom's Castile Soap Poster, David Thom & Co. Ltd.

Also published as an early picture postcard.

Thom is a lucky black cat of the kind commonly seen and probably cared for by the maidservants of the house.

final drying and airing of thick clothes. Soap had to be prepared before-hand: bought in large blocks, it was stored at home and cut into bars using a cheese-cutter type wire, then boiled down into a jelly-like solution ready for the wash tub. The manufacture of soap was a thriving industry in 19th century Britain, but Castile soap, traditionally imported from Spain was considered more refined and superior. The Castile name was used by Thom & Co to add a touch of quality to their product.

The cat's characteristically keen observance of cleanliness, grooming and washing – always seen by humans as a most desirable trait – was often pivotal to advertisements for scouring, laundering and household cleaning. The Thom's Castile Soap cat, in common with many others of his kind, cuts a comic figure. Humour had universal appeal and Thom's knowing wink is meant to assure buyers that he has found the right soap for the job.

Sunlight Soap. Lever Bros. Port Sunlight.

Free-standing advertising novelty for children – of all ages. However, the rhyme on the reverse may not merit top marks:

*Two little kittens were learning to spell,
As all good kittens should do,
But 'S' for SUNLIGHT,
So I've heard tell,
Was the only letter they knew.*

Hoffman's No. 1 Rice Starch logo.

The Hoffman logo of a cat washing his fur appeared on all their rice starch products sending a subliminal message of cleanliness and care for luxury fabrics.

A give-away blotter from Gospo, makers of White Cat soap and household cleansers. Gospo couldn't go wrong with their slogan 'Cats White, Homes Bright'. The picture of four lovely white kittens is probably from the studio of the fashionable society cat photographer E Landor. Gospo's White Cat products include GOS soap powder for washing up, laundry and general cleaning; this must have been one of the first domestic soap powders available. Their White Cat British Cleanser was an antiseptic scouring agent similar to 'Vim', a product of more recent times.

The numerous home-prepared methods for stiffening or starching clothes in the 19th and early twentieth century in the name of fashion, all sound alarming. Muslin was treated with isinglass (used to make jellies); a cotton dress could be stiffened by wringing out in sweetened

milk (!); and for heavier materials such as calico, a piece of glue boiled in a gallon of water was said to be effective.

However, fine lace was a particularly treasured fabric deserving of careful treatment with the rice starch. So who better to tell the Hoffman's story than a cat; clean, gentle and caring – attributes guaranteed to appeal to the most fastidious customer.

Hoffman's Rice Starch. Two collectable kitten picture postcards, c.1900. Hoffman's issued a series of these promotional postcards featuring different breeds of cat.

An idealised view of kitten transportation shows Persian kittens emerging from their travelling basket. Cats were routinely sent by rail to or from shows, or from breeders to new owners. Here these kittens have arrived safely, looking cute and perky, which unfortunately, was not always the case.

DYING TO MAKE DO

Home dyes were always popular as part of the 'make-do-and-mend' tradition, which for so many people was a way of life in times of hardship, wars, strikes and unemployment. In large families where youngsters had to wear their siblings cast offs, to change the colour of a garment could give it a renewed lease of life – if only in the eyes of the wearer. These were the new generation of brightly coloured aniline dyes which, by the 1860s, were replacing the subtler hued vegetable dyes so often subject to fading.

'Dolly' Tints and Dyes.

Promotional Picture Postcard

Diamond Dyes. Promotional trade card

Both trade cards were issued c.1890–1900 using humour along with cats. Dolly Tints claimed to *'brighten both home and clothing, in 12 beautiful shades, 1 penny each.'* The little bundle attached to the cat's tail is a Dolly Tint pack tied in a bag complete with a wooden stick to use when preparing. The cheeky boy makes a striking image in his yellow sou'wester cape as he clutches his cat and brolly. They are his insurance against stormy weather – or hard times – his black cat is a symbol of good luck. All that for a one penny 'Dolly' tint pack.

Diamond Dyes sold a colour-fast black dye for stockings and claimed that their *'brown and turkey red are new discoveries.'* It looks as if the terrified family kitten is getting a 'turkey red' makeover.

PUSS LIGHTS THE WAY

It seems that a cat and dog poised for a fight was seen as appropriate for sales of safety matches and It does look as if these aggressors are about to strike each other. The improved 'safety' match (only ignitable by striking on the box) was invented in 1855 by Johan Edvard Lundstrom, a Swede, who sold the British manufacturing rights to Bryant and May in the same year. Swedish brands continued to be imported and the wrappers shown here probably date from before the First World War.

Nightlights and candles were a familiar part of bed-time for children in 1910. Although by then, gas and to a lesser extent electricity had replaced candles for lighting – both for public and private use – there was still a demand for them, especially in rural areas.

Vulcan Brand Swedish Safety Matches.

An outer label for packs of six or a dozen boxes.

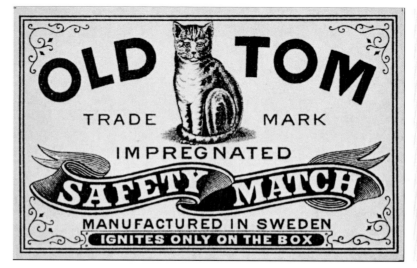

Old Tom Safety Matches. c.1900.

Another Swedish import. The choice of the 'Old Tom' image may turn on the ability of cats to see in the dark.

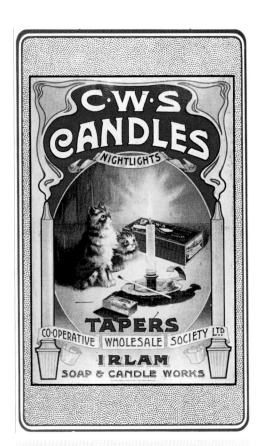

*C.W.S. Candles, Nightlights and Tapers.
1910.*

*A pair of fluffy kittens are neatly framed
in an ingenious art nouveau design of
candles and curling smoke. Fluffy kittens
are never threatening, always reassuring
for children. By kind permission of the Co-
operative Wholesale Society.*

PUSS AS THE HOUSEHOLD HELP

Pretty, playful, – and here to sell the
brand. Globe metal polish manufacturers
certainly took kittens to their heart. As
market leader, Globe produced many
novelty 'stand up' items featuring cats
and kittens as well as some outstanding
enamel signs and shop placards around
1890 onwards. Above, two thoroughbred
kittens in an expensive looking ornamental
gilt frame lend a touch of opulence. Globe

Globe Polish Die-Cut novelty item.

'Globe Polish Turns Work into Play'.

*A playful puss with a tin of Globe Polish.
Globe always associated their product
with the luxury market and chose the
longhaired cat to sell for them.*

Globe Polish.

A Die-Cut free standing novelty.

claim that their polish is non-explosive –
a strange concept for us today, but in an
age when ingredients were not so closely
monitored, it no doubt gave the buyer
confidence that the product was safe. A
German company, Fritz Schulz AG, was
the originator of Globe Polish paste and it
was later produced in the UK by Raimes
& Co. of London in 1912. After the First
World War, Globe Polish was taken over
by Reckitt and Colman who continued its
manufacture until 1962.

*'Ask For The "Globe" Polish and See That
You Get It'*

*A die-cut, free-standing novelty. The card
comes with a royal accolade: 'As used in
the households of H.M. The Queen and
most of the aristocracy and gentry'.*

Komo Brand Furniture Cream and Black Enamel for Fire Grates, c.1900.

Two cheerful die-cut moggies feature on a stand-up card. Each cat provides product information on the reverse. The cream cat assures the customer:

'Komo furniture polish extraordinary, will not finger mark!!' The Black enamel cat advises: 'It only requires one coat to impart a brilliant enamel black surface to Fire Grates, Iron or Woodwork, Gas Fittings, Bedsteads etc.'

In spite of the friendly help from two chatty cats, this is a stark reminder of just how much hard labour was needed in order to maintain a well-run house.

Maison Fevrier & Co. 1885–1900. Drapers and Outfitters.

A charming image of mother cat carrying baby while keeping junior safe on his lead. Using a lead or 'rein' as it was called was a common practice with human mothers up to the Second World War. This picture of mother and kittens is the work of British artist Helena Maguire and appeared on numerous greetings cards and later picture postcards in the UK.

These novelties were given away with purchases at grocery shops. The shopkeeper could be sure that the (usually female) customer, especially those with children, would take them away for show on a kitchen shelf or mantelpiece to serve as a product reminder. On the reverse, is the claim that Globe Polish was used in the households of Her Majesty Queen Victoria; these royal credentials are endorsed by Mr Sands, the Queen's former coachman who says:

'During the 53 years I was in Her Majesty's Service, I never met with any polish equal to the "Globe". It is the best I have ever tried.'

PUTTING ON THE STYLE

It is not at all clear why a cat was chosen over a dog for this particular promotion. Was it Puss's reputation for immaculate grooming? Economy was probably the deciding factor; the matrix of the cat may have been on the printer's shelf and he simply over-printed Hope's details.

O M Blynn, Chelsea. Boots and Shoes – Latest Styles.

A Bookmark, c.1880. Cats are a popular choice in advertisements both by shoemakers and for replacement soles and heels; no doubt because cats are seen as agile and surefooted.

Hope & Co. A three section fold-out sales leaflet.

Leonard. The Boys' Outfitter c1900 front and reverse.

The leaflet is die-cut and folded with a picture of a homely tabby and her two kittens, named 'Price' and 'Quality'. When opened flat, we see a dapper young man in his complete Hope outfit – bowler hat, gloves and walking stick.

THE COPY-CATS

Louis Wain picture postcard advertisement for Jacksons' Hats and Boots. c.1909

This lucky black cat is advertising Leonards, 'The Boys' Outfitters' in Ipswich. It was used for a number of other companies selling similar products, including the summer sales at Harry Loomes' drapery outlet in Colchester. A black cat is always useful for a sales drive so, as in the case of Hope's leaflet, the printer kept it to hand to be over-printed for the next client as the need arose. '*The dear boys **must** have Strong Clothing*

for their Hard Wear.' The elder of the two dear boys is wearing the ever popular Norfolk suit as he loads his Kodak camera. The younger, in spotless sailor collar is playing 'Diabolo', popular with children at the time and known as 'the stick trick' – it had a bobbin and a length of string fixed to a stick either end.

THE HATTERS' CATS

Binks was a 1920s cat-about-town who enjoyed a cosy life amongst the trilbies and fedoras at Bates, the famous hatters for gentlemen of distinction, on Jermyn Street, London. Out of loyalty to his firm, Binks always wore his own small silk top hat and when he finally left for the big hunting ground in the sky, his employers – unable to part with their beloved puss

– had him stuffed. Although the shop has moved to new premises, Binks still presides in pride of place in his top hat and (so un-politically correct!) smoking a cheroot. Every inch the boss-cat.

Louis Wain's comical cats may have been the inspiration for Binks' transformation from deceased cat to that of a permanent and popular addition to shop sales. Wain did several advertisements for Jacksons' hats and boots. Priced at 'ten and six' and 'three and nine', they were not the exclusive end of the market. All the better for us, as they are great fun and we can even read the titles on their song sheets, all well-known at the time:

'Has Anyone Seen Our Cat?', 'Meet Me At Midnight – Alone', 'Put Me Among The Girls', 'I Fear No Foe' and 'Come Into The Garden Maud'. They don't sing them like that any longer!

WARMTH WITH ELEGANCE

A brand of health-enhancing cloth woven from a mixture of wool and peat fibres was the inspiration of Gustave Jaeger, the originator of the Jaeger Wool Company. By 1880 Jaeger had published his volume *Health Culture* and was selling his products in London through an agent. His rallying cry 'Health Through Wool' stirred not only a generation; wool remained the popular choice for many British children and adults until the late 1950s when centrally heated homes began to come in. Doctor Jaeger's choice of the French name 'Rasurel' for his product was meant to imply well-being, confidence and support; all attributes guaranteed by the good 'Doctor' for those who bought his 'hygienic woollens'. Dr Jaeger believed that as we are animals, we should wear clothing produced from animals, such as wool, which is warm and highly absorbent. Cotton, he argued, lay wet and clammy upon the skin, causing chills.

An advertisement placed in the *Illustrated London News* in April 1903 pictures a family all dressed in:

'PURE WOOL and PEAT STOCKINET HYGIENIC UNDERWEAR.

Antiseptic. Absorbent. Unshrinkable. *Manufactured with yarns composed of **best pure, natural undyed Wool and Peat fibres**. To the benefits of wool, Dr. Rasurel has added the undeniable qualities of **Peat** which many experiments have proved is a **natural antiseptic**. All articles are made either with natural **brown peat** or with **bleached Peat**.'*

In 1884 that most respected journal, *The Lancet*, approved Dr Jaeger's wool blend and having made their own personal trials, confirmed:

'the clothing, made from wool and peat fibre is very absorbent and possesses antiseptic properties.'

'Health Through Wool' became a slogan wholeheartedly embraced by intellectuals of the aesthetic movement who raised it to the status of a religious faith. These adherents known as 'Woolleners' included such celebrities as Oscar Wilde and George Bernard Shaw – who had a

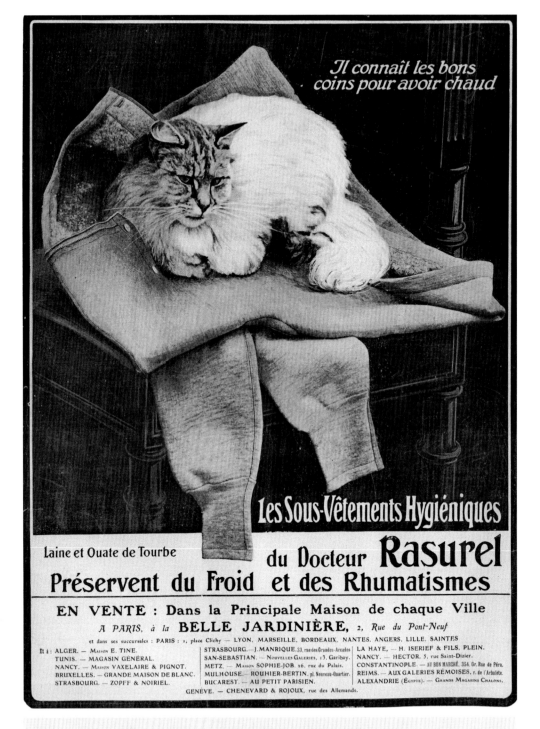

L'Illustration magazine, February 1910. Dr Rasurel's Hygienic Woollens.

'He Knows Where To Find The Cosiest Corner.' In 1910 the 'Cult of the Cat' is at its peak, Princess Helena Victoria is breeding Persians at Windsor Great Park, and longhaired cats are enjoying celebrity status. Here an exotic thoroughbred lends an aura of luxury – aimed at the quality end of the market.

whole suit made of it. Shaw was spotted striding along Regent Street in his sanitary wool suit:

*'a tall leggy figure with red hair, looking exactly like a forked radish.' ***

'Red flannel was readily discarded in favour of Dr Jaeger's cosier new-styled "Sanitary Wool" and the carriage trade flocked to his smart London outlet where they cleared the shelves.'

(* See Alison Adburgham, Shops and Shopping.)

'A Pleasant Christmas To You.'

'May The Joys Of The Season Never End In Smoke.'

SMOKE GETS IN YOUR EYES

Flor Fina Cigars issued trade cards overprinted with Christmas greetings so that customers could send them on with their own personal message. The two above were both used and inscribed by the senders. A novel idea and by using popular subjects such as cats, they were acceptable to send to the children of the family.

THE TALE OF THE BLACK CATS

Carreras bought into the 1920s craze for Egyptology; the opulence of golden tombs and cat goddess worship, naming their 'Craven A' cigarette brand 'Black Cat'. The company's headquarters at Camden in London, was architect-designed in art deco style with two giant bronze statues of cats (2.6 m tall) standing either side of the main entrance. Over the years the building went in to decline and was stripped of many of its decorative features including the cats.

Pet Cigarettes. Allen & Ginter cigarette card c.1885.

John Allen and Lewis Ginter founded the Richmond Virginia Tobacco Company and were first with the bright idea of enclosing a collectable card inside each pack. Allen & Ginter became part of the American Tobacco Company in 1890.

One went to the Carreras headquarters in Basildon, the other to the Carreras

Carreras Pipe Tobacco. Advertisement in Illustrated London News, October 1902, shows the 'Black Cat' brand trade mark endorsed by J M Barrie, then prospective author of Peter Pan.

factory in Spanish Town, Jamaica. In 1996 the original Carreras building in Camden was rescued and underwent complete restoration of its art deco features, including replicas of the two famous cat statues which now stand guard once more at the front entrance.

A beautiful pastel drawing of an elegant black Persian signed by 'Mac' was chosen to decorate Crawford's luxury biscuit brand. 'Mac' was the pseudonym of animal artist Lucy Dawson, famous for her much admired dog studies. In her 'Crawford's Pussy Cat' she skilfully captures the arresting loveliness of this black beauty with the golden eyes.

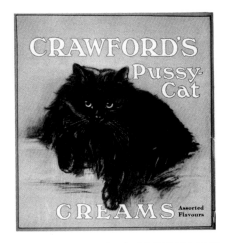

Crawford's Pussy-cat Creams biscuit tin illustration.

In 1871 when the Crystal Palace opened its doors to the first cat show, black was the colour then in vogue for the pedigree Persians on view. Show promoter Harrison Weir pays tribute to these handsome creatures and describes the points of the prize winning black, 'Minnie' who had all the coveted characteristics of the breed:

'A good rich, deep black; orange coloured eyes and long flowing hair, a grand mane and with a graceful carriage and a mild expression. Truly a very beautiful object, and very rare.'

Van Houten's Cocoa. From a series of 'collectable' trade cards.

Entitled 'The Little Pet's Breakfast' and featuring the family cat:

'We are such good friends pet, you and I, So a taste of the fare I'll let you try.'

On the reverse, Van Houten's claim to be 'unequalled for high quality and flavour, even better than a bank account is a fund of health and energy'. Fine for humans but not a drink that would appeal to cats, nevertheless, an appealing subject for Van Houten.

Duroyen et Ramette Cie.

French trade card c.1890. Retailers of chicory, coffee and drinking chocolate. 'Chicory at a thrifty price.'

Gail Borden Eagle Brand Condensed Milk. Trade Card 1893.

This picture of a little girl in a kitten disaster area would have charmed adults and children alike. However, Borden's milk was not all that it claimed: 'ideal in food preparation and for infants, 'unapproached by any other substitute for mother's milk'. In spite of Borden's glowing recommendation, tests proved that most brands of condensed milk had a high sugar content and no vitamin A or D, which led to obesity in babies as well as the possibility of rickets.

The USA investigating committee ruled that condensed milk must be labelled 'unsuitable for infants'. However, cats could still indulge in this delicacy, although the high sugar content would have made it difficult to digest.

Picture postcard c.1904. From H.M.& Co's 'Famous Posters in miniature'.

One of a pair of Nestlé advertising posters on the 'before' and 'after' theme. The matching poster shows the thin cat after it has grown fat on Nestlé milk

CATS' NIRVANA

When advertising their milk-based products, early manufacturers always took advantage of some ready-made sales 'purr-sons' – cats of course. The myth has survived over centuries that milk is good for them because they love it, so advertisers cashed in, but recent research has revealed the problems that many cats

Milkmaid Milk. Anglo-Swiss Condensed Milk Company late 1890s.

A Picture postcard published by Raphael Tuck, from their 'Celebrated Poster' series, c.1903. The Anglo-Swiss Company was taken over by Nestlé in 1905. The manufacturer claims that it is: 'too good for cats'!

The cats in this advertisement are in the style of the famous Theophile Alexandre Steinlen's cat poster for pure Vingeanne Sterilised milk which first appeared in 1894 and later modified by Steinlen himself for two advertisements for Nestlé.

experience digesting it. Unfortunately 'thin cat' would not have grown fat on any brand of condensed milk and it may well have caused bowel problems.

Mazawattee Tea Advertisement 1910. 'Derby Day' by cat artist Louis Wain.

Wain's cats are seen here at their most exuberant; off to enjoy an outing to the races on Derby Day, although it doesn't look as if much tea will be drunk.

Mazawattee tea Company, founded in 1878, was probably best known for the bespectacled granny and child image which appeared on many of their advertisements.

Bovril Display Placard. 1903.

The Royal Navy crew splice the mainbrace with the ship's mascot – a black cat – who awaits his share of the treat.

Robert Opie collection, Museum of Brands, Packaging and Advertising.

Bovril was first produced in 1871 in Canada as 'Johnston's Fluid Beef' made from meat extract with caramel, salt and spices. Johnston moved production to London in 1884 after a fire destroyed his Montreal factory. He changed the name of his fluid beef and patented it under the new name of Bovril. For the Victorians, beef tea had always been the staple diet for convalescents, the elderly or ailing children. But Bovril was a handy product, it could be spread on toast, added to soups and stews or taken as a warming, nutritious drink. It was even sold in theatre bars and Chocolate Bovril was available from slot machines. In his extensive and highly effective advertising campaigns, Johnson was able to challenge and see off his beef tea competitors. The reverse side of a Bovril advertising flyer of the early 1900s shows it did not pull its punches:

'Bovril is far superior to beef-tea, ask your doctor! Beef-tea is not nourishing as is commonly supposed. The strengthening parts of the meat are wasted in beef-tea – the albumen is coagulated and the fibrine is thrown away. Bovril contains all the nutritious, strengthening, building-up qualities of a meat diet. Over 1,000 British Hospitals and Infirmaries are using Bovril regularly'.

ENOUGH TO MAKE A CAT LAUGH

Picture Postcard of a poster advertising 'Charley's Aunt', a successful comedy show running at the London Crystal Palace Theatre in 1908 and familiar to us even today,

The sale of picture postcards reproduced from posters as mementos of a particular theatre production was a common practice up to the 1930s. 'Enough to Make a Cat Laugh' traded on the old saying, even though no cat was mentioned in the show. The *Oxford English Dictionary* gives a quotation as early as 1616: *'It would make any Mouse, Ratte, Catte or Dogge laugh to think what sport we shall have.'* A cat, along with other despised and persecuted animals,

suggests the original meaning; that it would take something extremely funny to cause them to laugh. Homeless dogs, like cats, scavenged to survive and had a similar rating. Pictures of cats and kittens were often used to promote theatre productions and, alongside *Charley's Aunt,* another new farce, *Baby Mine*, was at the Wimbledon Theatre.

A series of comic picture postcard cats – all entitled 'At The Play' – featured several musical comedies of 1908: *The Belle of Mayfair* led by Camille Clifford, creator of the fashionable swan shaped 'Gibson

Miss Hook of Holland, a picture postcard by artist William Ellam. A musical comedy starring Isabel Jay.

Reproduced from a theatre poster.

Baby Mine a farce presented by Weedon Grossmith at the Wimbledon Theatre in 1912.

Reproduced from a theatre poster.

Wellington Bromide Picture Postcard. Suppliers to the photographic trade.

Wellington bromides are an interesting example of a bygone era when picture postcards were sent to clients as a reminder to re-order the 'Wellington' brand 'Cream', 'Crayon' or 'Rough' bromide papers, and 'Xtra', 'Speedy' or 'Plate' glass negatives.

Girl' figure and *Miss Hook of Holland* with Isabel Jay in the leading role Local shops such as chemists, ironmongers and furniture suppliers were keen to use the picture postcard to promote their business. A humorous approach is taken by Wellington Bromide, circa 1910 with two kittens singing an old favourite from the same song sheet entitled '*Meet Me By Moonlight – Alone*'. The skilful adaptation of photographic methods to piece together a composition was often achieved afterwards in the design studio dark room.

PUSS MAKES HIS MARK

Drakes Bookstore Cat Bookmark. c.1890.

It seems only proper that this serious looking cat of obvious scholarly intellect is in charge of the Intelligence Office at Drakes Bookstore in Toledo USA; where the 'best of help' is supplied to their customers. Befittingly, he is a serious shorthaired tabby, not a frivolous fluffy feline.

A THOROUGHLY MODERN MOGGIE – The 1920s and 1930s

While cats were beginning to blaze new trails in to more specialised product areas no longer directly related to the home, such as Hutchinsons' Racing Cycle Tyres; their popularity as domestic pets

THE BAD GIRL OF THE FAMILY!

The Sphere December 1901.

A full-page advertisement for Strand Magazine Grand Double Christmas Number. Here we see artist Louis Wain's quirky cats getting down to some serious reading.

Picture postcard The Bad Girl of the Family! By Violet Roberts.

Roberts' wicked send up of Frederick Melville's heavily melodramatic play entitled The Bad Girl of the Family. The theme, that of the seduction of an innocent servant girl by a seedy, middle-aged philanderer was not seen as 'cool' and caused much hilarity among the 'Bright Young Things' of the 1920s.

had taken a downturn. For no obvious reason, dogs had become the more popular choice.

A clue is to be found in an observation made by Dutch author Friso Wiegersma about a pre-World War Two self-portrait by the art deco artist Tamora Lempicka behind the wheel of her car:

'She is the prototype of the woman of the time; beautiful, independent, enterprising and above all, "modern".'

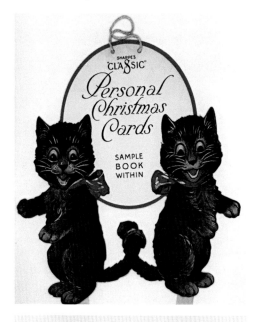

Sharpes Classic Personal Christmas Card Window display of 1925.

These fun loving cats are the siblings of those featured in the Comique Series of picture postcards published by Sharpes' Inter-Art Company. Much valuable picture postcard history was lost in the London bombing raids of the Second World War.

Following the horrors of the first World War, which led to considerable social change particularly for women, the word

Front Cover of Home Notes Christmas Annual 1927.

By Lawson Wood, a much-admired magazine illustrator and creator of the famous 'Grandpops Monkey' character. Throughout his life Wood was actively involved in animal welfare and, as a prolific picture postcard artist, delighted generations with his 'comic cats' series. He trained at the Slade School of Art, served in the First World War, and died in 1957.

'modern' represented the hopes of a new generation. The modern young woman was anxious to cast off the fashions and conventions of her parents along with the claustrophobic role of women; often delegated to look after elderly parents, tied to the Victorian tradition of home, hearth and – the living embodiment of the regime – the family cat!

THE TYRE WITH NINE LIVES

Hutchinson's Racing Cycle Tyres.

Series of Full Page Advertisements in Cycling Magazine for 1927 where black cats make the sales pitch.

Now we see for the first time, cats entering new markets by venturing into more technical sales areas. A series of advertisements which Hutchinson's ran to promote their market leading brand of tubular tyres featured stylised black cats. Tubular tyres were the latest development to replace the earlier 'wired on' type and a series of these full-page advertisements ran throughout 1927.

Hutchinson's make confident claims for their product: tenacity, speed, resilience, comfort and safety, all, it could be said, cat related. The Prestigious 'Tour de France' Road Race of 3,500 gruelling miles was won four times in succession on cycles using their 'All Black half-covered tubulars'. This must have been the inspiration for the novel black cat advertising campaign: 'The Tyre With <u>Nine</u> Lives'.

By the 1930s Glastonburys were confident market leaders. The hard-working fluffy kitten held pole position for charm and cuddly warmth and could not be bettered as ambassador for their Christmas range of fleece lined slippers. Advertisements had changed over the years; now more chatty and relaxed, a reflection of the continual shift in social attitudes which had taken place following World War One. Even the kitten is able to find his voice, says *'miaow'* and exclaims *'everyone's got Glastonburys but me'*. Aahh!

Clark, Son & Morland Ltd., advertised their ladies' slippers in Punch magazine, November 1936. The name 'Glastonburys' was replaced in 1950 with the now famous 'Morland' brand.

Maison Lyons Chocolates. Punch magazine, 11 February, 1925.

Such angelic kittens, but would you trust these two alone in your home?

THE LUXURY - LOVING CAT

Using the kittenly characteristic of curiosity, Maison Lyons finds a quotation from Thomas Emerson to sell their luxury chocolates to a discerning clientele – after all, they do cost four shillings a pound: *'Curiosity is lying in wait for every secret.'* – Thomas Emerson.

'The secret of Maison Lyons chocolates is worth the curiosity. They are good to behold, but their greater worth is within – every centre a delightful surprise!'

Maison Lyons was part of the Lyons Corner House concept. First opened in London in 1909, it combined tea shops, cafes (with light music played by a salon orchestra), a food hall, florist and confectioner all under one roof. Such was their success, smaller versions of the Corner House soon followed in large towns and cities throughout the UK. And still remembered, the smartly uniformed waitresses in white starched aprons and caps – nicknamed 'nippies'.

The Cat on the Bottle

Although there is very little information on the wife of Joseph Dubonnet she is said to have begun the long tradition of 'the cat on the bottle'. As a cat lover and owner, it was at her suggestion that an eye-catching picture of a cat was included on the first Dubonnet bottle label. Although there have been changes in style over the years, a cat image has remained there ever since.

However, it was the mosquito not the cat that acted as the catalyst for the invention of Dubonnet wine aperitif. The story goes that during the French campaigns of the 1830s in North Africa, malaria became a serious threat to the health of the troops. The deadly fever was carried by mosquitos and the only known weapon, a bitter tasting medicine extracted from cinchona bark known as quinine. French authorities were willing to offer cash incentives to anyone who could give the medicine a more palatable taste. Joseph Dubonnet found his perfect blend in 1846.

The Story of the Dubonnet Cat Poster

Adolphe Mouron, pseudonym 'Cassandre' and celebrated innovative designer of the art deco school, was working in Paris in the 1930s where he was the leading typographer of his day. His famous triptych style poster known as 'Dubonnet Man' was in three sections to reveal the man in the process of drinking. Dubonnet Man became a household name and in 1937 the idea was re-worked as a tribute by an unknown artist using the same triple module format and typography. This time round however, the idea of the Dubonnet 'cat on the bottle' was imaginatively introduced and he appears in lead role as circus strongman, trapeze artist and juggler.

Collette & 'Cat'

Dubonnet Wine Tonic Aperitif.

Art Deco Poster reduced as a magazine advertisement.

L'Illustration 2 October 1937.

Colette and her beloved 'Cat' endorse Perrier, 'the champagne of table waters'. L'Illustration 27 August 1938.

This drawing of Colette dining al-fresco on fruit and a bottle of Perrier was realised by the skilled illustrator and lithographer Luc-Albert Moreau.

Collette, the most famous and admired French writer of her day is pictured with her beloved Blue Chartreux cat* that she fell for at a Paris cat show. Colette's third husband, Maurice Goudeket told how she 'carried her off on the spot, like a bride!' Although they tried out several names, none seemed to fit and they decided that she just wanted to be called 'the Cat' as if she were the only one in the world. Later she earned the title of 'La dernière chatte' (the last cat) because Colette felt she could never be replaced in her affections. *Chartreux: a French Blue Shorthair breed thought to have been developed in the Middle Ages by the monks at the monastery of La Grande Chartreuse – famous for its liqueurs.

Dernière chatte was the model for 'Saha' the Russian Blue in Colette's novel *The Cat,* a psychological contest between young newly-wed husband and wife and his beloved cat. Cats had always been part of Colette's life; companions, comforters and source of inspiration. As a child she had wandered the Burgundy countryside with her brothers and sisters and 'a bloodthirsty gang of vagabond cats'. Her own cat Babou, 'black as Satan and as sinuous as an eel' raided the choicest strawberries from a neighbour's garden. She recalled how her grandfather, who was a confectioner, set out the wet slabs of chocolate to dry every night on the roof-terrace and in the morning each slab was imprinted with five little petals; the paw-marks of nocturnal cats.

At twenty, still a shy country girl she married a man fifteen years older than herself – Henri Gautier-Villars (nicknamed Willy) a publisher and something of a roué, who lived and worked in Paris. Parisian society was the setting she used for her 'belle epoque' novel Gigi, written fifty years later and made into a Hollywood movie. A delightful longhaired cat was introduced in to the film although there is no mention of it in the book.

Spotting that his young wife had talent, Willy set her to write spicy stories and to make sure she stuck at it he locked her in her room for several hours each day. These were the Claudine novels, the first ever written for a teenage readership. They flew off the shelves and made Willy rich and famous because he published them under his own name. He did however, give Colette two pets to keep her company; a French bulldog she called Toby and a grey Angora cat, Kiki-la-doucette (gentle Kiki). Kiki and Toby were her inspiration for *All Creatures Great and Small,* a dialogue between the two animals in which they discuss their own feelings towards one another and to their owners. A work of remarkable originality and a best seller, it was published along with a series of short sketches, *The Cats of Paris,* featuring the gift shop cat who sat in the window among the display of picture postcards. She was much admired by passers-by who went inside just to stroke her and never failed to leave with a purchase.

In 1906, after thirteen years of Willy, she finally rebelled and left him taking Toby and Kiki with her. Colette was already infamous for what she had written and when some of her stories were adapted for the theatre, who better than the author herself to take the stage? Although she became a professional actress she never stopped writing. Scandal was never far away and her theatrical career was defined by a very public six-year lesbian liaison with an aristocrat known as 'Missy'.

Colette was married for a second time to newspaper editor Henry de Jouvenel and a daughter was born, but the marriage crashed when her husband found that she – now aged 46, had seduced his handsome young stepson. Nevertheless, Colette it seems, had sown all of her wild oats and with her third husband, writer Maurice Goudeket, seventeen years her junior, she settled down to become a much-adored French national treasure. Goudeket published a poignant biography of her as he lovingly cared for her to the end of her life. As a Jew, he was under constant threat from the Gestapo during the occupation of France in World War Two and hid many times out on the rooftops of Paris. As Colette herself put it 'we lived under the threat of the doorbell.'

Sidonie-Gabrielle Colette gained numerous literary and civic honours over her lifetime, was awarded the Legion of Honour and was the first woman in France to be given a state funeral. In her declining years she continued to feed and care for many strays: a friend recalled Colette's 80th birthday at her home in St Tropez; summoning her cats to her with a kind of sing song musical refrain as they followed her in procession along the pathways bordered with purslane and amaryllis. 'Our perfect companions' said Colette, 'never have fewer than four feet.'

Bird's Custard. Picture Post, 16 December 1939.

Alfred Bird, 'Fellow of the Chemists Society' registered as a pharmacist in Birmingham in 1842 and went on to produce his 'eggless custard powder'. Sold worldwide, Bird's was particularly valued during the Second World War when eggs were on ration.

Christmas 1939 and in the Bird's advertisement things look normal and re-assuring. The confident little girl in her 'nippy' uniform bears pudding to table with her escort, the family cat who is obviously in control of kitchen duties. But war had been declared and for many people this may have been their last family Christmas at home before everything changed forever.

CATS LEAD ON
Post World War Two

From radar to refractories and plastics to electron microscopes; vital research made available in World War Two allowed industrial companies – some impressively large and with international status – to diversify. It therefore comes as a surprise to find that cats were often their chosen representatives. The overall increase in the number of cat images used in industrial and commercial advertisements in the 1950s and '60s reflects the wider public interest in cats as pets.

Coalite Smokeless Coal. An advertisement placed in numerous popular and technical magazines in the 1950s and '60s. Coalite claims to be:

'the ideal smokeless fuel for every type of grate, cooker, stove and boiler. It provides magnificent fires at low cost and being half the weight of coal it gives twice as many scuttles to the ton'.

On the home front, the 1950s and '60s saw the beginning of some long running domestic campaigns such as Kosset Carpets and Aga Cookers; the former

Philips Electrical Ltd. 1948.

An advertising campaign featuring similar cats, some in full colour, appeared in a range of post war trade magazines.

lasting well over twenty 'Kosset Cat' years and spanning three decades. Meanwhile, cats remained undaunted, and took on all these exciting new challenges without twitching a whisker.

Cats are placed central to hearth and home where the world is a better place now that it can be rid of the dirt and choking fogs suffered in the past. The pussies bask in a blaze of Coalite; the perfect fuel designed to meet the standards of the Clean Air Act of 1956.

Applying new technology developed in World War Two, Philips Electrical lost no time. In 1948 advertisements appeared using a cat to define the superiority of their new products in the electronics market. Their new optics range offered:

'such magnification a cat could stand astride the English Channel, its front paws in France, its hind legs in England. So great is the power of the Electron Microscope, that scientists can now study the secret organisms which hitherto, were far beyond the limits of even the best.'

The Aga Cooker Cats

In the years between 1948 and 1955 Aga ran a series of cat-themed advertisements in magazines such as *Punch*, *Ideal Home* and *House and Garden* where cats were used to promote both image and performance.

"Tender! Tender! There's nothing that won't turn tender in the Aga bottom oven."

Traditionally held views of cat characteristics were heavily drawn on; their attitude of superiority, their love of luxury, warmth, comfort and cosy domesticity. 'Lucky' black cats were often chosen – lucky to be living beside an Aga, as were their humans! Who better to endorse their owners' wise and tasteful choice of an Aga cooker than the family cat?

Dr Nils Gustaf Dalen, a Swedish engineer, was awarded the 1912 Nobel Prize for his contribution to maritime safety with his Solventil Solar Valve which enabled lighthouses and buoys to switch on and off automatically. In spite of being blinded in a tragic accident Dr Dalen went on to design and perfect the acclaimed Aga cooker.

Aga Heat Limited.

In Rudyard Kipling's 'Just So Story Book' style, a mother cat explains to her kittens the many secrets of how an Aga cooker functions and the amazing benefits to be gained.

Punch magazine, 16 April 1952.

GOING FOR GLAMOUR
The Kosset Carpet cats

For well over twenty years and spanning three decades, Kosset Carpet cats were the supreme luxury status symbol. The advertisements, mostly full-page colour, began in 1954 and went on into the late '70s using a number of thoroughbred silver chinchillas.

Although the silver line goes back as far as 1882, all can trace their ancestry to the first officially recorded silver Chinchilla 'Silver Lambkin', which laid claim a few years later to possessing the rare inhibitor gene which gives the white fur its unique silver lustre.

Everybody Loves Kosset.

House and Garden full-page advertisement. 1958.

As a result of the long running Kosset advertisements, the Persian Chinchilla soon shot to 'most popular breed' status in spite of the high maintenance required in daily grooming and the flattened nose characteristic which can cause respiratory problems.

Several of the Kosset cats went on to enjoy celebrity status, such as the beautiful Solomon who played the part of M's cat in the James Bond film *You Only Live Twice* and starred again in *Diamonds Are Forever.*

Knitting can be such fun with P & B wools

Patons & Baldwins Ltd.

Paton and Baldwin Ltd. P & B Wools. Everybody's Magazine 1950s.

'Knitting can be such fun.' Cats just love a muddle. A light-hearted and ingenious 'cat's cradle' aims to sell knitting as an enjoyable hobby.

PUSS CLIMBS UP THE POPULARITY POLL

The 1950s and '60s saw cats gaining in popularity once more and cat ownership growing rapidly. Keen cat lovers bought up publications covering all aspects of cat care, feeding, health and breeding as well as popular 'miscellanies' with pictures, stories and history. Cat shows became active again after a long wartime absence. In 1995 Mrs Lesley Pring, Honorary

Secretary of the Governing Council of the Cat Fancy, wrote in her article '*History of the Cat Fancy*':

'*The Fancy had great difficulty in surviving the Second World War and by the end there were very few pedigree cats left. Registration had fallen from 1000 a year up to 1939 to only 400 in 1940. But by the early 1950s registrations were increasing steadily.*'

"It makes me hopping mad," complained the Cat on Hot Bricks, "when they can't even keep the temperature constant from one minute to the next. What's wrong with this firm ! They ought to use oil fuel." All they've got to do is to contact Shell-Mex and B.P. Ltd., and get the best advice on controlled heat that anyone could come across in nine lifetimes."

CONTROLLED HEAT WITH OIL FUEL

SHELL INDUSTRIAL SERVICE BP

SHELL-MEX and BP Ltd.

Instant reader attention. From the old saying 'like a cat on hot bricks', this red hot moggy gives a fine performance. The 'Controlled Heat with Oil Fuel' advertisement was given a full page for maximum impact.

Journal of the Iron and Steel Institute. 1953.

'Behind the Ears'...

Keeping things clean—not just superficially but 'behind the ears' as well—must be someone's responsibility. If cleaning arrangements are one of your business or professional worries, you should get to know Teepol. This master detergent developed by Shell is now recognised as being the most effective and economical cleaning aid for use in commercial and industrial premises, and in municipal, institutional and public buildings of all kinds.

TEEPOL *is a SHELL contribution to improved public health*

 SHELL Shell Chemicals Limited, Norman House, 105-109 Strand, W.C.2. *Telephone :* Temple Bar 4455
(DISTRIBUTORS)

" TEEPOL" is a Registered Trade Mark

SHELL 'Teepol'. Courier Magazine (Trade) 1952'. Behind the Ears'...

A lovely striped tabby cat comes with his traditional message of cleanliness; not just superficially, but 'behind the ears' too, just like 'Teepol' does. Shell has developed a 'master detergent' and claims it to be 'the most economical cleaning aid for commercial, industrial and public premises'. When it's a cleaning job, puss is the expert.

It might well be concluded that at this point in time, every known situation and characteristic relating to a cat as a means of projecting a product image had been tried. Nevertheless, our felines continued undaunted, to sell to new customers some of the latest technology to emerge from World War Two.

If you wanted to make a jelly, either sweet fruit or savoury, at any time between 1400 (earliest record) and the mid-19th century you had a lengthy job ahead. First, produce your gelatine by the prolonged boiling of bones, particularly calves' feet; and the resulting gelatinous liquid could then be transformed – depending on your skill – into every variety of jelly for the table.

When you're eating Jell-O you'll wish you were a wildcat

because you'll be wild... simply wild about this jelly with the fruit-fruit-fruitier flavour!

Next time ask for **JELL-O**

only 9d.

It was not until 1845 that American, Peter Cooper patented his powdered 'Portable Gelatine'. Fifty years later, in 1897, New York cough syrup manufacturer Pearl B Waite and his wife May acquired the patent, put in a fruit flavour and marketed it under the name of Jell-O. But the Waites lacked the finances needed to promote it in a big way so they sold the rights to the Genesee Pure Food Company who launched it as 'America's Favourite Dessert.'

A COLD WAR CAT

Over the centuries eyes have held the power of possession; from the 'evil eye' of the old cunning woman to the mesmerist. United's cat is a predator with menacing jaws, his penetrating stare fixed on the enemy. He is the cat of darkness and calls to mind half-forgotten folklore of cats as witch's familiars gifted with the magic power to see in the dark.

Cats' eyes can also reflect; another useful feature which was the inspiration for Percy Shaw when he patented his Catseye Road Studs as a fog safety aid for motorists in 1934.

Multinational company United Aircraft, chose the cat to front its latest innovative radar technology, the Norden Search and Terrain Clearance System in the 1960s:

Cat's eyes on target

An elusive low-flying aircraft follows a course around hills and other hazards, pinpoints its target, and swoops in. The pilot "sees" his course and target clearly, even in midnight darkness or in spite of severe weather conditions, with Norden's Search and Terrain Clearance Radar.

This system, serving as "cat's eyes" for the Grumman A-6A Intruder in difficult flight environments, provides an electronic display of information supplied by advanced sensory equipment. Two viewing screens in the cockpit enable the pilot to determine targets and geographical features. The aircraft automatically pursues the desired approach, discharges its weapons, and leaves the target area. The pilot may easily alter course if the situation demands it.

Norden has developed a compact Terrain Clearance Radar System for military aircraft engaged in weapons delivery, reconnaissance, or resupply. It is another Norden contribution which strengthens the free world's defense by Extending Man's Capabilities. For further information, write:

United Aircraft
INTERNATIONAL
East Hartford 8, Connecticut, U.S.A.

SOLE FOREIGN REPRESENTATIVE FOR: Pratt & Whitney Aircraft, Hamilton Standard, Sikorsky Aircraft, Norden, United Aircraft of Canada Limited

Representative for Norden products in England:
Kelsey Ltd., Edinb House, Eastern Ave. West, Romford, Essex

United Aircraft.
Radar Navigation Systems.
Flight International. 25 July 1963.

CLOSELOY ROLLS
BY EXPERT ROLLMAKERS FOR EXPERT STEELMAKERS

steel-base horizontal rolls
m mill.

ARMSTRONG WHITWORTH (Metal Industries) **LTD**
Close Works, Gateshead 8, Co. Durham. Phone: Gateshead 71361

Closeloy Rolls. Journal of the Iron and Steel Institute. February 1965.

Closeloy makes rolled steel and tells us about it:

'Ocean liners or toy trains, cars or bottletops. Rolled steel is everywhere around us, but taken for granted – evidence enough that several experts have succeeded in their allotted tasks.'

The feline dustbin raider – yet another expert has succeeded in his allotted task.

for military aircraft engaged in weapons delivery, reconnaissance or resupply. The pilot 'sees' his course and target clearly, even in midnight darkness or severe weather conditions, the system serving as 'cats eyes' for the Grumman A-6A Intruder in difficult flight environments. Another Norden contribution which strengthens the free world's defense by extending man's capabilities.'

Don't trust to luck
in your choice of refractories

Best leave nothing to chance... better leave it to us. There's skill behind the selection of refractories, as much as in the making.

Get in touch—our knowledge is at your service—while a letter will secure for you a helpful series of leaflets. So don't trust to luck—put out the cat and contact us.

CONSETT IRON COMPANY LIMITED

CONSETT, COUNTY DURHAM. Telephone: Consett 341 (17 lines). Telegrams: Steel Consett Telex. Telex: 53172

Consett Iron Company Ltd.

A jaunty, happy-go-lucky black cat that could score a hit on any page. But he comes with a warning from Consett, don't trust to luck when you are replacing your old refractory. Take advice from Consett, the professionals who can place their skill and knowledge at your service. Put out the cat and contact Consett.

The Consett Iron Company was a major UK industry based in Consett County Durham. Founded in 1840 it became part of British Steel Corporation in 1967. Despite its impressive history, sadly there was no black cat to rescue Consett and the company closed in 1980.

Journal of the Iron and Steel Institute 1963.

This could also be viewed as another remarkable contribution from 'poor puss'... a performance well within his capabilities, but never with such poise and command.

THE GLAMOUR PUSS

'…of course, every cat is really the most beautiful woman in the room.'

English writer and biographer Edward Verrall Lucas, 1868–1938.

In 1895 Alfred Boucheron, founding father of the Boucheron diamond empire moved into number 26 Place Vendôme, Paris. He is alleged to have remarked that he chose the situation because it was in the sunniest spot and would make his display of diamonds sparkle. At the time he was already well established into exclusive high-end creative jewellery and was selling to the rich and famous – such as celebrity actress Sarah Bernhardt – as well as the crowned heads of Europe. Perhaps one of the company's most remarkable assignments came from the Indian Maharajah De Patiala who, in 1928, arrived with his retinue carrying six trunks full of precious gems to be made up into jewellery.

VLADIMIR THE BOUCHERON CAT

Vladimir began his modelling career in 1979 when he featured in a Boucheron advertising campaign and became a star overnight. He lived with his owner Gérard Boucheron. From a website there is a sighting of him:

'Gérard Boucheron's cat Vladimir was a much loved feature of the Place Vendôme boutique: he was perfectly at home weaving through displays and precious stones. Vladimir's presence in the private townhouse at 26 Place Vendôme added a genuine feeling of being in a family home. Considered to be a lucky cat and extremely affectionate he would seek out the client's gentle patting and stroking.'

There was more of Vladimir from an archived website, with a romantic description of him:

'Proud and majestic, the Persian cat conjures up an image of poetry. With its velvet paws wrapped in the secret of the night it panders to the desires of a disturbing liberty.'

It seems Vladimir was responsible for leaking indiscreet information regarding the forthcoming designs of some jewellery collections. Of course he did it all at night secretly, as cats do. The mysterious informant continues:

'Although he disappeared from the advertising campaigns, ten years later Vladimir still wanders with his starry eyes in the wings of the imagination of the famous jeweller.'

What a loving tribute to the memory of Vladimir, the cat of poetry, starry eyes, velvet wrapped paws! He must have been a very dear and cherished cat.

Vladimir went on to model Boucheron jewels in a series of magazine

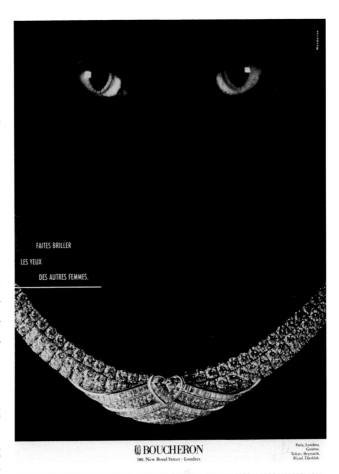

FAITES BRILLER
LES YEUX
DES AUTRES FEMMES.

⬡ BOUCHERON
180, New Bond Street · Londres

Paris, Londres, Genève, Tokyo, Beyrouth, Riyad, Djeddah.

Boucheron Diamonds. A series of advertisements featuring Persian cats, all using the caption:

'Faites briller les yeux des autres femmes'… 'Makes other women's eyes light up.'

Here Boucheron's own pet cat, Vladimir, features.

Country Life Magazine 1985.

advertisements in the 1980s but he always remained an affectionate family pet, fondly regarded by Boucheron clients. In January 2018 Boucheron celebrated its 160 years at Place Vendôme with a unique public exhibition of their work and history at the Monnaie de Paris, France's national Mint. Remarkably, Vladimir guided visitors around the exhibition with his own smartphone app!

INTO THE MILLENNIUM

At the end of the 20th century and beginning of the 21st, another phenomenon emerged – the Fiscal Feline, or City Cat. In these advertisements – and there were many others in similar

Know the moment

www.DLJdirect.co.uk
or call
0800 358 4477

deal direct

WE'LL save you pussy footing around and help you find the best time to buy and sell shares, by giving you extensive online access to the most up-to-date company data, which you're then free to analyse and use any way you like.

We'll also supply real-time information & pricing and help you set up programmable alerts. Not to mention instantly confirming your deal and sending you a hard copy, as well as providing personal phone support. All for a fraction of the price of conventional stockbrokers. So visit our website today and strike a better deal.

Deal direct with confidence.

DLJ Direct.

Do fund managers need cat characteristics? It could be argued that they need the skills to stalk their prey and the ability to make a fat juicy 'kill' at the right time: 'Know the moment, to save you a lot of pussyfooting around and help you find the best time to buy and sell shares'.

Financial Times. 28 September 1999

The best things come to those who don't wait.

The Equitable Life Assurance Society. 'The best things come to those who don't wait'.

Equitable offers a seductive opportunity for instant gratification. In this parody on human greed, the cat has caught the bird. With Equitable you too can 'catch the bird', and have everything you want... now. You don't have to wait. As Warren Buffet, the Oracle from Omaha said, 'If at first you succeed, quit trying'.

The Sunday Times 21 March 2000.

publications – some of Puss's negative attributes are utilised : self gratification and greed, traits also shared by human investors. However, customer care is also added in to the mix; investors can be as vulnerable as kittens. Much 'catty' wisdom is affirmed but all mention of a 'dead cat bounce' is of course carefully avoided. Advertisers have not chosen thoroughbreds for their advertisements, but have quite rightly stuck to the much-admired British short haired tabby; a

practical cat with common sense and a keen appetite for a good opportunity. It could be said, very similar to their clients.

CATS LED THE WAY

Poor Puss has come far since he first confronted his reflection in a shiny boot of the 1830s. When television entered our homes, cats soon began to feature in commercial breaks. In a study on consumer recall by Mintel International in the 1990s, fewer than half of the

Hitachi Home Monitoring.

An alert cat wonders who is watching him. Hitachi reassure us:

'It's nice to know your loved ones are safe at home. Wherever you are in the ubiquitous networked society of the near future, you'll be connected to everyone and everything anytime and anyplace. Even your cat.'

viewers brought to mind celebrity-led advertisements, while 70% remembered those featuring dogs. Cats however, topped the poll with an 82% recall. Since then many other species have joined in to ingratiate themselves into our subconscious mind. Animals can lift a product clear of class, wealth, race or religion. Many have followed in his paw prints but it was 'Poor Puss' who first led the way.

Ericsson Cordless Telephone. Make Yourself Heard.

'Now the whole family can see the beauty of digital sound'.

The cat's body language shows both curiosity and caution at first sight of this stylish piece of new technology. But Ericsson is confident: 'Whichever you choose, you are bound to get a 'phone that looks like nothing you have ever seen before'. And neither has the family cat.

Sunday Times Magazine, 11 July 1999.